Newswomen:
TWENTY-FIVE YEARS OF FRONT-PAGE JOURNALISM

Newswomen: Twenty-Five Years of Front-Page Journalism
Copyright © 2015 by The Sager Group LLC

Cataloging-in-Publication data for this book is available
from the Library of Congress.

ISBN-13: 978-0-9862679-4-9
ISBN-10: 0986267945

Cover Illustrated by Stravinski Pierre
Cover Designed by Stravinski Pierre and Siori Kitajima, SF AppWorks LLC
www.sfappworks.com
Formatted by Ovidiu Vlad
Published by The Sager Group LLC
www.TheSagerGroup.net
info@TheSagerGroup.net

𝔑𝔢𝔴𝔰𝔴𝔬𝔪𝔢𝔫:

TWENTY-FIVE YEARS OF FRONT-PAGE JOURNALISM

EDITED BY

JOYCE HOFFMANN

WITH INTERVIEWS BY KAYLEN RALPH AND JOANNA DEMKIEWICZ

THE SAGER GROUP

Artifex Te Adiuva

Table of Contents

Foreword

We were seniors studying journalism at the University of Missouri in the spring of 2013 when we first met Mike Sager. The Journalism school was sponsoring a two-day seminar on his company's second book, an anthology of long-form writing meant to be used as a text—*Next Wave: America's New Generation of Literary Journalists*. Students were excited about the book and the panel of young journalists who'd been flown in to talk about their stories and our chosen profession, proof certain that long-form journalism had not been killed by the Internet but ultimately enriched by it. The future seemed bright after all.

There was just one problem.

Of the nineteen writers featured in the collection, only three were women. And all of the writers flown in for the conference were men. Meanwhile, the conference room was packed with aspiring journalists, the majority of whom were women.

Someone in the audience asked the obvious question, "Where are all the women?"

After the program, we introduced ourselves to Mike, feeling inspired to do something about this institutional bias, and he caught our spark. This anthology—along with two more upcoming anthologies of literary long-form writing—is an attempt to answer that question. The truth is, women have been writing and producing great newspaper journalism for the past twenty-five years. There haven't been as many as men, but they are greatly accomplished, each in her own right. There just hasn't been a proper showcase for their work... until now.

At the same time Mike was envisioning these books, we decided to launch a long-form women's magazine in which we would be able to feature the kind of writing that women of our own generation would be celebrated and recognized for. Thus was born *The Riveter* magazine and TheRiveterMagazine.com.

Simultaneously working on this book and on *The Riveter* has given us a unique and important perspective on the past and has helped us move toward the future. It's important to us that this anthology features only women; we don't think our world (generally) or this industry (specifically) has achieved a place where a women-only anthology is unwarranted or unnecessary. Working on *The Riveter*, we often hear from college-aged women. It makes us so happy that they already recognize and understand what they're up against; we worked on this book for them, with the hope for a brighter future built on such a solid past.

Kaylen Ralph and Joanna Demkiewicz,
cofounders and coeditors, *The Riveter*

Introduction

By featuring the women whose stories are showcased in this collection, *Newswomen* affirms the value of the long and still-unfinished struggle to bring gender equity to American newsrooms. The seventeen stories reprinted in this volume were published on the front pages of major American newspapers. Many of these stories, and many others by the featured newswomen, claimed one or another of journalism's most coveted awards, including the Pulitzer Prize, the Goldsmith Investigative Reporting Prize, the Ernie Pyle Awards, and the Society of Professional Journalists Awards.

The quarter century in which this collection is framed marks what may have been the golden age of "modern" newswomen. Prior to this period, most women who chose journalism were ghettoized into what was inelegantly called "the hen coop," women's pages where their talents were largely squandered on fashion or fluff stories. The women featured in *Newswomen* are the descendants of these women; their integration into the other parts of the newsroom was engineered in large measure by the successful discrimination suits filed in the 1970s against leading news organizations, including the *New York Times*, *Newsweek* and the Associated Press. Straddling the millennium, this quarter century also covers a time period when America's newspapers achieved their greatest technical and influential advances, only to be undone by the transformational forces that have left newsrooms shuttered or depopulated, leaving the survivors to scratch their collective heads, in search of ways to carry on in the digital age.

The goal of this collection is to illuminate the accomplishments of newswomen in what might be called journalism's "post-hen-coop era." These stories demonstrate how women have established a presence on every newsroom beat—business, economy, science, medicine, crime, sports and war reporting.

Jacqui Banaszynski's 1987 account of the life and death of an AIDS-afflicted gay man in a Minnesota farming community is breathtaking in its depth. The series humanized gays who suffered from a frightening disease whose victims' lifestyles made them unsympathetic—and often feared—by average Americans. In revealing the intimate lives of a homosexual couple, Banaszynski gave readers of the St. Paul *Pioneer Press* an understanding of both the disease and gay life in America.

Eileen Welsome, a local reporter at the *Albuquerque Tribune*, spent more than a decade searching for the unwitting subjects of US government-sponsored human radiation experiments conducted by physicians soon after the end of World War II. She was the first to break the codes that rendered nameless the patients who were made human guinea pigs in this morally dubious medical research. The plutonium and other radioactive substances injected into random hospital patients predictably resulted in life-long health problems, most of which went unexplained to the patients themselves until Welsome found them.

Amy Harmon's exploration of the widening availability of genetic testing focused on a young woman whose family carried the genetic abnormality that caused Huntington's disease, an agonizing and fatal affliction that had devastated the lives of both her mother and her grandfather. Harmon's *New York Times* story explored the woman's decision to have her DNA tested and the emotional upheaval that followed as she wondered about what to do with her life before she faced the paralysis, brain damage, and painful death that awaited her.

Loretta Tofani's brief sojourn as a Salt Lake City retailer, a stab at "doing something different" after she left the *Philadelphia Inquirer* in 2003, soon took her right back to journalism, to a story that raised questions of conscience about the cheap Asian imports to which Americans have become addicted. Asia was familiar territory to her from her days as the *Inquirer*'s Beijing bureau chief. Selling Asian imports became the business model for her retailing adventure; however, on buying trips—especially those in China—the deplorable and dangerous working conditions she saw in the factories where her inventory was produced soon outraged her. In profiting from products manufactured in those settings, she felt complicit in the abusive practices that led to amputated limbs, cancer, renal failure, and other serious illnesses. She closed her store, reembraced journalism and pursued—at her own expense, and subsequently with grants—the story of "American Imports, Chinese Deaths," published in the *Salt Lake Tribune*.

Anne Hull traveled 2,600 miles from the high plains of central Mexico to coastal North Carolina with Mexican seasonal workers who trekked north each summer to labor in a crab shack in North Carolina. Her story in the *St. Petersburg Times* documented the lives of these migrants in their native villages, on their long annual pilgrimage, and in Roanoke Island, where an average crab picker cleaned about one thousand crabs a day during the six-month season—all in search of "*una vida mejor*," a better life.

This collection also features Edna Buchanan's landmark and wonderfully noir crime reporting out of Miami, and Christine Brennan's barrier- (and locker room-) busting sports reporting, two milieus dominated by male journalist for years. Teresa Carpenter's beautifully reported and written "Death of a Playmate," from the alt-weekly the *Village Voice*, went on to become the classic movie *Star 80*, starring Mariel Hemingway and Eric Roberts and directed by Bob Fosse. The tireless investigative efforts of Christine Pelisek, a crime reporter for the *LA Weekly*, unveiled the existence of a dormant serial killer who'd emerged from a decade-long hiatus to kill more women in South Central Los Angeles. Partly due to Pelisek's sleuthing, a suspect was found by police and brought to justice; two Lifetime Network films resulted, a feature and a documentary. In addition we have Lane DeGregory's detailed crime narrative about high school romance gone horribly wrong; Athelia Knight's investigation of life inside a Washington, DC, high school; Deborah Blum's examination of science's use of nonhuman primates for research; Julia Keller's reconstruction of the events surrounding a destructive tornado that hit the Midwest, and Andrea Elliott's story about a Brooklyn imam who helps his mostly immigrant-Muslim flock navigate the tricky cultural crosswinds of life in America.

Women have also brought praiseworthy insights to coverage of terrorism, warfare, and military life. Dana Priest wrote eye-popping stories about the CIA's secret prisons and counterterrorism operations. Corinne Reilly's series took readers inside a frontline military medical triage hospital in Kandahar, Afghanistan, and Diana Henriques uncovered military insurance scams carried out against naïve servicemen and women who fought the country's 21st century wars.

All of these stories are distinguished by brilliant writing, tireless research, and above all, a commitment to the kind of journalism that bears witness to people and issues that enlighten readers in ways that serve American democracy. Despite the inroads these stories represent and other noteworthy gender breakthroughs, too many gender disparities remain.

In 2013, women accounted for 36.3 percent of newsroom employees and were far more likely to hold news assistant and copy desk jobs than they were to occupy positions at the top of newsroom hierarchies, according to the Women's Media Center study on "The Status of Women in the U. S. Media 2014." At the nation's one hundred largest newspapers, women populated only 20 percent of the top managerial positions. The study concluded that men dominate the American media, "in print, on television and online across all media outlets and in all news topics." The Women's Media Center study also revealed that men had 63 percent of the bylines in the main news sections of America's ten top-selling newspapers. That result, perhaps coincidentally, mirrors the gender differential in American newsrooms. Op-ed page scores are considerably worse. Nationwide, women account for slightly more than a third of op-ed writers.

In 2014, among the ten Pulitzer prizes that were awarded to individual journalists and photographers, only one went to a woman. The 2015 Pulitzers awards marked a welcome turnaround. Five of the year's nine journalism-related prizes awarded to individuals went to women.

Whether the rounds of layoffs that have hit newsrooms in recent years have affected women in disproportionate numbers to men has yet to be measured, even though there is anecdotal information that suggests it might be the case. The most astonishing backward step was the awkward firing by the *New York Times* of its first female executive editor, Jill Abramson, whose tenure as executive editor lasted less than three years.

Yet, even as these uneven numbers still exist in newsrooms around the country, in classrooms around the country, the story is different. Anecdotally, 60 to 70 percent of journalism students today are women. With this collection, we hope to offer to students, readers, and educators a perspective on the great contributions women have already made to this vital industry.

Clearly, the future for women in journalism is brighter than ever. Let these outstanding women stand as beacons and inspiration. Having successfully fought for inclusion over the past quarter century, their pursuit of of excellence is the model they bequeath to coming generations of women who aspire to follow them.

Joyce Hoffmann

Editor's Note

Many of the articles included in this collection are excerpts from longer series. For their generous contributions of free reprint rights, The Sager Group would like to thank the *Washington Post*, the *Tampa Bay Times* (formerly the *St. Petersburg Times*,) the *Chicago Tribune*, the *Virginian-Pilot*, the *Salt Lake Tribune*, the *Sacramento Bee*, the *LA Weekly*, Jacqui Banaszynski, Christine Brennan, and Eileen Welsome.

The Author's Afterwords included after every chapter are the product of a collaboration between the interviewers and the authors. After a question and answer session, the answers were transcribed and then edited into an "as told to" format, faithfully preserving the quotations, contextual meaning and voices of the authors while tightening for space and flow.

Jacqui Banaszynski

Jacqui Banaszynski is a Pulitzer Prize-winning journalist who has traveled all seven continents for stories—from the cold of Antarctica to the warmest reaches of the human heart. She has covered beauty pageants and popes, AIDS and the Olympics, dogsled expeditions and refugee camps, labor disputes and social movements. She won the 1988 Pulitzer Prize for feature writing for an intimate series on a gay farm couple dying of AIDS. She was a finalist for the 1986 Pulitzer Prize in international reporting for her on-the-ground coverage of the sub-Saharan famine. She won the nation's top sports writing award for deadline work at the 1988 Summer Olympics in Seoul.

Writing wasn't Banaszynski's first career choice. She had aspirations to be an athlete but grew up before Title IX gave girls access to the field. She dreamed of being an astronaut or airline pilot but was handicapped by height and gender. She probably should have been an architect, but in her rural Wisconsin school district in the 1960s girls weren't allowed into shop classes, where she could have learned drafting.

Instead she joined the high school newspaper staff, got the keys to the school car, and followed her curiosity. It turned out OK.

Banaszynski spent thirty years as a reporter and editor at newspapers in the Upper Midwest and Pacific Northwest. She has reported and guided dozens of award-winning projects across a spectrum of topics and styles. She now occupies an endowed Knight Chair professorship at the Missouri School of Journalism. She is also a faculty fellow at the Poynter Institute. In 2008 she was named to the Society of Feature Journalists Hall of Fame.

AIDS in the Heartland

An intimate look at a gay couple in rural America
facing AIDS

Part 1

Death is no stranger to the heartland. It is as natural as the seasons, as inevitable as farm machinery breaking down and farmers' bodies giving out after too many years of too much work.

But when death comes in the guise of AIDS, it is a disturbingly unfamiliar visitor, one better known in the gay districts and drug houses of the big cities, one that shows no respect for the usual order of life in the country.

The visitor has come to rural Glenwood, Minnesota.

Dick Hanson, a well-known liberal political activist who homesteads his family's century-old farm south of Glenwood, was diagnosed last summer with acquired immune deficiency syndrome. His partner of five years, Bert Henningson, carries the AIDS virus.

In the year that Hanson has been living—and dying—with AIDS, he has hosted some cruel companions: blinding headaches and failing vision, relentless nausea and deep fatigue, falling blood counts and worrisome coughs, and sleepless, sweat-soaked nights.

He has watched as his strong body, toughened by thirty-seven years on the farm, shrinks and stoops like that of an old man. He has weathered the family shame and community fear, the prejudice and whispered condemnations. He has read the reality in his partner's eyes, heard the death sentence from the doctors, and seen the hopelessness confirmed by the statistics.

But the statistics tell only half the story—the half about dying.

Statistics fail to tell much about the people they represent. About people like Hanson—a farmer who has nourished life in the fields, a peace activist who has marched for a safer planet, an idealist and gay activist who has campaigned for social justice, and now an AIDS patient who refuses to abandon his own future, however long it lasts.

The statistics say nothing of the joys of a carefully tended vegetable garden and new kittens under the shed, of tender teasing and magic hugs. Of flowers that bloom brighter and birds that sing sweeter, and simple pleasures grown profound against the backdrop of a terminal illness. Of the powerful bond between two people who pledged for better or worse and meant it.

"Who is to judge the value of life, whether it's one day or one week or one year?" Hanson said. "I find the quality of life a lot more important than the length of life. " Much has been written about the death that comes with AIDS, but little has been said about the living. Hanson and Henningson want to change that. They have opened their homes and their hearts to tell the whole story—beginning to end.

This is the first chapter.

The tiny snapshot is fuzzy and stained with ink. Two men in white T-shirts and corduroys stand at the edge of a barnyard, their muscled arms around each other's shoulders, a puzzled bull watching them from a field. The picture is overexposed, but the effect is pleasing, as if that summer day in 1982 was washed with a bit too much sun.

A summer later, the same men—one bearded and one not, one tall and one short—pose on the farmhouse porch in a mock American Gothic. Their pitchforks are mean looking and caked with manure. But their attempted severity fails; dimples betray their humor.

They are pictured together often through the years, draped with ribbons and buttons at political rallies, playing with their golden retriever, Nels, and, most frequently, working in their lavish vegetable garden.

The pictures drop off abruptly after 1985. One of the few shows the taller man, picking petunias from his mother's grave. He is startlingly thin by now, as a friend said, "like Gandhi after a long fast." His sun-bleached hair has turned dark, his bronze skin pallid. His body seems slack, as if it's caving in on itself.

The stark evidence of Dick Hanson's deterioration mars the otherwise rich memories captured in the photo album. But Hanson said only this: "When you lose your body, you become so much closer to your spirit. It gives you more emphasis of what the spirit is, that we are more important than withering skin and bone."

Hanson sat with his partner, Bert Henningson, in the small room at Minneapolis' Red Door Clinic on April 8, 1986, waiting for the results of Hanson's AIDS screening test.

He wouldn't think about how tired he had been lately. He had spent his life hefting hay bales with ease but now was having trouble hauling potato sacks at the Glenwood factory where he worked part time. He had lost ten pounds, had chronic diarrhea, and slept all afternoon. The dishes stayed dirty in the sink, the dinner uncooked, until Henningson got home from teaching at the University of Minnesota-Morris. It must be the stress.

His parents had been forced off the farm, and now he and his brothers faced foreclosure. Two favorite uncles were ill. He and Henningson were bickering a lot, about the housework and farm chores and Hanson's dark mood.

He had put off having the AIDS test for months, and Henningson hadn't pushed too hard. Neither was eager to know.

Now, as the nurse entered the room with his test results, Hanson convinced himself the news would be good. It had been four years since he had indulged in casual weekend sex at the gay bathhouse in Minneapolis, since he and Henningson committed to each other. Sex outside their relationship had been limited and "safe," with no exchange of semen or blood. He had taken care of himself, eating homegrown food and working outdoors, and his farmer's body always had responded with energy and strength. Until now.

"I put my positive thinking mind on and thought I'd be negative," Hanson said. "Until I saw that red circle."

The reality hit him like a physical punch. As he slumped forward in shock, Henningson—typically pragmatic—asked the nurse to prepare another needle. He, too, must be tested. Then Henningson gathered Hanson in his arms and said, "I will never leave you, Dick."

Hanson is one of 210 Minnesotans and 36,000 Americans who have been diagnosed with AIDS since the disease was identified in 1981. More than half of those patients already have died, and doctors say it is only a matter of time for the rest. The statistics show that 80 to 90 percent of AIDS sufferers die within two years of diagnosis; the average time of survival is fourteen months after the first bout of pneumocystis, a form of pneumonia that brought Hanson to the brink of death last August and again in December.

"For a long time, I was just one of those statistics," Hanson said. "I was a very depressing person to be around. I wanted to get away from me."

He lost twenty more pounds in the two weeks after receiving his test results. One of his uncles died and, on the morning of the funeral, Hanson's mother died unexpectedly. Genevieve Hanson was seventy-five years old, a gentle but sturdy woman who was especially close to Dick, the third of her six children. He handled the arrangements, picking gospel hymns for the service and naming eight of her women friends as honorary pallbearers—a first in the history of their tiny country church.

But Hanson never made it to his mother's funeral. The day she was buried, he collapsed of exhaustion and fever. That night, Henningson drove him to Glenwood for the first of three hospitalizations—forty-two days' worth—in 1986.

"Dick was real morbid last summer," Henningson said. "He led people to believe it was curtains and was being very vague and dramatic. We all said to be hopeful, but it was as if something had gripped his psyche and was pulling him steadily downward week after week."

Hanson had given up, but Henningson refused to. He worked frantically to rekindle that spark of hope—and life. He read Hanson news articles about promising new AIDS drugs and stories of terminal cancer patients defying the odds. He brought home tapes about the power of positive thinking and fed Hanson healthy food. He talked to him steadily of politics and all the work that remained to be done.

He forced himself, and sometimes Hanson, to work in the garden, making it bigger than ever. They planted fifty-eight varieties of vegetables in an organic, high-yield plot and christened it the Hope Garden.

But Hanson returned to the hospital in August, dangerously ill with the dreaded pneumonia. His weight had dropped to 112 from his usual 160. He looked and walked like an old-man version of himself. "I had an out-of-body type experience there, and even thought I had died for a time," he said. "It was completely quiet and very calm and I thought, 'This is really nice.' I expected some contact with the next world. Then I had this conversation with God that it wasn't my time yet, and he sent me back."

Hanson was home in time to harvest the garden, and to freeze and can its bounty. He had regained some of his former spunk and was taking an interest again in the world around him.

"I'd be sitting next to him on the couch, holding his hand, and once in a while he'd get that little smile on his face and nod like there was something to hold on to," Henningson said. "And a small beam of life would emerge."

A month later, Hanson's spirits received another boost when he was honored at a massive fund-raising dinner. Its sponsors included Democratic-Farmer-Labor Party (DFL) notables—among them Governor Rudy Perpich, Lieutenant Governor Marlene Johnson, St. Paul mayor George Latimer, Minneapolis mayor Don Fraser and congressmen Bruce Vento and Martin

Sabo—and radical political activists Hanson had worked with over the years, farmers who had stood with him to fight farm foreclosures and the West Central power line, women who remembered his support during the early years of the women's movement, members of the gay and lesbian community, and other AIDS sufferers. What started as a farewell party, a eulogy of sorts, turned into a celebration of Hanson's life. Folk singer Larry Long played songs on an Indian medicine man's healing flute. Friends gathered in a faith circle to will their strength to Hanson. Dozens of people lined up to embrace Hanson and Henningson. For most, it was the first time they had touched an AIDS patient.

"People are coming through on this thing and people are decent," Hanson said. "We find people in all walks of life who are with us in this struggle . . . It's that kind of thing that makes it all worth it."

So when the pneumonia came back in December, this time with more force, Hanson was ready to fight. "The doctor didn't give him any odds," Henningson said. Hanson was put on a respirator, funeral arrangements were discussed, estranged relatives were called to his bedside.

"He wrote me a note," Henningson said. "'When can I get out of here?' He and I had never lied to each other, and I wasn't about to start. I said, 'You might be getting out of here in two or three days, but it might be God you're going to see. But there is a slim chance, so if you'll just fight . . .'"

People from Hanson's AIDS support group stayed at the hospital round the clock, in shifts, talking to him and holding his hand as he drifted in and out of a coma. Friends brought Christmas to the stark hospital room: cards papered the walls and a giant photograph of Hanson's Christmas tree, the one left back at the farmhouse, was hung.

The rest was up to Hanson.

"I put myself in God's healing cocoon of love and had my miracle," he said. "I call it my Christmas miracle."

He was released from intensive care on Christmas Eve day and since has devoted his life to carrying a seldom-heard message of hope to other AIDS patients, to give them—and himself—a reason to live as science races to find a cure.

"I'd like to think that God has a special purpose for my life," he said. His smile under the thinning beard is sheepish; faith is personal, and easily misunderstood.

"I don't want to come across like Oral Roberts, but . . . I believe that God can grant miracles. He has in the past and does now and will in the future. And maybe I can be one of those miracles, the one who proves the experts wrong."

Hanson has spent his life on the front line of underdog causes—always liberal, often revolutionary, and sometimes unpopular.

"Somewhere along the line Dick was exposed to social issues and taught that we can make a difference," said Mary Stackpool, a neighbor and fellow political activist. "That's what Dick has been all about—showing that one person can make a difference."

Hanson put it in terms less grand: "You kind of have to be an eternal optimist to be a farmer. There's something that grows more each year than what you put into the farm . . . I've always been involved in trying to change things for the better."

He was born into the national prosperity of 1950 and grew up through the social turmoil of the 1960s. A fifth-grade teacher sparked his enthusiasm in John F. Kennedy's presidential campaign. He was thirteen when his father joined the radical National Farmers Organization, took the family to picket at the Land O'Lakes plant in nearby Alexandria and participated in a notorious milk-dumping action.

He later led rural campaigns for Eugene McCarthy, George McGovern, Mark Dayton, and his current hero, Jesse Jackson. He led protests against the Vietnam War and was a conscientious objector. He organized rival factions to try to stop construction of the high voltage power line that snakes through western Minnesota.

He was an early member of the farm activist group Groundswell, fighting to stop a neighbor's foreclosure one day, his own family's the next. The 473-acre Hanson farm has been whittled to 40 by bankruptcy; Hanson and Henningson are struggling to salvage the farmhouse and some surrounding wetlands.

He has been arrested five times, staged a fast to draw attention to the power line protest and stood at the podium of the 1980 DFL district convention to announce—for the first time publicly—that he was gay. That same year, he was elected one of the first openly gay members of the Democratic National Committee and, in 1984, made an unsuccessful bid for the party's nomination for Congress from the Second District. In 1983, he and Henningson were photographed in their fields for a 1983 *Newsweek* magazine story about gays responding to the AIDS crisis; neither knew at the time they carried the virus.

"He just throws himself into a cause and will spare nothing," Stackpool said. "He will expose himself totally to bring out the desired good."

Now the cause is AIDS. The struggle is more personal, the threat more direct. But for Hanson, it has become yet another opportunity to make a difference.

"He's handling this just as he would anything else-with strength and lots of courage and hope," said Amy Lee, another longtime friend and fellow activist. "And with that pioneering spirit, if there's anything he can do, any way he can help other victims, any time he can speak—he'll go for it."

Hanson has become one of the state's most visible AIDS patients. He and Henningson are frequently interviewed for news stories, were the subject of a recent four-part series on KCMT-TV in Alexandria, and speak at AIDS education seminars in churches and schools throughout the state. Last month, Hanson addressed the state senate's special informational meeting on AIDS.

"I want to take the mask off the statistics and say we are human beings and we have feelings," he said. "I want to say there is life after AIDS."

Rather than retreat to the anonymity of the big city, as many AIDS sufferers do, Hanson has maintained a high political profile in Pope County. He is chairman of the DFL Party in Senate District 15. He and Henningson continue to do business with area merchants and worship weekly at the country church of Hanson's childhood, Barsness Lutheran.

"I've always been a very public person, and I've had no regrets," Hanson said. "One thing my dad always emphasized was the principle that honesty was the most important thing in life."

Hanson and Henningson use their story to personalize the AIDS epidemic and to debunk some of the stereotypes and myths about AIDS and its victims. They are farmers who have milked cows, slopped hogs, and baled hay like everyone else. Their politics and sexual orientation may disturb some. But their voices and values are more familiar, and perhaps better understood, than those of some of their urban counterparts.

"It makes people aware that it can happen here," said Sharon Larson, director of nursing at Glacial Ridge Hospital in Glenwood.

That honesty has carried a price. A conservative Baptist minister from Glenwood criticized their lifestyle at a community forum and again in a column in the *Pope County Tribune*. Some of Hanson's relatives were upset by the Alexandria television show and demanded he keep his troubling news to himself. There have been rumblings in his church from people concerned about taking communion with him, and a minor disturbance erupted in a Glenwood school when his niece was teased about him.

But his connections also carry clout.

"It brings it a little closer home to the guys in the capitol who control the purse strings," a fellow AIDS patient said.

When they speak, Hanson and Henningson touch on a variety of topics: the need for national health insurance to guarantee equitable care, the cruelty of policies that force AIDS patients into poverty before they are eligible for medical assistance, the need for flex-time jobs so AIDS sufferers can continue to be productive, the imperative of safe sex.

They also stress the personal aspects of the disease: the need for patients to be touched rather than shunned, the importance of support from family and friends, and, most dear to Hanson, the healing powers of hope.

"I know there are some who die because they give up," he said. "They have no hope, no reason to fight. Everything they're faced with is so desperate and dismal . . . I believe the biggest obstacle for us who have AIDS or an AIDS-related complex is fighting the fear and anxiety we have over the whole thing. Every positive thing, every bit of hope is something to hold on to."

Next month, Hanson and Henningson will celebrate five years together, perhaps with a gathering of friends and an exchange of rings. They exchanged vows privately that first summer while sitting in their car under the prairie night.

"We asked the blessing of the spirit above," Hanson said. "It was a pretty final thing."

At first blush, they seem an unlikely couple.

"Bert the scholar and Dick the activist . . . In some ways they're just worlds apart," Stackpool said. "But politics brought them together, and now they take delight in those differences and in their special traits. They've figured out things many married couples never come close to figuring out."

Henningson is bookish and intense, a PhD in international trade, a professor and essayist. He is a doer and organizer. He charts the monthly household budget on his Apple computer, itemizing everything from mortgage payments to medicine to cat food. He sets a hearty dinner table, which is cleared and washed as soon as the last bit of food is gone. He buries himself in his work during the week, becomes reclusive when he retreats to the farm on weekends, and has worked hard over the years to control an explosive temper.

Hanson is more social, an easygoing, nonstop talker with a starburst of interests. He spent twelve years detouring through social activism before finally earning a bachelor's degree in political science at the university's Morris campus. He has a political junkie's memory for names, dates, and events, thrills in company and is quick to offer refreshments, having inherited his mother's belief in friendship through food.

But they also have much in common.

Henningson, forty, grew up on a farm near Graceville, in neighboring Big Stone County. His life paralleled Hanson's in many respects: the radical farm movement, antiwar protests, involvement in liberal political campaigns.

Both suppressed their homosexuality until they were almost thirty. Hanson kept so active with politics and the farm that he didn't have time for a social life. After acknowledging his homosexuality, his sexual life involved weekend excursions to the Twin Cities for anonymous encounters at the gay bathhouse.

"I had to taste all the fruit in the orchard," he said. "I had some real special relationships, but if they suggested it just be us I felt trapped, like they were closing in on me."

Henningson threw himself into graduate school, tried marriage, and took on a demanding career in Washington, DC, as an aide to former US Rep. Richard Nolan. He divorced and returned to Minnesota, where he enrolled in a human sexuality program at the University of Minnesota. He had three homosexual involvements before meeting Hanson at a political convention.

"There were some major forces working in the universe that were compelling us together," Henningson said. "I don't know that we even had much to say about it. I've always believed in serendipity, but I also feel you have to give serendipity a little help. So I didn't sit back and wait for Dick to call—I called him."

Any doubts Hanson had about their relationship were squelched by his mother. She visited the farmhouse one Sunday morning with freshly baked caramel rolls, which she served Hanson and Henningson in bed. Henningson was accepted as part of the family, moved to the farm, and eventually assumed financial responsibility for the family's farm operations.

"It was so good to work together, to sweat together, to farrow those sows and help the sows have those little piglets," Henningson said. "We literally worked dawn to dusk."

That hard but somewhat idyllic life has been altered drastically by AIDS. Hanson does what he can, when he can, perhaps baking cookies or doing the laundry. But the burden of earning an income, running the house, and caring for Hanson has fallen heavily on Henningson's shoulders.

Hanson's medical bills—totaling more than $50,000 so far—are covered by welfare. Henningson's temporary job at the state Department of Agriculture, where he writes farm policy proposals, pays their personal bills, helps pay their apartment rent in the Twin Cities so Hanson can be near medical care during the week, and allows them to keep the farmhouse.

"Dick's optimism is fine," Henningson said. "But you have to help optimism along now and then with a little spade work. I ended up doing all of the work with no help. What could have happened is that I could have grown resentful and blamed the victim.

"But I tried to put myself in his shoes—having pneumonia twice—and with all my anger and short temper, could I live with that? Could I even get through that? I'd probably have the strength to go to a field and dig a hole and when the time came crawl in and bury myself. But I don't know if I'd have the strength to do what he did."

So, their commitment to each other remains absolute, perhaps strengthened by facing a crisis together.

"When you know that somebody's going to stand by you, and when they prove that they will, when they go through what Bert's gone through this past year in putting up with me... you just know it's very, very special what you have," Hanson said.

Each week, Hanson checks in at the AIDS clinic at Hennepin County Medical Center. He and Henningson make the three-hour drive to Minneapolis every Monday and spend their week in the Twin Cities. Henningson has work through June at the Agriculture Department. Hanson's full-time job is AIDS.

He has his blood tested to determine his white blood cell count his body's natural defense system. It often is below 1,000; a healthy person's count would be closer to 5,000.

He has a physical exam, chats with two or three doctors, gives encouragement to fellow patients, and collects hugs from the nursing staff. He is a favorite with the social workers, who tease him about his lack of interest in the women who flock to his examination room each week for a visit.

He does weekly inhalation therapy, breathing an antibiotic into his lungs to ward off the dreaded pneumonia. Then he buses to St. Paul for a long, healing massage from one of several local massage therapists who donate time to AIDS patients.

Thursday mornings find him at the University of Minnesota Hospital and Clinic for eye treatments. Doctors inject medicine directly into his eyeball to thwart a virus that is attacking his vision. Sometimes the needle punctures a blood vessel, leaving Hanson with bright red patches in his eyes.

On Thursday nights, he and Henningson attend an AIDS support group meeting, where as many as thirty patients, relatives, and friends gather to share comfort and information.

For eight months, Hanson has taken AZT, or azidothymidine, an experimental drug believed to prolong life for AIDS sufferers. He takes other drugs to counter the nausea caused by AZT's high toxicity, and he is watched closely for bone marrow suppression.

He uses various underground treatments, all with his doctor's knowledge.

He rubs solvent on his skin to try to stimulate a response from his immune system, and spreads a home-brewed cholesterol agent on his toast, hoping it will help render the virus inert.

He watches his diet to prevent diarrhea and takes various prescription drugs for depression and anxiety.

His spare time, what there is of it, is devoured by long waits for the bus or slow walks to his various appointments. He naps often to keep his energy level up and spends evenings watching the Twins on TV. Reading has become painful for him, straining his eyes and making him dizzy.

"It comes back and back and back many times," he said. "Is this my total life? Has the illness become such an all-encompassing thing that my life will never be judged by anything but this brand of AIDS?"

Weekends are spent on the farm, where Hanson often can be found kneeling in his flowerbeds. The impatiens, moss roses, and sweet Williams are planted especially thick this summer; Hanson was eager to see their cheerful pinks and reds cover the crumbling stone foundation of the old farmhouse. He insists on having fresh flowers in the house every day, even dandelions and thistles. Once, after pranksters broke the peony bushes in the church cemetery, Hanson gathered up the broken blossoms and took them home, placing them around the house in shallow bowls of water.

Or he can be found singing in the empty silo, practicing hymns for Sunday's church service. His voice is sweet and natural, with a good range. It is inherited, he says, from his mother, who sang to him when he was in the womb and tuned in opera on the radio in the farm kitchen when he was a youngster. He has sung for his brothers' weddings but is better, he says, at funerals.

On hot summer nights, he and Henningson sleep in twin beds in a screened porch upstairs. The room is kept cool by towering shade trees and constant breezes blowing off the marsh that winds in front of the house. From there, the men note the comings and goings of their neighbors: egrets and blue herons, Canada geese that feed on what Henningson calls Green Scum Pond, a doe and her buff-colored fawn. There is an owl in the nearby woods, a peregrine falcon nesting in the farmhouse eaves, and an unseen loon that sings to them at dusk.

If the weekend is slow, the weather is mild, and his energy is high, Hanson can be found in a dinghy somewhere on Lake Minnewaska, the sparkling centerpiece of Pope County. He's a skilled fisherman and remembers weekends when he would haul home a catch of 200 pan fish for one of his mother's famous fries.

"I find that going out in the garden is a good way to get away from things, or going fishing, or just visiting with people and talking," he said. "I don't want my whole life to be branded by AIDS."

Hanson awakes in the Minneapolis apartment on a recent morning to the sound of his mother's voice.

"It wasn't part of any dream," he said. "Just her voice, crystal clear, calling."

He has been running a fever for several days and suffering headaches. His white blood cell count has dropped precipitously. His chatter, usually cheerful, is tinged with fear.

"I got pretty emotional about it," he said. "But Bert held me and said, 'Don't be afraid. Don't fight it.' And I remember a year ago when I was so sick, and she was reaching to me, and I was so scared I was almost pushing her away. And Bert said not to fight it, to let her comfort me even if she's reaching to me on a level we don't understand . . .

"There are days I think I'm just going to get out of this, put this whole thing behind me and get a job and go on with my life again. Then I have a rough day like this and I have to look at things much more realistically."

Hanson seldom talks of death. When his health is stable, there seems little point. He has beaten the odds before and will, he says, again.

"Intermittently, there has been some denial," said his physician, Dr. Margaret Simpson, director of the sexually transmitted disease clinic at Hennepin County Medical Center. "That's not too surprising. When you're feeling good, it's easy to think this isn't true.

"But he's deteriorating again, and it's worrisome. I don't make predictions, but I think now in terms of weeks and months rather than months and years."

Hanson senses that urgency. But he remains a fighter. His attitude, he says, is not one of delusion but of defiance.

"I think I'll know when the time is right and it's coming," he said. "Should it be, I'm ready to meet my maker. But I'm not ready to give up and say there's nothing that will turn around so I can live."

A week later, Hanson is in the hospital. The headaches are worse, and doctors do a painful spinal tap to determine if the AIDS virus has entered his brain. His white blood cell count is dangerously low, but a transfusion is too risky.

It is the first hospitalization in six months, and only an overnight stay for tests, but it evokes painful memories of the past and fears for the future.

Henningson telephones Hanson's sister.

"I told Mary it may be only three or four months and we have to respond to him accordingly," he said. "Not treat him as someone who's going to die, but accord him the time and attention you want. We can't just say, 'See you next week.' It's not a matter of dealing with certitude anymore, but a great deal of uncertainty about where it's going to lead."

Hanson is quiet this evening and seems distracted. The Twins game plays silently on the hospital room TV, but relief pitcher Jeff Reardon is losing and Hanson pays only passing interest. He gets up once during the evening to vomit and occasionally presses his hand to his temple. But he never mentions the nausea, the throbbing headache, or the pain from the spinal tap.

Henningson sits next to him on the bed and thumbs through their photo album, recalling lighter times. Suddenly, Hanson waves his hand vaguely, at the room, at his life. "I'll miss all this," he confided. "I'll just miss all these wonderful people."

Then he and Henningson discuss—gently—the logistics of his death. Should he be placed in a nursing home if he becomes invalid? Should life-sustaining measures be used if he falls into a coma again? Should he donate his body to research?

The morbid conversation is held in matter-of-fact tones and seems to soothe Hanson. It is Henningson's way of pulling out the emotions, the soft rage and futility that Hanson otherwise would keep tucked inside.

"Talking about things like that helps you understand your mortality, that it may not be much longer," Henningson said. "And that helps relieve your fears. Dick's fears are not so much for himself as for me. Will I live out here all by myself? Will I find someone else? I say don't worry about that, it's out of your control."

But Henningson, too, is shaken. He sits at the window next to Hanson's hospital bed, and holds his hand. Finally, he abandons the diversionary talk and cries. He is worried about losing the farm, about the political hassles involved in getting housing assistance, about getting a job after his contract with the state expires, about not having enough time left with Hanson.

And he can't help but worry about the AIDS virus in his body and his own health prospects. Although he guards his health carefully and is optimistic about medical progress on the AIDS front, he fears that the stress of caring for Hanson is taking its toll. He watches Hanson and wonders if he is watching his own future.

Then he comforts himself with a wish.

"I want to be cremated and have my ashes thrown in Big Stone Lake. And from there I would flow to the Minnesota River, down to the Mississippi River, all the way to the Gulf. And I'll hit the Gulf Stream and travel the world.

"And I told Dick if he'd like to be cremated, they could put him in Lake Minnewaska, and he would flow to the Chippewa River and then into the Minnesota and the Mississippi and to the Gulf and around the world. And at some point we would merge and we'd be together forever."

He stops, perhaps embarrassed.

"You can't control what happens to people after they're dead," he said. "But even if it doesn't happen, it's a lovely, consoling thought."

June 21, 1987

Author's Afterword

I was an overly curious little girl growing up in the 1950s and '60s in rural, old-world America. Who knows if you're born with curiosity or you're introduced to it, but I remember my mother always telling me I asked too many questions, and I remember my father paying me a quarter if I would stop talking for fifteen minutes at a time.

Growing up, there weren't a lot of opportunities for women of my generation, careerwise. As it happened, though, the high school put out the official, legal community newspaper, so the high school journalism class was really, really special for lots of reasons. We covered the community. The newspaper was a place to which I gravitated, and it just seemed to work for me. Even back then it was stressful, but in a kind of fun, joyful way. So I started doing that when I was fourteen. The writing part was always hard for me, but the reporting part was always like, "Really, I get to do this? Cool."

I don't think any journalist who's worth his or her salt or trying to do the job well doesn't face obstacles. Everybody faces obstacles, whether it's the lawyer who won't give you access to the people you want to interview, or the politician who won't answer your questions honestly. Sometimes you're in a war zone where you might get killed. Or in a developing nation, stepping into a rickety airplane that's about to fly over the jungle. That's what we journalists do; we face the obstacles. And then we surmount the obstacles. If you want a story badly enough, anyway.

As a young woman in the professional world I faced obstacles, yes. When I started, there were very few women in news positions. Women were in features, or they covered society news, or they were on the women's pages—not including, of course, those incredible women who stepped into newsrooms during World War II when the men were off at war. Of course, once the men came home most of those women got pushed back out of the newsrooms. That was the late 1940s. It wasn't until the late sixties and early seventies that women started making headway again.

When I was young, there was sexual harassment, there was sexual discrimination, there were come-ons from sources. You had to be quick on your feet about how you dealt with sources, editors, and colleagues who didn't take you seriously. And you had to learn how to deal with those individuals who treated you like a sex object and not a professional doing her job. You had to be ready to deal with that. And you had to fight the doubts of men who thought women could not do the same jobs in the newsroom as men.

I can't say my sex was as big a barrier as the women who were fifteen years older than me, because they're the ones who really fought those battles. They kicked the door open. My generation, our job was to walk through the door and do something once you got into the room. It wasn't like there weren't women around. It wasn't like there weren't strong women around. But it wasn't at all like we were accepted as equal players with the boys. We had to fight for it. We had to be like, "Wherever you want to send me, I'll do the best job; I'll get there first." Back then, in general, the few women in the newsrooms would bond and kind of band together. We would say to each other, "We're going to change the newsroom culture. We're going to make a difference." In some cases we were all on the same page, and in some cases we weren't. All women are not the same person, of course. Mostly, our relationships were supportive, but sometimes, the relationships among women were very negative and competitive. It takes all kinds, and we all reacted differently.

I think journalists have a reputation for being arrogant, but I think the truth is we're not very good at talking about ourselves. We're the people who wanted to ask a million questions. We're not always good at answering them.

What I am most attached to when I look at my career overall is the sense that I have tried to do this work with passion for its purpose, dedication to its craft, and a real compassion for the people I have met along the way. It's not like I'm a big walking hug. I have just as much edge and snark as any journalist. But I really care about the people I meet and the stories I've written. What happens to those folks matters to me. And I hope that shows in my work.

There's no question working in journalism has made me more aware of other people's realities, other people's views, and other people's values. It has allowed me to grow larger than the small screen of the perspectives with which I entered young adulthood.

Journalism is one profession where your work can help to make you a better person, a wiser person. For example, after being in a situation where I had to talk frankly about death with two men dying of AIDS, after thinking about death and reading and learning about it, I found that I was better prepared when death visited my family. Through journalism I've met all kinds of people who find themselves in all kinds of positions. I've learned that they all share a common humanity, and this has helped me be nonjudgmental about my family and friends, to understand that frankly, shit happens. The sense of perspective I've gained is enormous.

Deborah Blum

Deborah Blum, a Pulitzer Prize-winning science journalist, author, and blogger, is the Helen Firstbrook Franklin Professor of Journalism at the University of Wisconsin-Madison.

Author of five books and a popular guide to science writing, her most recent publication, *The Poisoner's Handbook*, was a *New York Times* paperback best seller and became a PBS documentary on *American Experience* in January 2013. Previous books *include Ghost Hunters: William James and the Scientific Search for Life after Death* (2006); *Love at Goon Park: Harry Harlow and the Science of Affection*, a 2002 finalist for the *Los Angeles Times* Book Prize; *Sex on the Brain* (1997); and *The Monkey Wars* (1994). She is also coeditor of *A Field Guide for Science Writers*, published in a second edition in 2006.

Blum writes a monthly environmental chemistry blog for the *New York Times* called "Poison Pen." She also blogs about toxic compounds at *Wired*; her blog "Elemental" was named one of the top 25 blogs of 2013 by *Time*. She has written for a wide range of other publications including *Scientific American*, Slate, *Tin House*, the Atavist, *Wall Street Journal*, *The Guardian*, *Los Angeles Times*, and *Discover*. Before joining the university in 1997, she was a science writer for the *Sacramento Bee*, where she won the Pulitzer in 1992 for her reporting on ethical issues in primate research. Her work has been anthologized in *Best American Science Writing*, *Best American Science and Nature Writing*, and *The Open Laboratory: Best Science On-Line*. She was the 2014 guest editor of *Best America Science and Nature Writing*, published by Houghton Mifflin.

Blum is currently at work on a book for Penguin Press on the history of poisonous food.

Monkey Wars

Behind the scenes of the animal rights debate

Part 1

On the days when he's scheduled to kill, Allen Merritt summons up his ghosts. They come to him from the shadows of a twenty-year-old memory. Eleven human babies, from his first year out of medical school. All born prematurely. All lost within one week when their lungs failed.

"We were virtually helpless," said Merritt, now head of the neonatal intensive care unit at the University of California, Davis Medical Center. " There's nothing worse than being a new physician and standing there watching babies die. It's a strong motivator to make things different." On this cool morning, he needs that memory. The experiment he's doing is deceptively simple: a test of a new chemical to help premature babies breathe. But it's no clinical arrangement of glass tubes. He's trying the drug on two tiny rhesus monkeys, each weighing barely one-third of a pound. At the end of the experiment, he plans to cut their lungs apart, to see how it worked.

Even his ghosts don't make that easy. Nestled in a towel on a surgical table, eyes shut, hands curled, the monkeys look unnervingly human. "The link between people and monkeys is very close," Merritt said. "Much closer than some people would like to think. There's a real sense of sadness, that we can only get the information we need if we kill them."

Once, there was no such need to justify. Once, American researchers could go through two hundred thousand monkeys a year, without question. Now, the numbers are less. Perhaps twenty thousand monkeys will die every year, out of an estimated forty thousand used in experiments. But the pressures are greater.

These days, it seems that if researchers plan one little study slicing the toes off squirrel monkeys, siphoning blood from rhesus macaques, hiding baby monkeys from their mothers, they face not just questions, but picket signs, lawsuits, and death threats phoned in at night.

The middle ground in the war over research with monkeys and apes has become so narrow as to be nearly invisible. And even that is eroding.

Intelligent, agile, fast, but not fast enough, these nonhuman primates are rapidly being driven from the planet, lost to heavy trapping and vanishing rain forests. Of sixty-three primate species in Asia where most research monkeys come from, only one is not listed as vulnerable.

Primate researchers believe they are making the hard choice, using nonhuman primates for medical research because they must, because no other animal so closely mirrors the human body and brain. During the 1950s, American scientists did kill hundreds of thousands of monkeys for polio research, using the animals' organs to grow virus, dissecting their brains to track the spread of the infection. But out of those experiments came a polio vaccine. Using monkeys, scientists have created vaccines for measles, learned to fight leprosy, developed antirejection drugs that make organ transplants possible.

Outside the well-guarded laboratory wall, that choice can seem less obvious. Animal rights advocates draw a dark description of research. They point out that AIDS researchers have used endangered chimpanzees, without, so far, managing to help people dying of the disease. Further, conservationists fear that the research is introducing dangerous infection into the country's chimpanzee breeding program, badly needed to help counter the loss of wild animals.

"They're guzzling up money and animals and for what?" asked Shirley McGreal, head of the nonprofit International Primate Protection League. "Why not use those resources in helping sick people, why infect healthy animals?"

Her argument is that of animal advocates across the country, that scientists are sacrificing our genetic next-of-kin for their own curiosity, dubious medical gains, and countless tax dollars.

No one is sure exactly how much money scientists spend experimenting on monkeys, although the National Institutes of Health alone allocates almost $40 million annually to its primate research programs, including one in Davis. Overall, more than half of NIH's research grants, approaching $5 billion, involve at least some animal research.

Rats and mice are the most abundant, some fifteen million are used in experiments every year.

For people such as McGreal, these are animals in a very wrong place. McGreal's long-term goal for monkeys is simple: out of the laboratory, back into what remains of the rain forests.

"I used to think that we could persuade those people to understand what we do," said Frederick King, director of the Yerkes Regional Primate Research Center in Atlanta. "But it's impossible. And that's why I no longer describe this as a battle. I describe it as a war."

The rift is so sharp that it is beginning to reshape science itself.

"Science has organized," marveled Alex Pacheco, founder of the country's most powerful animal rights group, People for the Ethical Treatment of Animals. "Researchers are outlobbying us and outspending us. They've become so aggressive that it puts new pressure on us. We're going to have to fight tougher too."

In the past year, researchers have made it clear just how much they dislike the role of victim. If Pacheco wants to call scientists "sadistic bastards," which he does frequently, then Fred King is more than ready to counter with his description of PETA: "Fanatic, fringe, one of the most despicable organizations in the country."

But beyond name-calling, the research community is realizing its political power. Its lobbyists are pushing for laws that would heavily penalize protesters who interfere with research projects. And this year, to the fury of animal rights groups, primate researchers were able to win a special exemption from public records laws, shielding their plans for captive monkey care.

For researchers, the attention focused on them is an almost dizzying turnabout. Not so long ago, they could have hung their monkey care plans as banners across streets and no one would have read them.

"When I first started, twenty years ago, monkeys were twenty-five dollars each," said Roy Henrickson, chief of lab animal care at the University of California, Berkeley. "You'd use one once and you'd throw it away. I'd talk to lab vets who were under pressure about dogs and I'd say, I'm sure glad I'm in nonhuman primates. Nobody cares about them."

He can date the change precisely, back to 1981, the year Pacheco went undercover in the laboratory of Edward Taub. Taub was a specialist in nerve damage, working in Silver Springs, MD. To explore the effects of ruined nerves, he took seventeen rhesus monkeys and sliced apart nerves close to the spinal column, crippling their limbs. Then he studied the way they coped with the damage.

Pacheco left the laboratory with an enduring mistrust of scientists and an armload of inflammatory photographs: monkeys wrenched into vices, packed into filthy cages. Monkeys who, with no feeling in their hands, had gnawed their fingers to the bone. Some of the wounds were oozing with infection, darkening with gangrene.

Many believe those battered monkeys were the fuse, lighting the current, combative cycle of animal rights. In the fury over the Silver Springs monkeys, Pacheco was able to build People for the Ethical Treatment of Animals into a national force, and across the country, the movement gained power. Today, membership in animal advocacy groups tops twelve million; the thirty largest organizations report a combined annual income approaching $70 million.

And primate researchers have suddenly found themselves under scrutiny of the most hostile kind.

There are experiments, such as Allen Merritt's work to salvage premature infants, that the critics will sometimes reluctantly accept. The compound that Merritt is testing on young monkeys is a kind of lubricant for the lungs, a slippery ooze that coats the tissues within, allowing them to flex as air comes in and out.

Without the ooze, called surfactant, the tissues don't stretch. They rip. The problem for premature babies is that the body doesn't develop surfactant until late in fetal development, some thirty-five weeks into a pregnancy. Although artificial surfactants are now available, Merritt doesn't believe they're good enough. Two-thirds of the tiniest premature babies, weighing less than a pound at birth, still die as their lungs shred. He's trying to improve the medicine.

"There could be a scientific defense for doing that, even though it's extremely cruel," said Elliot Katz, head of In Defense of Animals, a national animal rights group, headquartered in San Rafael, California.

But Katz finds most of the work indefensible. He can rapidly cite examples of a different sort, a US Air Force experiment, which involved draining 40 percent of the blood from rhesus macaques and then spinning them on a centrifuge, to simulate injured astronauts; a New York University study of addiction, in which monkeys were strapped into metal boxes and forced to inhale concentrated cocaine fumes.

Last year, animal advocates rallied against a proposed study at the Seattle center, a plan to take thirteen baby rhesus macaques from their mothers and try to drive them crazy through isolation, keeping them caged away from their mothers and without company. The scientists acknowledged that they might drive the monkeys to self-mutilation; rhesus macaques do badly in isolation, rocking, pulling out their hair, sometimes tearing their skin open.

This year, protesters have been holding candlelight vigils outside the home of a researcher at a Maryland military facility, the Uniformed Services

University of the Health Sciences. That project involves cutting the toes from kittens and young squirrel monkeys and then, after they've wobbled into adjustment, killing them to look at their brains.

In both cases, there are scientific explanations. The Washington scientists wanted to analyze the chemistry of a troubled brain, saying that it could benefit people with mental illness. The Maryland researchers are brain-mapping, drafting a careful picture of how the mind reorganizes itself to cope with crippling injury.

But these are not, and may never be, explanations acceptable to those crusading for animal rights. "This is just an example of someone doing something horrible to animals because he can get paid for it," said Laurie Raymond, of Seattle's Progressive Animal Welfare Society, which campaigned against the baby monkey experiment and takes credit for the fact that it failed to get federal funding.

Researchers say they are tired of telling the public about their work, documenting it in public records, and having that very openness used against them. The Washington protesters learned about the baby monkey experiment through a meeting of the university's animal care committee, which is public. The Maryland work came to light through a listing of military-funded research, which is public.

When the US Department of Agriculture, which inspects research facilities annually, complained about the housekeeping at the Tulane Regional Primate Research Center in Louisiana, the director wrote the agency a furious letter. Didn't administrators realize that the report was public and made scientists look bad?

"The point I am making is that USDA, without intending to do so, is playing into the hands of the animal rights/anti-vivisectionists whose stated goal is to abolish animal research," wrote center head Peter Gerone, arguing that the complaints could have been handled privately. "If you are trying to placate the animal rights activists by nitpicking inspections... you will only serve to do us irreparable harm."

When Arnold Arluke, a sociologist at Boston's Northeastern University, spent six years studying lab workers and drafted a report saying that some actually felt guilty about killing animals, he found himself suddenly under pressure. "I was told putting that information out would be like giving ammunition to the enemy," he said.

He titled his first talk "Guilt Among Animal Researchers." The manager of the laboratory where he spoke changed guilt to stress. When he published that in a journal, the editors thought that stress was too controversial. They changed the title to "Uneasiness Among Lab Workers." When he gave another talk at a pharmaceutical company, he was told uneasiness was too strong. They changed the title to "How to Deal with Your Feelings." Arluke figures his next talk will be untitled.

"People in animal research don't even want to tell others what they do," he said. One woman I talked to was standing in line at a grocery store, and when she told the person next to her what she did, the woman started yelling at her, 'You should be ashamed of yourself.'"

And when new lab animal care rules were published this year, it was clear that researchers were no longer willing to freely hand over every record of operation.

The new regulations resulted from congressional changes in 1985 to the Animal Welfare Act. They included a special provision for the care of laboratory primates; legislators wanted scientists to recognize that these were sociable, intelligent animals.

The provision, perhaps the most controversial in the entire act, regarded the psychological well-being of primates. When the USDA began drafting rules in response to the new law, it received a record thirty-five thousand letters of comment. And fourteen thousand consisted of a written shouting match over how to make primates happy. It took six years before the agency could come up with rules that the research community could accept.

Originally, the USDA proposed firm standards: laboratories would have to give monkeys bigger cages, let them share space, provide them with puzzles and toys from a list.

Researchers argued that was unreasonable: every monkey species was different; the rigid standards might satisfy one animal and make another miserable. Now, each institution is asked to do what it thinks best for its monkeys. USDA inspectors will be free to study, criticize, and ask for changes in those plans.

But animal rights groups will not. Research lobbyists persuaded the USDA to bypass the federal Freedom of Information Act; the president of the American Society of Primatologists told the agency that making the plans public would be like giving a road map to terrorists. Under the new rules, the plans will be kept at the individual institutions rather than filed with the federal government, as has been standard practice. That makes them institutional property, exempt from any requests for federal records.

Tom Wolfle, director of the Institute for Laboratory Animal Resources in Washington, DC, the federal government's chief advisory division on animal issues, said the research community simply needed some clear space. "The idea was to prevent unreasonable criticism by uninformed people," he said.

Advocacy groups have sued the government over the new rules, saying they unlawfully shut the public out of research that it pays for. "In the
end, they just handed everything back to the researchers and said, here, it's
all yours," said Christine Stevens, an executive with the nonprofit Animal
Welfare Institute.

Stevens, daughter of a Michigan physiology researcher, finds this the
ultimate contradiction, as well as foolish and short-sighted. She thinks that
science, of all professions, should be one of open ideas.

On this point, she has some unlikely allies. Frederick King, of Yerkes, no
friend to the animal rights movement, is also unhappy with the research community's tendency to withdraw. "I don't know about the law," he said, "but our
plans for taking care of our primates will be open.

"We are using taxpayers' money. In my judgment, we have an obligation
to tell the public what we're about. And the fact that we haven't done that, I
think this is one of the greatest mistakes over the last half-century, hell, the
last century, that scientists have made."

Against that conflict, Allen Merritt's decision to make public an experiment in which he kills monkeys was not an easy one. His wife worried that
antiresearch fanatics would stalk their home. His supervisors worried that
animal lovers would be alienated; one administrator even called the Davis primate center, suggesting that Merritt's work should not be publicly linked to
the medical school's pediatrics department.

But Merritt, like King, believes that his profession will only lose if it
remains hidden from the public. "People need to understand what we're doing.
If I were to take a new drug first to a nursery, and unforeseen complication
occurred and a baby died—who would accept that?"

So, on a breezy morning, he opens the way to the final test of lung-lubri-
cating surfactants that he will do this year, a twenty-four-hour countdown for
two baby monkeys. Those hours are critical to whether these drugs work. If
human premature babies last from their first morning to the next one, their
survival odds soar.

The tiny monkeys—one male, one female—taken by C-section, are hurried into an intensive care unit, dried and warmed with a blow drier, put onto
folded towels, hooked up to ventilators, heart monitors, intravenous drip lines.
During the experiment, they will never be conscious, never open their eyes.

"OK, let's treat," Merritt says. His technician gently lifts the tube from the
ventilator, which carries oxygen into the monkey's lungs. A white mist of surfactant fills the tube, spraying into the lungs. And then, through the night, the
medical team watches and waits.

The next morning, they decide to kill the female early. An intravenous line going into her leg is starting to cause bleeding problems. The monkey is twitching a little in her unconsciousness, as if in pain. Merritt sees no point in dragging her through the experiment's official end.

But the male keeps breathing. As the sun brightens to midday, the scientists inject a lethal dose of anesthesia. Still, the monkey's chest keeps moving, up and down, up and down with the push of the ventilator. But, behind him, the heart monitor shows only a straight green line.

For a few seconds, before they shut the machines down and begin the lung dissection, Allen Merritt stands quietly by the small dead monkey, marshaling the ghosts of the babies he couldn't save, a long time ago.

November 24, 1991

Author's Afterword

Around the time I was in college, I started thinking about my career path. I told myself I wanted to be a writer, I wanted to be paid for it, and I wanted to pursue a lifetime of figuring out how things worked. The "how things worked" part is what pushed me into being a science writer.

As a journalism major at the University of Georgia in Athens, I joined the school paper, the *Red and Black*. It was there I discovered another thing about journalism that I'd never thought about before: I really hate it when people say no to me. I don't know what it is about my character, but when someone says no to me, I love to try to figure out how to get around it. In journalism, of course, you hear the word no quite a bit, so once I actually started *doing* journalism, I realized what a good fit this job was for me. People were *always* saying no, and I was *always* figuring out how to get what I wanted. It's a great motivation. I think it just clicked for me.

When I graduated from the University of Georgia, during the seventies, I had two job offers. One was a police reporting job at this small paper in north Georgia—I was totally afraid of that. And then I had a copyediting offer at a larger paper in south Georgia. I went to talk to our career adviser at the school, and he told me to take the copyediting job because, "Everyone knows that after a few years you'll get married and have children, so we really need to save reporting jobs for men."

Well, that was it. I was so angry I walked out of there and called the paper in north Georgia and took the reporting job. People who had been in journalism a long time weren't used to women doing that job. Think about it—I was covering cops in north Georgia! It's weird because I'm a late twentieth-century journalist . . . but you still felt like you were kind of carving a path.

From there, I did what everyone did in those days: I worked my way up. I spent a year there and then went to another small daily. Then I went to the *St. Petersburg Times*—and then I went to graduate school because I realized I wanted to be a science writer.

The "Monkey Wars" series was a whole litany of everyone saying no to me at every turn. I spent a year filing public record act requests for information on primate research. So when I first called everyone up, they'd say "No we won't talk to you. Why would we do that?"

So what you do is you start out at the periphery, talking to the people out there. The information they give you brings you closer to the inner circle, and you just keep going. Pretty soon the people you're trying to interview, the people at the center of your investigation, realize that you've talked to all of these people who know them—and that all these people are talking about them. Eventually, these central figures realize they have a vested interest in talking to you. What happened to me in my primate investigation was something like that. I backed off and went out a few more degrees of separation and circled back around. Like everything, good reporting needs a strategy. The way between two points is not always direct, and it's not short. You take the route you have to take. Usually it's through a back door.

As a journalist, I try to develop a relationship of trust with my sources. I'm really honest. One time my husband, who's also a journalist, was listening to me do an interview. My source asked me, "Am I going to like this story?" And I said, "Well, I can't promise you that."

Later my husband said to me, "I don't know why anyone ever talks to you because you never say, 'Yes, I'm sure you'll like the story.'" But I never do, because I feel like one of the things I like to do, even with people who are skittish, is to try and build a relationship with trust. I don't BS them. I don't booby trap them. I'm really honest about where I think I'm going. A lot of the time I'll tell them as much as I can. I'll say, "Here's the story I'm working on, here's what I'm trying to do, here's what I think I need to know, here's who else I've talked to." So I try to give them a sense of comfort in talking to me. I'll let them know that "any questions you need to ask me I'm happy to answer." I do a lot of that. Also, just knowing how to read people is important before you even get to your questions.

Journalism has made me infinitely curious; it's an outward-looking profession where you get paid by someone else to learn. Right now, I write this monthly column for the *New York Times* called "Poison Pen". It's all about environmental chemistry regulation; it has changed the way I think about the way we regulate. It's really interesting for me because my graduate degree was environmental reporting with a specialty in chemistry. It's like I finally got the job I went to grad school for.

I guess I'm also proud to say I'm the 2014 guest editor of the Houghton Mifflin series *Best American Science and Nature Writing*. I'm only the fourth woman to edit that book in fourteen years. If you look at the contributor list, it's about 75 percent male.

After I got to the St. Pete Times, which is now the *Tampa Bay Times*, one of my former editors in Georgia organized a panel at the Georgia Press Association called "Women in Journalism." I was on that panel, and I remember saying that I really looked forward to the day when we don't have to have panels on women in journalism. It says to me, we still haven't accomplished what we need to accomplish. Here we are today, a bunch of years later. There are a lot of ways we've moved it forward, but it's not finished. It's OK to say, "It's not good enough."

In general, I think women interview people really well, and we give journalism a good reputation. We're really solid and nice and forthright about how we do it, and I think that's good for the reputations of journalists. Women are smart in the way we do our research and organize our material. We ask really good questions. And again, not to stereotype—because clearly men have done all those things and continue to do them—but when I sit down with a group of female journalists, I always leave the table thinking, "This is such a smart group." I don't know why, but there are just a lot of really talented women writers—not just amazing reporters, but phenomenal writers.

We've made much fuss over so many male writers through the years; we need to admire and make more of a fuss over women writers. I think one of the things that are important is that we're looking at journalism not as a trade but as a profession. Women are really good professionals.

Christine Brennan

Christine Brennan, a *USA Today* columnist, has twice been named one of the nation's top ten sports columnists by the Associated Press Sports Editors. She is also a commentator for ABC News, ESPN, and NPR. Her national bestseller, *Inside Edge: A Revealing Journey into the Secret World of Figure Skating*, was named one of the top one hundred sports books of all time by Sports Illustrated. Brennan lives in Washington, DC.

Best Seat in the House

How a young sports fanatic became the first woman
to cross the locker room barrier

"Two tickets to a Cleveland Indians game," the announcer was saying on the Saturday morning radio show on WSPD in Toledo, Ohio, "for the person who knows the answer to this trivia question."

All six of us were at the kitchen table on a typically chaotic, noisy Saturday morning in late May of 1969. I had my head buried in the newspaper, poring over baseball standings. I don't think my parents or my siblings heard the question, but I did.

"Who were the two pitchers involved in the only double no-hitter in baseball history?" the man on the radio asked.

"I know the answer to that," I said, as much to myself as to anyone else. "Fred Toney and James Vaughn."

It was in one of the baseball books I was reading. Having just turned eleven, I already was smitten with baseball, with our minor-league Mud Hens and with all the major-league teams surrounding us: the Cubs and White Sox in Chicago, the Tigers in Detroit, the Indians in Cleveland, the Reds in Cincinnati. Unlike so many children in other parts of the country, I didn't have to pick one team to cheer for. I had a half dozen in my big Midwestern backyard. But those weren't the only teams I followed. When I tried to fall asleep at night, I didn't count sheep. I recited World Series teams, going backward from 1968, until I didn't know them anymore.

My father turned to look at me.

"You want to call in?" Dad asked.

I shook my head no. I pictured a sports fan, a man, already at his phone somewhere else in Toledo, dialing in, answering correctly, winning the tickets.

We listened for a few moments.

"We still don't have any callers," the radio announcer said.

Dad looked at me and smiled. I pushed my chair away from the table and walked to the phone. I still thought I would be too late. I picked up the phone and looked at my father, then at my mother. They nodded approvingly without saying a word. I dialed the number.

A man answered at the radio station. I recognized his voice. It was the announcer. Everyone in the kitchen fell silent. Mom reached for the kitchen radio and twisted the knob to turn down the sound so I wouldn't get distracted, then ran to their bedroom to listen.

"So," the announcer asked, "you know the answer?"

"Yes," I said in the firmest eleven-year-old voice I could muster. "Fred Toney and James Vaughn."

"Oh, we've got a young fan here," the announcer chuckled. "And what teams did they play for?"

He was adding another question, right then, on the air. It wasn't a problem. I knew the answer.

"The Cincinnati Reds and the Chicago Cubs," I replied

"You're right! You win the tickets! What's your name?"

"Christine Brennan," I said.

Silence.

"Oh," the announcer said. "You're a girl."

My first press box was in our family room, ten feet from the television. Every Saturday morning during baseball season, I pulled mom's manual Olympia typewriter off a closet shelf, set it on a small table, and typed up a three- or four-paragraph preview of the NBC "Major League Game of the Week." My brother, Jim, who was four years younger than I was, would do research, looking up statistics in the *Toledo Blade* sports section. He was very thorough for a seven-year-old, giving me all the information I asked for. We wrote about the starting pitchers, about who was hitting well, about what to expect in the game. My stories had a circulation of six—five not counting me: my father, a former high school tackle and shot putter who once had a tryout with the Chicago Bears; my mother; and my siblings. There were four Brennan children; I was born in May of 1958, my sister, Kate, in November of 1959, my brother, Jim, in June of 1962, and my sister, Amy, in August of 1967.

Those little stories flew off my fingertips. I had read hundreds of articles about baseball in the *Blade*, the *Toledo Times*, and the *Detroit Free Press*. I also had some previous writing experience. My parents gave me a diary for

Christmas of 1968. It had blue and green floral print on the cover and a lock that I never used. My first entry, on January 1, 1969, was typical of what I believed my diary would be: "Woke up late after staying up last night to wait for New Year. After lunch, went to the Sports Arena to ice skate. After that, watched the Rose Bowl and Orange Bowl. In the Rose Bowl, Ohio State won over USC, 27–16. In the Orange Bowl, Penn State won over Kansas, 15–14."

I sounded like a stringer for the Associated Press.

Barely a day went by when I did not report in my diary the score of a University of Toledo Rockets basketball game, or an NFL play-off game, or, when spring came, the score of a Toledo Mud Hens or a Detroit Tigers game or the Saturday "Game of the Week." My entries also covered the daily activities of a girl turning eleven: memorizing words, going to class at the Toledo Museum of Art, skating on someone's frozen backyard.

My entry for February 28 was particularly memorable:

"Today I begged my Dad to try to get tickets for the Rockets' game tomorrow against Miami. It is Steve Mix's last game. Daddy will try to get tickets."

Steve Mix was the first big sports superstar I idolized. He was the University of Toledo basketball team's six-seven, 220-pound center. With his broad shoulders and tree-trunk arms, Mix lumbered through the key and under the basket like a giant, and we loved him for it.

"The Mixmaster!" Dad would yell, his deep voice booming above the crowd, as Mix grabbed a rebound and threw his elbows side to side, churning like a blender to protect the ball. I would look up and smile at my father, a big block of a man at six feet and two hundred pounds, with a quarter-inch crew cut and black-rimmed glasses.

And when Mix laid in a basket, rolling it off his fingertips as he blew through the lane "like a freight train," as Dad said, we cheered mightily.

The Rockets won the Mid-American Conference championship in the 1966–67 season, going 23–2 and making NCAA Tournament, which was quite a feat because only twenty-three teams qualified for the tournament that year. Mix and his teammates cut down the net after they clinched their spot in the tournament, and the next morning, I was stunned to see it hanging off a kitchen cabinet in the home of one of my friends whose father was a University of Toledo professor with connections to the team. We were living in the well-manicured, middle-class enclave of Old Orchard in West Toledo, just across busy Bancroft Street from the university. The old Field House where the basketball team played—no one called it the men's team because there was no women's team that we knew of back then—was a five-minute walk from our home. Dad and I had gone to a few games that season, but not the one that clinched the title. Instead, I listened to every minute of that crucial game on the radio. Seeing that net the next day made it real to me.

We went to a few games that year, Dad and I, and on occasion, Kate and Jim. We went to several more the next, which was the 1968–69 season. Mix was a senior that season, and the March 1 game was Toledo's last, our final chance to see him play. My father did find two tickets; he bought them from a student—and we joined the crush of spectators streaming into the Field House. The building held just four thousand fans. It was hard to say if the more remarkable quality about the old barn of a gym was heat or the acoustics. Let's call it a tie. It was the hottest, loudest place I had ever been.

Dad and I found our seats in the last row, just under the ceiling at the top of the student section. We were a long way from the court. "But we're here!" Dad said, turning to me with a big smile. "That's the important thing. We can smell it."

We could smell, see, and hear every second of Mix's finale. I don't remember how many points he scored. I do remember breathing in every moment of the event as if it were pure oxygen. I kept looking around the gym, taking mental pictures of every significant moment. I could feel my heart racing. This was, I would later come to understand, the adrenaline rush of the big event: so many people gathered in one place, and us with them, for a grand, two-hour high-wire act. Nothing that happened within the confines of the usual routine of my young life could match this. Nothing even came close.

When the horn sounded near the end of the game, which Toledo lost, 70–65, Dad nudged me and motioned for me to look toward the Toledo bench.

"They're taking him out," Dad said.

Steve Mix was walking slowly toward the Rockets bench down on the floor many rows below us. Coach Bob Nichols shook his hand. His teammates patted him on the back. Someone handed him a towel. Mix sat down hard.

"And thus a great career comes to an end," Dad said.

I looked at Dad. I tried to blink back tears. Dad smiled at me. I thought I saw a tear forming in his eye too.

Dad introduced me to sports when I was four, during the 1962 World Series between the New York Yankees and the San Francisco Giants. While watching the first game of the series on our black-and-white television, I made a pronouncement that Mom recorded in my baby book: "Yogi Bear is going to catch. When he gets the ball, he'll steal it, as he does the picnic baskets."

The next summer, I used one of Dad's old gloves when we first played catch in our backyard. Dad immediately taught me how to throw the ball properly, firing it from behind my right ear without the slightest hint of the motion that has come to be known as "throwing like a girl." I don't remember hearing anyone use those words until late in elementary school; certainly my father or mother never used them. Nor did the boys I played ball with every spring and summer day in our neighborhood. I was the only girl who regularly played with them—and I threw like they did.

Then something wonderful happened. As my eighth birthday approached, I asked for my own baseball mitt. Dad went to a sporting goods store and bought a light brown, perfectly smooth, pristine Rawlings glove. Written in script on the palm of the glove was the name Tony Cloninger, with a drawing of a man throwing a baseball. Imprinted nearby were these words: "The Finest in the Field!"

I didn't know who Tony Cloninger was, so I checked the sports section to find out. He was a right-handed pitcher for the Atlanta Braves who was to gain fame later that year, 1966, for hitting two grand slams in one game against the San Francisco Giants. Unfortunately, I never saw him play in person or on TV. Cloninger existed only in newspaper photos, on baseball cards, in the box scores, and in the palm of my glove.

When Dad gave me the glove, I held it to my face and inhaled deeply. All the boys did that with their gloves, so I did it too. My glove smelled new and fresh and natural. This was the scent of baseball. I used my new mitt every day that summer, playing with the boys in the neighborhood in the morning and afternoon, then with my father when he came home from work in the evening and it stayed light until after nine o'clock.

I took to sports naturally when I was a little girl because I never really was little. My mother said I was born size 6X and kept growing. I was the only Brownie Scout, Mom said, who outgrew her dress in the second grade, when at the age of seven, I was already four and a half feet tall and weighed more than seventy pounds. By the time I was nine, I was five feet tall and one hundred pounds. What was bad for Brownies, however, was good for sports. While the boys were ambivalent or downright inhospitable to most girls who wanted to play with them, they specifically asked me to join them and sometimes picked me first when we chose sides.

With my dark brown hair cut in the simplest of pageboys, I was the tomboy of the neighborhood. I broke my arm falling out of a tree when I was seven. That same year, I asked for G. I. Joe, not Barbie, for Christmas—and that's what Santa brought. While Kate was innately drawn to Mom's side at the stove, I obliviously walked by them—Mom, Kate, and the stove—as if they were invisible on my way outside to play catch.

Because I played with the boys all day, I wanted to look like they did, so I wore baggy T-shirts and grass-stained shorts and pedal pushers. When we went swimming in the pool that Mom and Dad had had built in our backyard, I often swam topless. Not that it matters, not at that age. I was five or six at the time. If the boys could swim topless, I said to Mom and Dad, why couldn't I? They smiled and told me it was fine. I was seven or eight when I switched to a girl's bathing suit. This required no family intervention; it just happened like most things do when parents don't push their children, by my mother buying me a girl's suit and my one day putting it on.

In those days, I was clamoring for as much from sports as I could get. I kept asking for more trips to the backyard to play catch with Dad, kept hoping for more visits to the University of Toledo for a basketball or football game, kept wanting more time in front of the television or beside the radio with my father to understand the game better. I desperately wanted to learn to keep score of baseball games, to understand the sport's strange numbering system— the catcher was 2, the shortstop was 6, the center fielder, 8.

Dad wasn't pushing me to do this. I was asking, and Dad happily obliged. I wondered years later if Dad thought of me as his first son, and he laughed and shook his head. "No, you wanted to play sports and learn about sports, and you were a happy child, so your mother and I thought that was just fine. We wanted you to do what you wanted to do."

If Dad wasn't home, I turned to my best friend, David Hansen. David was my first running mate—a triplet with a brother, Douglas, and a sister, Laurie. We became such good friends that they labeled me the "the Fourth Triplet." A title I believe I hold for life. They all called me Christy back then. I would later become Chris or Christine to everyone else, but not to the Hansens, and especially not to David. Nearly forty years later, when I talk to David, I'm still Christy Brennan, which is fine with me. David and I spent our summer days trading baseball cards, fiddling with his transistor radio dial trying to tune in the Chicago Cubs from two hundred miles away, and racing around the block on our new bikes. One day we got the great idea to attach a rope to the collar of the Hansens' large boxer, McDuff, so he could drag us around the block on our skateboards as if we were waterskiing. There were more skinned knees in the neighborhood that summer than any year before or since.

David Hansen and I had just about everything in common. Our mothers always wondered if we would eventually get married. (We did not.) David was ten months older, but we were the same height as kids, perfectly compatible for playing sports all day long. My first sleepover, when I was seven, was not at a girl's house, but at David's. We slept in sleeping bags in the Hansens' basement. It didn't take me long to get there: we lived two doors apart on Barrington Drive in Old Orchard. David and his siblings and I and mine played in our neighborhood Monday through Friday, then we went to art classes together at the museum Saturday mornings and to church Sunday mornings. I sometimes missed a Sunday, but the triplets never did. They couldn't. Their father was our minister at Christ Presbyterian Church.

There was only one boy in the neighborhood taller than I was back then, Clifford Siegel. Clifford was the triplets' age, a year ahead of me in school, and he lived with his grandparents just a few doors down from our home. One day, he stood on the sidewalk, refusing to move as I barreled toward him.

"You better move!" I yelled.

"I dare you to hit me!" Clifford yelled back.

I did.

I flew off my bike one way, Clifford flew another way. But we both bounced up, dusted ourselves off, and within an hour were meeting up with the other kids at Goddard Field, a grassy expanse two blocks from our homes, playing baseball once again. If we weren't pretending we were Mickey Mantle when we were up to bat, we were Al Kaline, the great Detroit Tiger. Other days, we played kickball, or running bases, or tag, or someone brought a kite and we ran so fast we sometimes fell trying to coax it off the ground. Goddard Field was right across Bancroft Street from the University of Toledo's soaring, limestone Gothic clock tower. We told time by the black hands on the clock; when the hour hand reached six, we dashed those two blocks home for dinner, often to meet again in an hour or so to ride bikes or play another sport, assuming that Dad wasn't home yet and ready to play catch with me.

Professional Baseball turned one hundred in the spring of 1969; I turned eleven. We watched the weekly games on TV, but mostly, baseball came into our home through the radio. Dad already had taught me every last detail of how to keep score; then, just in time for the Toledo Mud Hens season, he bought me a ringed, blue baseball score book. I would plug in a radio on the end table beside the sofa in our living room, then close the doors to our family room and kitchen, where everyone else was doing chores, homework, or watching TV. There I'd sit, night after night, by myself, listening to the Mud Hens on WCWA 1230 AM. I had my pencil and the score book on my lap and my well-worn copy of the Blade's special Mud Hens pullout section, with all the players' pictures and biographies, at my side. Occasionally I switched to the Detroit Tigers game on the radio, but even though they had won the World Series the year before, I preferred the Mud Hens, who were the Tigers' Triple-A, International League farm club. They were ours.

I listened to those games from places that felt far away, cities like Syracuse and Rochester and Richmond. I pictured what the stadiums might look like, heard the sounds coming from them through the radio—one day I was sure I heard a hot dog vendor's yell—and, for that night, I wished I could be there. Dad soon let me in on a little secret: many of the Hens' road games were re-creations. The crowd noise and crack of the bat were produced in a studio, he said, and the announcer simply was reading the play-by-play coming over a ticker. Alas, the hot dog vendor probably never existed. I was surprised by Dad's news, but hardly crushed. I began to listen more intently to see if I could tell the difference between a real away game and a re-created one. The big giveaway was the sound of the crowd noise; after an inning in which it sounded the same no matter who was up to bat or what the batter did, junior sleuth that I was, I knew it was fake.

My mind wandered those evenings sitting on the sofa by myself. I never knew what other team's players looked like. I didn't know what color their uniforms were. There was no way to know if the radio announcer didn't mention it; the local TV station never went on the road with the Mud Hens, so there were no game highlights to be seen. It was still a full decade before the launch of ESPN, even longer before the arrival of local sports cable stations. I had to rely on the stories and black-and-white photos in the newspaper to tell me what the game must have looked like. That, and my imagination. Years later, a sportswriting colleague told me that he had the same problem. When his favorite major-leaguer was traded, he wrote to ask him a simple question: "what number are you wearing with your new team?"

The newspaper sports section then became my guide, and many days, I grew impatient waiting for it. We subscribed to the afternoon *Blade*, and it arrived around 4 p. m., sometimes 4:30. So eager was I to start in on the box scores and the wire reports of the previous night's major-league games that I sometimes stood quietly in our foyer, waiting for the thunk on the doorstep.

Even after listening to the entire Mud Hens game the previous night, I devoured the newspaper stories the next day. I realized I actually was more interested in reading about a game after I had spent the night listening to it. Even at this early age, I was intrigued to see how writers described it, what they choose to emphasize. I pored over the box scores and analyzed the International League standings to see who had gained a game or who had fallen back. I did the same for the Tigers and the other major-league teams, but I spent most of the time on the Mud Hens.

A few years later, the television show M*A*S*H and its nutty Corporal Klinger, played by Toledoan Jamie Farr, introduced the nation to the Mud Hens. People came to realize then what I was understanding in the 1960s, that our Mud Hens were the very essence of minor-league ball. They had been around forever and had a colorful history. Dad told me the great Casey Stengel even had been Toledo's manager in the late 1920s and early 1930s. Back in the late 1800s, the team had been alternately known as the Blue Stockings, the Toledos (the Toledo Toledos?), the Maumees (for the river that runs through the town), and the Swamp Angels. For a while, their stadium was located in a marshland inhabited by ducklike birds. Amused by these creatures that occasionally joined them in the outfield, opposing players began calling them "mud hens."

In 1896, this became the team's permanent nickname. What a godsend this would become a century later when merchandisers inherited the earth and people wanted offbeat souvenirs like hats with a hen on them.

The man who brought the Mud Hens to life for me in our living room every night in 1969 was Frank Gilhooley, a local sportscaster with a rich, jolly voice. He was the Hens' radio play-by-play man. There was a language to sports, and I began to learn it from him. One night, Gilhooley mentioned "the hot corner." I didn't know what that was. I waited for him to use the term again, to see if I could figure it out, but before he did, Dad walked into the living room.

"What's the hot corner, Dad?"

If this question surprised him, coming out of the blue as it did, he didn't miss a beat. "That's another term for third base."

I thought about that for a moment.

"Because the ball can come off the bat of a hitter really fast down there at third?"

"Exactly," Dad replied.

Another time, Gilhooley talked about a double play going 6-4-3, and, because Dad had taught me how to keep score, I knew that meant the play went from the shortstop to the second baseman to the first baseman.

One night, Gilhooley announced a contest to name an all-time Mud Hens roster, position by position. A couple weeks later, he took time away from calling the game to read one submission.

As he read the names, I listened very carefully: "Tom Timmermann. Ike Brown. Bob Christian. Don Pepper..."

Every name he read was a player who had been with the team that year or the year before, when the Hens won the International League pennant. Brown and Timmermann were playing in the game I was listening to that night.

As the list was being read over the air, my father walked into the room. He stopped and stood over me, listening intently with me as Gilhooley finished.

"Must be from a young fan," Gilhooley said to his listeners.

I could hear a smile in his voice.

"But there's no name on it," he said, "so we'll never know who sent it in."

I don't remember what Gilhooley said next, although I do know he chuckled. I looked straight ahead. My father started to leave the room.

"Dad?"

My voice stopped him.

"That was me."

As I thought about it years later, I didn't put my name on that piece of paper because, at eleven, I thought voting for an all-star team was the same as voting in an election. I thought you were supposed to remain anonymous. I remember feeling embarrassed until Dad looked down at me and smiled.

"You know that was yours," he said softly. "That's all that matters."

From that moment on, I put my name on anything I ever wrote.

As for my all-time Hens, they didn't fare too badly.

Pitcher Tom Timmermann and infielder Ike Brown were called up by the Detroit Tigers on the same day later that season. They both played their first major-league game on the road, in Yankee stadium. Timmermann, who was six-foot-four and wore thick, black-framed glasses, played for Detroit and Cleveland for parts of six seasons. In 1970, he had twenty-seven saves as a relief pitcher for Detroit and was named Tiger of the Year. Brown, who always seemed to be laughing on his way out of the dugout, played for the Tigers for portions of six seasons.

Outfielder Bob Christian led the Mud Hens in hitting in 1968 with a .317 average. He was in his early twenties, but every picture I saw of him made him look younger. He had a sweet smile. Christian played parts of three seasons in the majors with Detroit and the Chicago White Sox, and I followed him in the box scores. But in February 1974, I opened the paper and was shocked to read that he had died of leukemia. He was twenty-eight.

I found out about Don Pepper many years later. While covering a golf tournament, I stopped LPGA star Dottie Pepper to ask if she was related to the Hens' old first baseman.

"Related?" she said. "I'm his daughter."

May, 2006

Author's Afterword

As a girl growing up in the suburbs of Toledo in the '60s and '70s, I just loved news. I couldn't get enough of watching the news on TV, and we had the radio on all the time listening to the news at the top of the hour. My parents loved news, so I loved news. I loved writing every day in my diary. I loved sports, but I never thought I would be a sportswriter as a girl growing up, because there were no female sports role models—I never saw a woman doing sports on TV, never read a woman's sports byline until I got to Northwestern University.

But I loved the news, couldn't wait to get my hands on the sports section whenever we'd be on vacation, couldn't wait for the *Toledo Blade* to plunk onto our doorstep (it was an afternoon paper) to read all the box scores and sports news. So I was a news junkie, and I just thought it would be the coolest thing to work in a newspaper. I was the editor of my high school newspaper, went to Northwestern, got my undergrad and master's in journalism from Northwestern in '80 and then '81 . . . and then just followed my heart and my passion.

As far as obstacles, being a woman in a man's world, the whole issue of getting into men's locker rooms is well documented in the ESPN documentary *Let Them Wear Towels*. It's a must-see when it comes to telling the story of women's struggle to report sports. I'm in that. Locker rooms were still closed to women in the NFL and college football in the '80s when I started, but that quickly was resolved in the NFL in 1985, when the NFL issued an edict that all locker rooms would be open to women. At that time the *Washington Post* assigned me to cover Washington's NFL team—I don't use its nickname anymore; I think it's offensive. But anyway, that made me the first woman assigned to cover an NFL team. There were a lot of stories written about it back then, but it's ancient history now. In sports, everything is great for women— equal—it has been for years, decades now. We have equal access into locker rooms and other areas where we do the interviews.

I'm very proud of being able to fight for women to get into the business. I started a scholarship internship program with the Association for Women in Sports Media that has now supported more than 130 women. There are those in the mainstream sports media, some of them my friends, who wonder why I write so much about women's sports. In both 2004 and 2005, I went from the men's NCAA basketball final game to the women's NCAA final the next evening. Several other writers did this in 2005, when it was a drive from St. Louis to Indianapolis, but as best as I could tell, I was on my own going from San

Antonio to New Orleans in 2004. When I told my colleagues in the pressroom at that men's Final Four what I was doing, most looked at me as if I had said I was heading to Iceland; it was fine if I wanted to go, but they certainly didn't want to go with me.

It makes no sense to me why so many reporters won't cover women's sports. Newspapers are losing readers by the hundreds of thousands. Wouldn't it be logical to try to attract new readers through the sports section, which has always been an entry point to the newspaper? And aren't new sports section readers by definition likely to be women and girls?

When I was growing up loving sports, I read about male athletes almost exclusively and never thought to wonder why there was so little coverage of the few women's sports that existed back then. Today, however, girls have dozens of female sports role models, yet the sports media aren't doing a very good job reporting on them. The stories on women's sports can be few and far between, and buried deep in the sports section. This in turn doesn't entice those girls to read the sports section. And then we in the newspaper business scratch our heads and wonder how we're ever going to attract new readers . . . .

So, when my male columnist friends wonder aloud why I write so much about women's sports, I give them my standard reply: "I know you won't, but I'm happy to."

Edna Buchanan

Edna Buchanan was the crime reporter for the *Miami Herald* for eighteen years, covering more than five thousand violent deaths, three thousand of them homicides, as well as kidnappings, riots, fatal fires, and major plane crashes. Among her many awards, she won the Pulitzer Prize for reporting and the George Polk Award for Career Achievement in Journalism, as well as international acclaim for her classic true-crime memoirs, *The Corpse Had a Familiar Face* and *Never Let Them See You Cry*. Buchanan's first novel of suspense, *Nobody Lives Forever*, received an Edgar nomination. The author of eighteen books, which have been translated into eleven languages, she has also written numerous short stories, articles, essays, and book reviews. Buchanan lives in Miami Beach, Florida, America's hottest beat.

McDuffie

A police cover-up of a beating death sparks riots
in Miami, Florida

The phone rang at my desk on Friday, December 21, 1979. Life would never be the same again.

That call set into motion events that ended in shocking headlines worldwide, changing the face of Miami forever. Hearts would break, including mine. Eighteen men and women would die and three hundred and fifty people, some of them children, would be hurt. Six hundred people would be arrested and property destruction would exceed $100 million.

The voice on the phone was familiar. It told me that a black motorcyclist was either dead or about to die, brutalized by white Public Safety Department (PSD) officers after a chase. They beat him with their heavy metal flashlights, called Kel-Lites, then faked a traffic accident to explain his fatal injuries, said my source. That was all.

It sounded insane—insane enough to be true. That's how it often seems to be in Miami; the more unbelievable the story, the more likely it is true. We spend a great deal of our time continually checking out rumors, calls, and whispers.

I asked at the medical examiner's office if there was a black motorcyclist in the morgue, a man fatally injured in a police chase.

No, they said, but one was on the way. He had just died at Jackson Memorial Hospital. His name was Arthur Lee McDuffie. He was thirty-three.

I called PSD internal affairs. They investigate when a civilian is hurt during an encounter with police. The commander was familiar with the case, he said, and nothing was amiss. The man simply had an accident trying to outrun the police.

At 1:51 a. m., according to the police story, a patrol sergeant tried to stop McDuffie for a traffic violation. He ran. More than a dozen patrol cars had joined the chase or were on the way, as the pursuit took them to speeds of one hundred miles an hour, across the city limits into Miami. There, they said, the cyclist's Kawasaki 900 crashed at sixty-five miles an hour. His safety helmet flew off on impact, they said. Arthur McDuffie staggered to his feet and tried to escape, forcing them to subdue and restrain him as he fought, the officers said.

I telephoned Dr. Ronald Wright at the morgue, to alert him before the autopsy that perhaps this was no routine accident. Downtown, at PSD headquarters, I listened to a tape of the eight-minute chase. It ended at 1:59 a. m., near a Miami expressway ramp. "We have him..." says the sergeant who launched the pursuit. Slightly more than two minutes later, now breathless, the sergeant asks for an ambulance.

On the accident report, I saw the names of the officers involved. A few sprang off the page. I had last seen those names a year earlier—in a *Herald* series on police brutality.

One of them, Michael Watts, was a study in contrasts. An honored Officer of the Month in 1976 for interrupting the rape of a woman hitchhiker and arresting sex killer Robert Can, Watts had also been accused more than once of assaulting motorists he stopped for traffic violations. One driver required brain surgery as a result. Another, guilty of having an expired inspection sticker, complained that Watts had dragged her out of her car by her boots, bouncing her head on the pavement. Internal Affairs had investigated all the complaints against him.

They sustained none.

One night months earlier I had received a call from a concerned cop who was a friend of Watts's. The cop said a supervisor, aware that Watts had difficulty in dealing with blacks, had deliberately transferred him to the predominantly black Central District. Watts was upset, the officer told me, and predicted that in his new assignment he would either "kill or be killed." The officer dared not be quoted. There was little I could do at the time.

The McDuffie accident report listed the name of the towing company that removed the dead man's wrecked orange-and-black Kawasaki. I went to find it.

When I asked for Arthur McDuffie's motorcycle, an employee at Barbon Towing picked up a clipboard. "Sign here," he said. "We were wondering when somebody was going to pick it up."

No investigation was under way. If there was one, the machine would have been seized as the prime piece of evidence. I told the man I had not come to claim it, but just to take a look. He shrugged and showed it to me.

I am no accident investigator. I have written about hundreds of traffic accidents, but I am no expert. It seemed odd, however, that every piece of glass and plastic on the machine was shattered—the speedometer, all of the gauges, all of the lights.

The scuffed and blood-smeared white motorcycle helmet worn by Arthur McDuffie was at the medical examiner's office. The chin strap was missing, cleanly severed, as if it had been sliced rather than torn. Chief medical examiner Dr. Joseph H. Davis was to leave for an island vacation that Saturday morning, but he postponed his departure after my call to Ronald Wright the night before; he wanted to be present for the autopsy on Arthur McDuffie. I did too, but they would not allow me to watch, so I waited.

The doctors reported their findings afterward, to police officers from Internal Affairs. I sat in on the session. Arthur McDuffie's skull had been shattered like an egg. The fatal fracture, directly between the eyes, was typical of the type of injury suffered when a motorcycle rider hurtles over the handlebars head first, smashing into a solid object, such as a pole or a bridge abutment. There were, the doctors acknowledged, other "blunt-impact" injuries that could have been inflicted by police Kel-Lites. But, as they pointed out, it is an established fact that already fatally injured people often come up swinging and have to be subdued. There were approximately ten head wounds.

I drove out to the crash scene near a windy expressway entrance ramp and walked around looking. For what, I didn't know. One thing I did not see: there was nothing that the motorcycle—or Arthur McDuffie's head—could have hit.

No pole, no bridge abutment, not even a curb.

I left the place where Arthur McDuffie began to die to see where he had lived. He and his sister had shared a modest northwest section home. The house was crowded with grieving family who welcomed me. They, too, had visited the accident scene. His mother, Eula Mae, had combed the pavement for clues to her son's death. She had found the broken frame from his eyeglasses, the chin strap from his helmet, and part of a police sharpshooter's badge, apparently lost from a uniform during a scuffle.

The family made no accusations. They did not know what happened; they were bewildered. Aside from traffic violations, including a suspended driver's license, Arthur McDuffie had never been in trouble with the law. In fact, he had been a policeman himself, in the military. He had also been named the outstanding member of his Marine platoon and the president of the marching band at Booker T. Washington High School in Miami.

One wall of the well-kept living room was covered with plaques. They all had Arthur McDuffie's name engraved on them: awards for achievement—his insurance company sales team had sold more policies than any other in the firm. When I later described Arthur McDuffie in stories as an insurance executive, it drew fire from some quarters. It was startling how many people, not only police officers, raised that question, inferring that the *Herald* had deliberately overstated or "whitewashed" McDuffie's status and accomplishments. Many people would have preferred that Arthur McDuffie be out of work, with a spotty reputation and a long criminal record. He was not.

Arthur McDuffie was being groomed for promotion at Coastal States Life Insurance. He was also a notary public and moonlighted on weekends, driving trucks and operating a car wash with the help of unemployed neighborhood youngsters, whom he also trained in house painting. With their help he had painted the Range Funeral Home, where his burial was now being arranged.

I borrowed a photo of McDuffie; handsome and well-dressed, he was smiling. The divorced father of three children, eighteen months to eight years old, Arthur McDuffie had been romancing his ex-wife, his childhood sweetheart. They planned to remarry.

Before I left, I held Eula Mae McDuffie's hand in mine and promised to find out what really happened to her son. As I drove back to the *Herald*, I kicked myself. Why did I say that? Maybe because she was crying. How could I ever keep that promise? Especially after the medical examiners' conclusions that it could all have happened just the way police said. Maybe it did. The worst possible scenario was personally difficult to accept. I know better than most that it is risky business, very risky business, to lead police on a high-speed chase. What looks like fun and games in *Smokey and the Bandit* is not. In the movies, police cars take to the air and sail off bridges. They splash into rivers, bays, and ditches; they spin into spectacular chain-reaction crashes. No harm done; everyone walks away.

In real life, a thirty-second pursuit is a long chase. Adrenaline kicks in and takes over. One minute seems endless. Eight minutes is an interminably long high-speed chase. When the cops do catch you, they are mad as hell.

You are likely to get hurt.

But knowing all that and accepting that police officers are all too human, it is shocking to even suspect that cops might kill over a traffic offense and then launch a massive conspiracy to cover up their crime. I did not want it to be true. And it seemed unlikely when you considered the logistics. At least a dozen people would have to know. How high up could such a conspiracy go? It would not be easy to persuade that many cops to agree on anything, much less on how to cover up a killing.

Emery Zerick, that crusty, long-time Miami Beach detective, told me many things over the years. One of them was, "When a cop gets in trouble, the other cops all run like thieves." The fabled brotherhood of the men behind the badge, the men in blue, all for one and one for all, is a myth. I have seen proof of that dozens of times since.

So if the worst is true, I thought, how can they be hanging in so tight? Wouldn't they all be sweating by now? I left messages at the station for all the officers listed on the accident report. None returned my calls.

I did not learn until months later that the officers knew what I was doing and were monitoring my progress.

Saturday night, l called the home of Charlie Black, an assistant chief in charge of the police division, which includes the detective bureaus.

Charlie Black has a fondness for leather jackets. His eyes are heavy-lidded over pale ice-blue, and he has a presence—he is tough and he looks ba-a-a-d. In my book, he is not. A straight-talking veteran street cop, he has always told me the truth and been up front, even when it was not to his advantage. I asked him about Arthur McDuffie—a total blank. The chief had never heard of Arthur McDuffie—six days after the accident.

Provoked, Chief Black drove directly to the home of his homicide captain, Marshall Frank, to find out why he had not been informed.

A short time later, my home phone rang. Both the chief and the captain were on the line. Arthur McDuffie was news to the captain, too. He had never heard the name. My dinner burned beyond recognition in the kitchen while they both asked me questions and more questions.

The *Herald* newsroom Christmas party was the following day. I missed it. I worked late, writing the story; when I finished I was in no mood to party. An inexperienced editor worked the desk that night. She sharply questioned my descriptions of the helmet strap, the damage to the motorcycle, and the accident scene. "Who can we attribute this to?" she demanded.

We don't have to, I explained, they are fact. I saw them myself. I was having trouble getting this story in the newspaper. Dr. Wright was able to corroborate some of the details. Those that could not be attributed to any outside authority were cut, and I was told to lead the story by reporting that Internal Affairs was investigating the matter.

The story repeated the police version of the accident, the medical examiners' substantiation that it could indeed have happened that way, the backgrounds of some of the officers, and the bewilderment of the McDuffie family. It quoted the dead man's sister, Dorothy, who described her brother as an intelligent man who would not fight police officers.

I learned much later that two of the cops involved were waiting outside the *Herald* that winter morning for a copy of the final edition. In the dark before dawn, they took it to a secluded spot to study the story. They concluded that they might be safe, that they still might be able to pull it off.

They were wrong. It was not a strong story, but it was enough.

It was published on Monday morning, December 24, Christmas Eve. Later in the day, a Miami police officer went to one of his superiors. He had witnessed the beating. The accident, he said, was a fabrication.

My editors also became more interested in the case that day. Now they wanted photos of McDuffie's Kawasaki. But it was no longer at Barbon Towing. Police had seized it. A homicide investigation had begun. It was the prime piece of evidence in the case. Captain Frank, who had been totally unaware that the motorcycle and its rider existed until I told him, now refused to let our photographers shoot or even see it, despite my protests.

On Christmas Day, some of the officers were relieved of duty with pay, pending the outcome of the investigation.

The next day was Wednesday. Officer Charles Veverka, twenty-nine, went to see Captain Frank. He had something to say. Dark-haired, articulate, and boyishly appealing, Veverka was the officer who wrote the accident report. It was fiction, he confirmed. There had been no accident. He falsified the report. It wasn't his idea, he said. He was only following orders.

Veverka, a second-generation policeman and the son of a lieutenant on the same department, told his story. He had been checking out a routine burglar alarm in a warehouse district when it all began.

It was nearly 2:00 a. m., a quiet night. Miami streets, under the eerie orange glow of sodium-vapor lights, were nearly deserted. Blocks away, other officers and a sergeant were talking to a tearful young woman who said she had been raped, when an orange-and-black Kawasaki rolled into their line of vision. At the corner, the rider "popped a wheelie," a daredevil antic that lifts the front wheel off the pavement.

The stunt prompted the sergeant to chase the cycle, red lights flashing, siren screaming. Another officer piled into his patrol car to follow. More joined in, including Veverka, who heard the chase via radio and raced to take part. The boredom of a long and uneventful night was broken. Soon nearly every car in the district, as well as some city officers, had joined the wolf pack.

Desperate to lose them, the cyclist succeeded at one point but was spotted again as he rounded a building. An officer fired several shots. That was enough to stop him. The cyclist decelerated and slowed down. He pulled over near the shadows of an expressway ramp, a ramp that would have led to almost certain escape had he used it. Patrol cars screeched to stops. To the man on the motorcycle, it must have looked as if every cop in the world was arriving.

Officer Veverka reached Arthur McDuffie first. The boyish cop who confessed claimed that the 138-pound cyclist, who had just stopped to surrender, took a swing at him. Another version later was that McDuffie simply said, "You got me, I give up."

Whatever happened, Veverka admittedly threw and landed a punch. Suddenly he and his prisoner were the core of a mob. McDuffie, his wrists handcuffed behind him, was torn from Veverka's grasp.

A police officer described the scene later, "It looked like a cartoon, with arms and legs flying out of a pile of dust. They looked like a bunch of animals fighting for meat. His [McDuffie's] face looked like it was sprayed with a can of red paint."

Veverka claims he tried to pull his prisoner free of the pack, but heavy flashlights, fists, and nightsticks were swinging wildly. Hit on the arm and spattered by McDuffie's blood, he says he stepped back.

The prisoner was helpless on the pavement when a Latin officer swung back over his head with both arms, to smash down a two-handed blow with his big metal flashlight. It connected right between the eyes of Arthur McDuffie. One young cop asked another if he knew how to break legs. Then he demonstrated, rapping the dying man's limbs with his nightstick.

A paramedics' rescue van approached, and somebody warned the others to break it up. City of Miami officers who watched the beating but took no part were told, "You didn't see nothing."

Another PSD sergeant arrived, took in the scene, and quickly began to orchestrate a cover-up. Officers smashed all the glass and plastic on the cycle with nightsticks and flashlights, kicked it over, then drove a police car over it. One cop repeatedly pounded McDuffie's helmet on the pavement. Another spotted McDuffie's wristwatch in the grass, pulled his service revolver, and shattered it with a bullet. Arthur McDuffie's keys and identification were hurled up onto a nearby roof, and Veverka was instructed to write a report on the "accident."

After hospital officials reported that McDuffie was in a hopeless coma, two officers drove to Barbon Towing before dawn. The yard was closed and padlocked. The two cops vaulted a fence and battered the motorcycle with concrete blocks to make the damage appear serious enough to explain a dead rider. In the days ahead, the officers repeatedly cautioned each other to "stick to the story."

Veverka confessed on Wednesday, December 26. That night, medical examiners and state attorney's office investigators visited the scene of the accident for the first time, ten days after it took place. With high-intensity fire department lights, they turned darkness into day, and in that brilliant glare they also discovered what was not there—there was no bridge abutment, no pole, no concrete pillar on which Arthur McDuffie could have smashed his skull.

The death was declared a homicide that night. It was official.

The story, stripped across page one in the morning paper, reported that there had been no "accident," that the police reports were faked.

Carol King Guralnick, Lady Law, now in private practice with her husband, plunged into the case with full fervor—representing the McDuffie family. Active in civil rights causes, the couple already represented a black school-teacher beaten by PSD narcotics detectives who raided the wrong house. Carol called a press conference for the McDuffies. An investigator from the state attorney's office disrupted it as it began. He flashed a subpoena and, as McDuffie's mother wept, seized the items she had found during her pitiful search at the scene. He also confiscated her son's bloodied clothes, returned to the family by hospital officials.

Carol called for immediate intervention by a federal task force. She asked for "an outside in-depth analysis of the inner workings of the Metro Public Safety Department and the Miami Police Department." The request was direct-ed to President Carter, the FBI, the Justice Department, Florida's senators and congressmen, and Senator Edward Kennedy, head of the Senate Judiciary Committee. "The police," she said, "simply cannot police themselves."

She also announced plans to file a multimillion-dollar wrongful-death action against the county, the department, and the officers involved.

It was an election year and the zealous top assistants to the state attorney rushed to file criminal charges. On Friday, December 28, one week after the initial telephone tip to me, Captain Frank arrested five PSD officers, four of them on manslaughter charges. All four had records of commendations for good work, balanced by histories of brutality complaints and lawsuits. The sergeant who initiated the chase had once been pulled off the street for "weak leadership." A commander had warned that if he persisted in his ways, some-body who wore a badge "would go to jail." The fifth suspect, charged with being an accessory and fabricating evidence, was Sergeant Skip Evans, the man who masterminded the "accident." He is also the husband of a fresh-faced and friendly Miami Beach policewoman named Patricia. They had been sweethearts since grade school, and she was pregnant at the time of his arrest. She had been my friend for years.

Arthur McDuffie's funeral was the following day.

Hundreds came to see him off to what his preacher promised would be a better world. The promise did little to console the dead man's loved ones. His mother screamed, and his little girl, tearful in white ruffles, called out "Daddy!" as a Marine honor guard bore the flag-draped casket into the church.

Mourners filled the Jordan Crove Missionary Baptist Church and overflowed into the street outside. Hundreds filed by the open casket. Arthur McDuffie wore his Marine uniform. The brass buttons shone. His hands were folded peacefully. A dozen men and women fainted during the emotionally charged service.

Carol King Guralnick sat with the family, hugging the dead man's weeping child. The choir sang "I'll Fly Away," as the engines of a local motorcycle club present to escort the hearse thundered outside the church.

"Oh, Lord," the Reverend Joe Lewis prayed, "we need you here in Miami today."

The good reverend's words were as true as any ever spoken.

The Southern Christian Leadership Conference and the Achievers of Greater Miami marched three hundred strong that day. With NAACP members and local black leaders among them, they carried a black casket, symbolic of McDuffie's death. They also carried signs:

WHY?????
WHO'S GOING TO POLICE THE POLICE?
JUSTICE NOW!

The manslaughter charges did not satisfy them. They wanted police officers charged with murder. Mingling among marchers and mourners were agents from the Community Relations unit of the Justice Department.

A month later the manslaughter charges against Officer Alex Marrero, believed to have struck the fatal blow, were upgraded to second-degree murder. Jailers kept him in isolation to protect him from other prisoners. His family and friends charged that Marrero was the victim of discrimination and distributed a hundred thousand fliers appealing for public support.

McDuffie coverage passed out of my hands to reporters on the courthouse beat as the case traveled through the system to its inevitable climax. I still had plenty to write about. The year 1979 had been the most violent in Dade County history. The body count continued to mount. Cocaine cowboys were invading public places, spraying bullets wildly, unconcerned about who else got in the way as they tried to kill their intended victims. More citizens were arming themselves against crime and then using the guns to shoot loved ones.

The large Jamaican, Haitian, and Latin influx included people overwhelmed and depressed by culture shock, inflation, the job market, and wage disputes. It made them more susceptible to losing their cool—in other words, trigger happy.

Killings were sparked by traffic arguments, lack of parking spaces, and radios played too loud. Various authorities blamed drugs, guns, the economy, and sunspots. There were 360 dead by the year's end.

Little did anyone suspect that 1979 would soon be looked back on as the good old days.

In 1980 there would be 569 murders in Dade County.

In 1981 there would be 622.

And elated officials called it good news when the annual murder toll dropped back down to 538 in 1982.

Little did we know.

At the stroke of midnight Miamians greeted the new decade in the same way they had ended the old: with a fusillade of gunfire. Somehow it had become traditional for celebrants to empty their weapons into the air at midnight. And more and more people had guns.

Thousands of bullets slammed into houses and cars and blacked out entire neighborhoods as they hit power transformers and streetlights. Some even struck an airplane in flight. Downtown Miami sounded like World War III. In prior years as many as half a dozen people were wounded, some were killed; this time, incredibly, nobody died. A twin-engine Cessna hit in the tail section by bullets fired from the ground, landed safely, its five passengers unhurt. Miami was lucky.

It didn't last. Shortly after midnight police reported one suicide and five unsuccessful attempts by residents reluctant to face the New Year. Three murders were logged by 3:00 p. m., New Year's Day, 1980. I had plenty to do.

Not long after the McDuffie arrests, I chatted with some PSD detectives. They lamented, as usual, their sagging morale. Worse than it had ever been, they said. They blamed it all on the unhappy events of the past year, the ill-considered wrong house raid on the schoolteacher's home, the cocaine scandal among homicide detectives, and the McDuffie case.

I did my best to cheer them up. "At least no policeman was charged with rape last year," I said brightly.

"What about the highway patrolman who attacked the little girl?" a detective said glumly.

"Highway patrolman? What highway patrolman?"

"The one who molested the little girl in his patrol car."

He could recall few details, except that it had occurred several months earlier and that PSD detectives had arrested the trooper. How could we miss that story? How did it slip so quietly and neatly through the system with no media attention?

PSD rape squad detectives were deliberately vague and displeased at my interest. The case was closed, they said. They did not want to discuss it. It all happened months and months ago.

When I insisted on hand-searching their arrest logs for the entire year, they divulged the trooper's name—Willie Thomas Jones—but warned me to let well enough alone. Justice had been served.

Curiosity drove me to the Justice Building, where I pored over the case file. The trooper had pled no contest to lewd and lascivious assault on a child. He could have been sentenced to fifteen years in prison; instead, he got probation—on condition that he undergo treatment and pay for the eleven-year-old girl's psychiatric care. An adjudication of guilt was withheld; he would have no criminal record.

The judge had wished the trooper "a lot of luck" in the record and said he might even terminate the probation early.

Little was mentioned about the young girl.

I found her living in Columbia, South Carolina, where her mother was finishing college. The child was no precociously pubescent Lolita-type; she looked more nine than eleven. Her main interest was not parties or boys, but the French horn.

Always shy, she had regressed to babyhood since her encounter with the trooper. She clung to her mother, wet the bed, and suffered nightmares. Withdrawn and depressed, she was still in treatment. They had never received a dime to pay for it, a condition of the trooper's probation.

The little girl's mother had been told that the disgraced trooper had been fired and would never be allowed to wear a badge again.

It was not true. On the day of his arrest, Trooper Jones was permitted to quietly resign from the Highway Patrol. On his arrest forms, detectives listed his occupation as unemployed. Released in his own custody, he never had to post bond.

His personnel file in Tallahassee, the state capital, reflected that Trooper Jones had resigned to enter private business and that his record was excellent.

That is what any would-be employers—including police departments—would be told upon checking his references.

While the case was pending, he had failed a polygraph test and was evaluated as "borderline psychotic." A psychiatrist said he strongly suspected that other such crimes had taken place. Four doctors agreed that he was a mentally disordered sex offender.

Then the judge wished him luck and put him on probation.

He was doing much better now. In fact he had been pronounced cured after a few free group rap sessions at Jackson Memorial Hospital.

The little girl's mother said she had been told that the trooper would plead guilty and go to a mental institution. She and her family had been urged by prosecutors and police to keep silent. They said it was for the child's protection.

It did not appear that the little girl was the one who had been protected.

Neither the trooper nor his attorney would talk to me—at all. The little girl's mother, however, was relieved. She had been troubled about the way the case was handled and was suffering from guilt herself, because she had always instructed her child to trust and obey police officers.

The little girl had been stopped by the trooper as she walked home from elementary school. On duty, in uniform, he told her she was suspected of stealing candy and would have to be searched. He ordered her into the backseat of his patrol car and took her to a desolate area for the search.

The little black girl, sexually molested by a white policeman, was never taken to the rape center and was questioned only by white policemen.

The story I wrote infuriated the judge. He called it "yellow journalism" and denounced me in open court. To prove that everything he did was proper and that the trooper was treated just like any other defendant, the judge appointed Dade County's respected former state attorney, Richard Gerstein, to investigate the entire matter.

After a three-month probe, Gerstein delivered his report. It called the case "a tragedy and a miscarriage of justice" and the police response "insensitive, indifferent, and incomplete." He found that two judges had been lobbied for leniency and that the detective and the prosecutor, who was a former police officer, worked to protect the trooper, not the little girl. "Nobody seemed to care about the plight of this victim," Gerstein reported.

We were right.

Now the judge blamed the prosecutor and the detectives, saying they had misrepresented the facts of the case to him. He sent Gerstein's report to the federal grand jury for further investigation.

During that time, Miami's black community suffered another humiliation. An all-white jury convicted Dade County's first black school superintendent, Johnny Jones, for using taxpayers' money to buy 24-karat-gold plumbing fixtures for his vacation home. Eventually he would win his appeal because blacks were excluded from the jury.

Racial tensions continued to mount.

A Miami judge granted a change of venue in the McDuffie case, calling it a "time bomb I don't want to go off in my courtroom or this community." The case was transferred to Tampa, on Florida's west coast. Black groups in Tampa protested, predicting that no justice would be found there. Miami blacks organized fish fries and barbecues to raise money so that Arthur McDuffie's family could attend the lengthy trial.

Officer Veverka and another young officer had agreed to testify for the prosecution. The immunity they had been granted was not enough; they still wanted to be cops and were bitter at being fired. Police work was his life's dream, Veverka protested, complaining that he was ordered to write the false reports.

The trial began in Tampa in April 1980. It took six weeks. I did not attend, although it wasn't as though they didn't want me. In fact, I was busy dodging defense subpoenas.

From the start I had been aware that I could be subpoenaed and knew that I had to protect the identity of my source, the tipster who told me about Arthur McDuffie. In the months prior to the trial, people speculated about who it might have been. Whenever anyone asked if it was an anonymous caller, I simply smiled and said nothing. Some took that as an acknowledgment, which was exactly what I hoped the attorneys would think. If they didn't bother to subpoena me, it would be simpler.

Ed Carhart, the man who had convicted the Miami cops in the case of Wanda Jean, was no longer a prosecutor. Now in private practice, he was defending one of the McDuffie cops and wanted to question me under oath. If a judge ordered me to identify my source, I could go to jail for refusing.

One afternoon an editor warned me to get out of the building because a subpoena server was in the hallways looking for me. I ducked out the back door—and didn't know where to go. I couldn't go home, they'd probably look for me there too. I couldn't drive away, somebody might be watching my car. So, I ankled over to Omni, a vertical mall a block away, browsed in a store, and bought a pair of yellow shorts on sale. It was the first chance I'd had to go shopping in months.

When I got back to the newsroom, executive editor John McMullan wanted to see me. He took the initial notes I had scribbled on the case and locked them in his safe. Anyone who made a legal attempt to seize them would have to arrest him first. A born fighter, I think he almost hoped they would try it. Then he suggested that I get out of town—out of the country, in fact. The *Herald*, he said, would send me to the Bahamas to hide out.

I may be the only *Herald* employee, possibly the only newspaper reporter in history, to refuse management's offer of a trip to the Bahamas. Running away seemed repugnant to me. I didn't do anything wrong; Miami is my home. Who would water my plants, feed the cats, walk my dog? Besides, who knows what stories I would miss. Hell no, I wouldn't go.

McMullan was incredulous.

I stayed cautious and stopped answering my door. Eventually, once the trial was under way, a sleazy process server oozed up to my front porch and caught me at the door. The *Herald* lawyers challenged the subpoena and won. For some legal reason never clear to me, I did not have to go. I think the trial had already progressed too far for me to be called as a witness.

In the interim, the *Miami News* reported the attempt to subpoena me, prompting my source to call and say, "Don't go to jail. If you have to, you can tell them who I am."

Despite the kind offer, I would not have done it anyway. It's a matter of principle and ethics. I am still relieved it never came to that. I would not have liked jail.

Captain Frank and Dr. Wright both testified that they first heard about McDuffie from me. Reporters covering the trial called from Tampa to interview me about the case. It all seemed bizarre.

Something quite revealing happened at about that time. People generally seemed to believe that my source was an anonymous caller, so somebody decided to use that to his own advantage. An impostor began to claim he was my tipster.

Former Officer Charles Veverka, now employed as a night watchman, was still hoping to be a cop again. Trying hard to project an earnest all-American-boy image, he called me to deliver another confession. He was my anonymous caller, he said. Tortured by his conscience, he had tipped me off so that the entire conspiracy would unravel.

I was unimpressed.

"No, Charlie," I said. "It wasn't you."

He suggested that I didn't remember his voice because it had been so many months ago. And, oh yes, he said, he had tried to disguise it at the time. Good try, but no cigar. It was not Charles Veverka who telephoned the tip about that fatal night. It was a friend, someone I have known for more than sixteen years. It was not even a police officer. It was not even a man; it was a woman.

TV news coverage of the trial focused, of course, on the most colorful, shocking, and damning testimony. The brief time allotted on the nightly news only permits use of high drama. I remember seeing again and again on TV a husky policeman in suit and tie, both hands raised high over his head as though wielding an axe, demonstrating how the brutish hammer-like blows were struck.

Gene Miller, the *Herald's* best, reported on the trial. His daily stories from Tampa covered both sides thoroughly. They were not all front-page. On TV, every story is front-page, and lots of people, particularly in low-income neighborhoods, get all their news from TV. What they saw may have convinced them that convictions were certain.

The defense attorneys were all high-powered, top-flight. They said that McDuffie fought and resisted and had to be subdued. One officer won a directed verdict of acquittal after six weeks. The fate of the other four was in the hands of an all-male, all-white jury. The Mariel boatlift was under way at the time, and back in Miami, a crush of Cuban refugees, many of them vicious criminals and mental patients, were arriving; across the nation, Mount Saint Helens was rumbling and about to erupt.

It was Saturday. I was at the office and doubted a verdict could be reached before Monday. After all, there were four defendants charged with a total of thirteen crimes ranging from murder to falsifying police reports. There had been half a dozen lawyers and weeks of testimony. The jurors would need time to digest and weigh all they had seen and heard.

I was wrong.

The jury took two hours and forty-four minutes to acquit everybody of everything.

Defendant Michael Watts sobbed. So did Eula Mae McDuffie as she stumbled out of the courtroom in tears and outrage. "God will take care of them," she said.

The news flashed to Miami in minutes. The timing could not have been worse—three o'clock on a hot, sunny Saturday afternoon. I was concerned. I knew the mood on the street.

I called PSD Director Bobby Jones.

"What are we going to do about tonight?" I envisioned trouble—but nothing like the trouble we got. I was afraid somebody might shoot at some cops.

"What do you mean?" he said.

"Don't you think there'll be problems?"

"Our Safe Streets officers are out there," he said reassuringly. "They'll keep things under control."

Rocks and bottles began to fly within two hours. Some of our photographers rolled out onto the street in their radio-equipped cars. I was checking reports of a shooting, a deranged Mariel refugee shot down by a cop outside a Miami mental health clinic, when I heard garbled shouts. They came from a two-way radio across the room, on the photo desk.

It was Battle Vaughn and two other photographers, Bill Frakes and Michel DuCille. It sounded like they were in trouble, yelling for help. I stood up, straining to hear. The man at the photo desk was chatting on the telephone. Looking annoyed at the racket from the radio, he absently reached over and turned down the volume.

I ran to the desk, reached over his shoulder and turned it up full blast, as the man on the telephone blinked in surprise. The photographers were pinned down, being shot at, their windshield smashed. They were under attack by a mob in Liberty City at the edge of the Miami city limits, where jurisdiction is a toss-up between county and city. I made emergency calls to both—and to the fire department rescue squad.

With Battle at the wheel, they escaped without serious injuries but were shaken and cut by flying glass. The *Herald* car had lost its windows and sustained major body damage, torn by bullets and battered by concrete blocks and rocks. It was still early. Traffic could have been diverted, those streets should have been blocked off, but it was the weekend—nobody stepped forward, nobody took command, nobody gave the order.

And as dusk approached, innocent people began to drive down those streets.

Most had not heard the verdict. Some had never even heard of Arthur McDuffie.

Three young people—two men from Pottstown, Pennsylvania, and a woman—on their way home from a day at the beach, drove unknowingly into the area where our photographers had been attacked. A mob was waiting. A brick smashed the windshield, hit the driver, and the car careened out of control. It struck a seventy-three-year-old black man and an eleven-year-old black girl who was playing in front of her house. It pinned her against the building. Her head was injured, her lungs punctured, and her left leg torn off.

The three young whites were dragged from the car and battered with whatever the crowd could lay hands on. The men were shot, stabbed, and run over repeatedly. One died, his brother was maimed, and permanently brain damaged. The young woman with them escaped death, rescued by a stranger. A black man shoved her into a taxicab that took her to a hospital.

A short time later, Benny Higdon, a twenty-one-year-old father of three, drove his aging Dodge Dart into the same neighborhood.

With him was his pregnant wife's fifteen-year-old brother and the boy's best friend, also fifteen. Homeward bound after a day of fishing, they were dragged from their car. All three were battered to death. The mob used rocks, boards, fists, feet, and a newspaper rack. As the three lay dying in the street, the mob forced an ambulance to turn back. Two Miami police sergeants finally careened down the block in a speeding paddy wagon. Braving a hail of rocks and bottles, they loaded the three victims into the wagon and fled to a hospital. It was too late.

Higdon worked at a local bakery. He had just moved his family out of the small mountain town in Alabama where he had worked as a coal miner. They had come to Miami seeking a better life.

Those savage deaths were just the beginning.

A middle-aged hotel maid on her way home from work was burned to death in her car because she was white. A car driven by an elderly butcher was pounded by rocks. He swerved and slammed into a wall. A crowd turned the car over, set it afire, and jabbed at the man with sticks when he tried to crawl out. He burned to death.

During the mob madness, one police officer found a grotesquely mutilated corpse in the street. He loaded it into his squad car for safekeeping until he could take it to the morgue later.

Policeman Frank Rossi, en route to work, jumped from his car and ran to help a young white couple being dragged from their van by a mob near an expressway ramp. The young couple escaped, but Rossi was badly hurt. In the hospital emergency room, lying on an examining table, he asked a nurse for a telephone and dialed my number at the *Herald*. He wanted to describe what was happening, what was going on out there. His life was saved, he said, because he was not wearing his brown uniform shirt. His attackers did not know he was a cop.

Two black men walked into a fast-food chicken outlet at closing time. A Latin couple was mopping the floors and cleaning up. "This is for McDuffie," the two men said and shot them both.

There were reports that the mob was taking over public buildings, so *Miami Herald* security, unmanned and sparsely manned, took action. Fearing that rioters might try to invade the *Herald* building, security personnel locked all but the employees' entrance.

That entrance leads up a narrow hallway, on an incline, to an elevator. I have been told that the chief of security sent out to a supermarket for several cases of Wesson oil; the plan was—if the rioters came—to pour the oil down the hall until it was too slippery for a mob to make it uphill to the elevator. We were lucky. No mob came to the *Herald* that night, only a cop.

Security said a policeman wanted to see me at the employees' entrance. It was Marshall Frank, the homicide captain who had investigated the McDuffie case. I took the back elevator down to meet him. PSD police headquarters was under siege, and he feared for the safety of his men.

The shift commander had called him to report that rioters were breaking into the building. Reports were sketchy. He had raced from his North Dade home intending to join his detectives. As he turned off the I-95 expressway near headquarters, a black man ran up the exit ramp excitedly waving his arms and shouting a warning, "Get back! Get back!"

"It's all right, I'm police," the captain said and swung off the exit anyway. He saw his mistake at once. People were running everywhere in the dark. An overturned car was burning.

A powerful voice, another policeman, bellowed "Turn back! Now! Now!" from an overpass above. He turned, struck by the urgency of the shouts, and saw what appeared to be a sniper leveling a gun at him. He wheeled the car around and got out. As he did, he saw miragelike in the distance what appeared to be a platoon of Miami police in riot gear advancing, marching in military formation.

Frantic to know the fate of his men and the scope of what was happening in the city where he has lived all his life, the veteran cop knew of only one place to find out: the *Miami Herald.*

"How bad is it?" he said, his face grim.

"Bad."

Violence and bloodshed were sweeping south through the city, into Coconut Grove and South Miami. Fires were being set. Looting had begun. Some bodies, burned in their cars, would not be recovered until the next day. Cops under fire were making heroic forays into the riot area, snatching the dead and injured off the street. Many of the heroes were Vietnam combat veterans.

Nothing taught in a police academy could prepare a man or woman for the streets of Miami that night.

Cut off from headquarters and his department, Marshall Frank had instinctively turned to the *Herald.* I felt somehow moved by that, even though I knew he simply wanted to assess the situation by monitoring our radios. In the past, we had been adversaries, on opposite sides; in crisis, we had everything in common. We cared—we had both taken part in the events that led to this. We did the best we could.

I was scared; everything was out of control. It was all coming down around us. We boarded the slow and creaky elevator to the newsroom and simultaneously stepped into each other's arms, hugging tight through the rest of the ride.

At our police desk, the radio traffic was chaotic.

What was to have been a solemn candlelight vigil turned into an ugly mob that took over the Metro Justice Building and surrounded the Public Safety Department headquarters. The thinly spread weekend staff was trapped. Taken by surprise, all the cops inside could do was barricade themselves behind furniture. Their handguns would be a last resort when the building was overwhelmed. Nobody knew where to find the key to the locked cabinets where the tear gas and riot gear were stored. Nobody was prepared.

One man, Michael Cosgrove, a baby-faced City of Miami police major and a Vietnam War hero, took command and saved the county's ass that night. It was Cosgrove's army that Marshall Frank had seen advancing.

He rallied seventy vastly outnumbered city cops and led them to the rescue. In riot gear, they marched down the street, cleared thousands of demonstrators, retook the Justice Building and saved PSD headquarters, along with the county cops trapped inside. He and his men went on to rescue people who would have died that night without them.

More than 270 injured were treated at Jackson Memorial Hospital. Casualties would rise to 350 over the next three days. Surgeons and support staff were called in from home. The emergency room and the trauma team had been prepared for a routine Miami Saturday night, but not for this.

At the height of the chaos and confusion in the emergency room, a nurse broke down and shouted, "You can thank Edna Buchanan for this!"

I was not there, another reporter heard it and told me.

I don't feel guilty about anything that happened. I am not to blame. It wasn't me who got caught up in an adrenaline-crazed chase. I didn't kill Arthur McDuffie or lie to cover it up. I was only the bad-news messenger, the reporter who found out and wrote the story. I still think about it. If it happened again, what could I do differently? I still don't know.

I do know that Miami was a time bomb. Out on those sweltering streets, in the softness of the night, if you were close to the city, you could hear it ticking. Even if Arthur McDuffie had remained an unknown traffic statistic, something or someone else would have struck the match that lit the fuse.

My conscience is clear, but that does not mean there was no pain. One of the McDuffie jurors, asked later if he felt McDuffie's death should have been left a traffic accident, replied, "The people killed in the riot would probably think so."

The next day, Sunday, was bright and beautiful. I drove the 1.2-mile stretch of causeway west to the *Herald* from my island home. To the east, toward the sea, the fronds of stately royal palms were etched against the brilliant blue of a cloudless sky. To the west, over Miami, the sky was black—Miami was burning. The pall of dense smoke was visible for fifteen miles. It hung like a shroud over the city I love. I had to stop at the side of the road to fight the tears.

If you are a woman in this business, you must never let them see you cry.

Dozens of fires erupted at intersections. Firefighters were forced back by gunfire. Businesses and stores burned unchecked. "It's absolutely unreal," said Miami fire inspector George Bilberry. "They're burning down the whole goddamn north end of town."

Late Sunday, fifteen major blazes still raged out of control. Snipers fired rifles at rescue helicopters. The looting and burning went on for three days. Public schools were closed, and an 8:00 p. m.–6:00 a. m. curfew was established. The National Guard was brought in, eleven hundred strong, to establish order on Miami's turbulent streets. They were quickly joined by twenty-five hundred more guardsmen. It was life in a war zone. Police issued frequent advisories to motorists on safe routes to travel and the streets to avoid to stay alive. Cops went for days and nights without going home, without hot meals, without sleep. It took its toll.

I was in the newsroom Sunday when word came of another death: a Miami police lieutenant. His patrol car slammed up against a tree. He was slumped over the steering wheel. At first they thought a sniper killed him, but medics found no bullet wound. He had died, without warning, of a massive heart attack.

It was Ed McDermott.

The sad and quiet Irish cop—tall, husky, with a stomach as flat as a board —forty-eight years old. Dead.

You must never let them see you cry.

After the National Guard moved in, the US attorney announced immediate action in the McDuffie case. A federal grand jury was impaneled to investigate possible violations of Arthur McDuffie's civil rights.

President Carter visited Miami, and blacks threw bottles at his limousine. Teddy Kennedy, then a presidential contender, asked for a full report on the case. Fidel Castro seized the opportunity to accuse the United States of promoting human rights abroad but not practicing them at home. Attorney General Benjamin Civiletti announced plans to intensify a probe into police brutality in Miami.

Within weeks, the federal grand jury indicted former trooper Willie Thomas Jones for violating the rights of the little girl in his patrol car. Jones was arrested, then released pending trial. But there was no trial. He fled— leaving behind his wife and three small children. He would remain a federal fugitive for years.

In July, after two months of investigation and testimony, the federal grand jury handed down its first and only civil rights indictment in the McDuffie case.

The defendant: Charles Veverka.

That was a surprise. Many people were indignant; one of the toughest jobs in proving police misconduct is persuading cops to testify against each other. Veverka was the first to tell the truth and did testify against the others. Now the government had gone after the state's key witness. What message would this send to police departments across the country?

Others, however, believed that the indictment was deserved, that Veverka only told the truth to save himself as he saw the conspiracy beginning to fall apart. He was the cop who reached Arthur McDuffie first that night; had he handled his prisoner professionally, the man might have survived. Instead, Veverka hit him, perhaps setting off the spark for the attack that followed.

His trial was moved to Atlanta, then to San Antonio, Texas. Rumors were that perhaps if he was convicted, other indictments might follow, but they did not. Veverka was acquitted.

Nobody was ever convicted of anything for the death of Arthur McDuffie. But a lot of people paid.

AFTERMATH

The death toll was eighteen, including Lieutenant Edward McDermott, counted as a riot casualty. The property damage in Miami was estimated at $100 million. The damage to the city's reputation was incalculable.

One of the acquitted McDuffie cops, Michael Watts, later tried to kill himself—with a motorcycle. He rolled it into his apartment and let it run, filling the room with deadly exhaust fumes. The attempt failed when his motorcycle ran out of gas and his ex-wife arrived and found him unconscious.

The Dade County Public Safety Department took away the heavy metal Kel-Lites and gave their officers harmless plastic flashlights. The PSD then put the wrong-house narcotics raid, McDuffie, the riot, and the cocaine scandal all behind it, changing its name to the Metro-Dade Police Department.

Chief Charlie Black, who launched an immediate homicide probe upon hearing of McDuffie's death, was later demoted to captain. The reason given was that acting director Bobby Jones, who had accepted the permanent job, had to build his own management team. And Marshall Frank, the homicide captain with a photographic memory for murder cases, was transferred to a desk job in the civil process bureau. The stated reason: career development.

The baby-faced war hero, Michael Cosgrove, who saved the county the night the riots began, was promoted to assistant chief. But in 1984 he was demoted to captain, ostracized, and forced out of the department after an unblemished seventeen-year career. Politics, Miami style: he was perceived as being loyal to his chief, who had been abruptly fired in a 2:00 a. m. phone call from the city manager.

Cosgrove, the hero, had the last laugh: the city manager's turn came, and he got fired. Beleaguered city politicians, faced with a police department in trouble, pleaded with Cosgrove to return as chief.

He said no.

A fugitive for four years and eight months, former trooper Willie Thomas Jones quietly surrendered in Miami, saying he was "tired of running." In April of 1985 he pleaded guilty and was sentenced to a year in federal prison. He wept at the sentencing.

So did the victim's mother, now a social worker. She has forgiven him, she said, for molesting her daughter, now a painfully shy high school senior who has yet to go out on her first date.

The county settled with the McDuffie family for $1 million.

Their lawyer, the woman who said she believed in destiny, never did become a judge.

Carol King Guralnick, the beautiful, brilliant, and rich Lady Law, was at the wheel of her sunshine yellow Ferrari when it broke down on a Miami street. Exasperated, she left the stalled sports car with the LADY LAW tag. She walked toward a gas station across the street for help and stepped into the path of a van. She was thirty-four.

The young widow of riot victim Benny Higdon had her baby, a little girl he never saw. Left at age twenty-one with four children to raise alone, she sued the county and the city for negligence in her husband's death. She lost. The case was thrown out, and she got nothing.

And Charles Veverka's dream of becoming a cop again came true. He got a job with North Bay Village, a small force with twenty-five officers. He did fine, for a time. He even took part in having another Village cop arrested on cocaine charges. But then Veverka got in trouble again. He was accused of kicking a handcuffed prisoner, a black man, in the groin during an elevator ride at police headquarters. Aboard the same elevator was a witness to what occurred, a county crime-lab technician with a long and spotless record. A religious and idealistic man, he was torn between lying to investigators and handing up a fellow police officer. After a meeting with prosecutors, who threatened to charge him and ruin his career if he did not tell the truth, he went home, put a gun to his head, and shot himself to death.

Without a witness, the charges of kicking the black man were dropped, but Veverka resigned from his police job under pressure.

Michael Watts, completely recovered from his suicide attempt, also pinned on a badge again, as a cop with the North Lauderdale police department.

A record, a single, was released: "The Ballad of Arthur McDuffie." It was never a hit.

1987

Author's Afterword

When I was four years old, I learned to read by reading newspapers. I would sit at the kitchen table with my grandmother, who spoke Polish, and I would read her stories from paper. The third page of the *New York Daily News* had all these crime stories. She thought that I was making them up, that something was wrong with me. That was when I met all the dark princes of my childhood—Willy Sutton, bank robbers, Lucky Luciano, the mob boss who organized the mob, the Mad Bomber...

The great thing about it was that in my adulthood, when I became a reporter and worked for the *Miami Herald*, I got to meet Willy "the Actor" Sutton. Willy Sutton was a bank robber. A folk hero to a lot of people on the eastern seaboard. A film crew from one of the networks was supposed to do an interview with him; he had never done an interview before. I got a tip. My plan was to try and find him and steal the interview first. I got to the interview spot early. Sure enough, his car pulls up and I walked up to him and he thought I was the person there to meet him for the interview. I suggested we go to another place, where they would never find him. So I did this long interview with him and called in the story, dictated it over the phone, got on the plane back to Miami. By the time the film crew was flying back to Miami, wondering what had happened to their interview, our story was out in the bulldog edition, Sutton's picture on the front page in color.

Sutton was one of these dark heroes of my childhood, which probably made me want to go into police reporting, but I didn't know it at the time. I never had a journalism course; it just came naturally because I had been reading so many newspapers every day since I was a little girl.

I guess my big break, or my start in the business, came after I'd moved to Florida. I joined a creative writing class, and one of the guys in the class was an editor at a small newspaper in Miami Beach. With his support, I went in there and I took a writing test. And then before I knew it, the guy was saying, "Congratulations, you're a journalist."

Five years at that little paper was great. At times I was the only reporter on staff. I got to do everything. I interviewed movie stars, covered the police beat, went to court, covered the city commission. Sometimes I wrote the letters to the editor because nobody else wrote in. I had these two assumed names. They were having a feud with each other, writing back and forth, zinging each other in the letters page. I guess that was my early beginning with fiction.

Of everything I did, I really liked the police stories best. It seemed like that was what I should be doing full time. The cops weren't used to having a female reporter coming around. It was very schizophrenic; one day they might love you because they did something good and they wanted to make sure you got it in the paper, and the next day they might slam the door on you or push you out into a storm because they don't want to tell you anything. A lot of them were pretty lewd and crude—these were cops and we were in the 1950s and 1960s. Women's rights had scarcely been heard of at this point. So I did what you had to do—I learned how to deal with them. I just kept coming back, and eventually they began to consider me a piece of the furniture. My editors were always hoping they would arrest me so they could write editorials about freedom of information . . . this little paper, they always loved to write editorials and they never had anything that big to write about; they were secretly hoping I'd be hauled off to jail so they could write editorials and try to get me out. Luckily, the lawyer was so good, I never did have to go.

The cops were always mean to me, sure, but a few times they gave me awards for helping solve cases. Probably the thing I was most proud of was winning the Pulitzer, because when I won the Pulitzer, a lone reporter hadn't won it for a long time; often the award would be shared by a staff of a newspaper for their joint coverage of a big disaster or joint work on a big investigative project.

My Pulitzer was given on the basis of ten stories that I did that year. In all, I'd probably written more than two hundred and fifty that year. At one point at the *Herald*, some of the other reporters, all men, got mad because I was doing so many stories. I was making them look bad. One day one of the male reporters came and said he wanted to take me to lunch, and I said, "Well I don't go to lunch. How can you go to lunch when we have a deadline for the first edition?" It was clear that all of them thought I had *diarrhea of the typewriter*. I was making them look bad.

But journalism was never like work for me. There was nothing I wanted to do more. I think I was born to do it. It's interesting, but some of the better detectives I've known through the years have been women. Women look at things in different ways; they have a better eye for detail than men. Cops and reporters kind of share the same skill set.

I've always loved fiction, but every day of my life I miss the newsroom, I miss the reporting. There's nothing like it, and truth is really stranger than fiction. You can make up the screwiest thing you could possibly make up for a novel, but it's never going to be as crazy as something that really happened.

Teresa Carpenter

Teresa Carpenter is a Pulitzer Prize-winning, bestselling American author. She was born in Independence, Missouri, and lives with her husband Steven Levy (author of *Hackers* and *In the Plex*) in New York's Greenwich Village. Her work on the crime beat of the *Village Voice* won the 1981 Pulitzer prize for feature writing for her account of the death of *Playboy* centerfold Dorothy Stratten. Carpenter is also the recipient of two Clarion awards, a Page One award and The Front Page award. The Stratten article was the inspiration for a television movie starring Jamie Lee Curtis and also the basis for a feature film, *Star 80*, directed by Bob Fosse and starring Eric Roberts and Mariel Hemingway. The movie is considered a modern classic. Carpenter is the author of four books: *Missing Beauty* (1988), *Mob Girl* (1992), *Without a Doubt* (1997), and *The Miss Stone Affair* (2003). She is also editor of *New York Diaries: 1609-2009* (2012.)

Death of a Playmate

Dorothy Stratten was the focus of the dreams
and ambitions of three men—one killed her

It is shortly past four in the afternoon and Hugh Hefner glides wordlessly into the library of his Playboy Mansion West. He is wearing pajamas and looking somber in green silk. The incongruous spectacle of a sybarite in mourning. To date, his public profession of grief has been contained in a press release: "The death of Dorothy Stratten comes as a shock to us all... As Playboy's Playmate of the Year with a film and a television career of increasing importance, her professional future was a bright one. But equally sad to us is the fact that her loss takes from us all a very special member of the Playboy family."

That's all. A dispassionate eulogy from which one might conclude that Miss Stratten died in her sleep of pneumonia. One, certainly, which masked the turmoil her death created within the Playboy organization. During the morning hours after Stratten was found nude in a West Los Angeles apartment, her face blasted away by 12-gauge buckshot, editors scrambled to pull her photos from the upcoming October issue. It could not be done. The issues were already run. So they pulled her ethereal blond image from the cover of the 1981 Playmate Calendar and promptly scrapped a Christmas promotion featuring her posed in the buff with Hefner. Other playmates, of course, have expired violently. Wilhelmina Rietveld took a massive overdose of barbiturates in 1973. Claudia Jennings, known as "Queen of the B-Movies," was crushed to death last fall in her Volkswagen convertible. Both caused grief and chagrin to the self-serious "family" of playmates whose aura does not admit the possibility of shaving nicks and bladder infections, let alone death.

But the loss of Dorothy Stratten sent Hefner and his family into seclusion, at least from the press. For one thing, Playboy has been earnestly trying to

avoid any bad national publicity that might threaten its application for a casi-
no license in Atlantic City. But beyond that, Dorothy Stratten was a corporate
treasure. She was not just any playmate but the "Eighties' First Playmate of the
Year," who, as *Playboy* trumpeted in June, was on her way to becoming "one of
the few emerging film goddesses of the new decade."

She gave rise to extravagant comparisons with Marilyn Monroe,
although unlike Monroe, she was no cripple. She was delighted with her success and wanted more of it. Far from being brutalized by Hollywood, she was
coddled by it. Her screen roles were all minor ones. A fleeting walk-on as a
bunny in *Americathon*. A small running part as a roller nymph in *Skatetown
U.S.A.* She played the most perfect woman in the universe in an episode of *Buck
Rogers in the 25th Century*. She was surely more successful in a shorter period
of time than any other playmate in the history of the empire. "*Playboy* has not
really had a star," says Stratten's erstwhile agent David Wilder. "They thought
she was going to be the biggest thing they ever had."

No wonder Hefner grieves.

"The major reason that I'm . . . that we're both sittin' here," says Hefner,
"that I wanted to talk about it, is because there is still a great tendency . . . for
this thing to fall into the classic cliché of 'smalltown girl comes to *Playboy*,
comes to Hollywood, life in the fast lane,' and that was somehow related to
her death. And that is not what really happened. A very sick guy saw his meal
ticket and his connection to power, whatever, slipping away. And it was that
that made him kill her."

The "very sick guy" is Paul Snider, Dorothy Stratten's husband, the man
who became her mentor. He is the one who plucked her from a Dairy Queen
in Vancouver, British Columbia, and pushed her into the path of *Playboy*
during the Great Playmate Hunt in 1978. Later, as she moved out of his class,
he became a millstone, and Stratten's prickliest problem was not coping with
celebrity but discarding a husband she had outgrown. When Paul Snider
balked at being discarded, he became her nemesis. And on August 14 of this
year he apparently took her life and his own with a 12-gauge shotgun.

It is not so difficult to see why Snider became an embarrassment. Since the
murder he has been excoriated by Hefner and others as a cheap hustler, but
such moral indignation always rings a little false in Hollywood. Snider's main
sin was that he lacked scope.

Snider grew up in Vancouver's East End, a tough area of the city steeped
in machismo. His parents split up when he was a boy and he had to fend for
himself from the time he quit school in the seventh grade. Embarrassed by

being skinny, he took up bodybuilding in his late teens and within a year had fleshed out his upper torso. His dark hair and mustache were groomed impeccably and women on the nightclub circuit found him attractive. The two things it seemed he could never get enough of were women and money. For a time he was the successful promoter of automobile and cycle shows at the Pacific National Exhibition. But legitimate enterprises didn't bring him enough to support his expensive tastes and he took to procuring women. He wore mink, drove a black Corvette, and flaunted a bejeweled Star of David around his neck. About town he was known as the Jewish Pimp.

Among the heavy gang types in Vancouver, known as the Rounder Crowd, Paul Snider was regarded with scorn. A punk who always seemed to be missing the big score. "He never touched [the drug trade]," said one Rounder who knew him then. "Nobody trusted him that much and he was scared to death of drugs. He finally lost a lot of money to loan sharks and the Rounder Crowd hung him by his ankles from the thirtieth floor of a hotel. He had to leave town."

Snider split for Los Angeles where he acquired a gold limousine and worked his girls on the fringes of Beverly Hills. He was enamored of Hollywood's dated appeal and styled his girls to conform with a 1950s notion of glamour. At various times he toyed with the idea of becoming a star, or perhaps even a director or a producer. He tried to pry his way into powerful circles, but without much success. At length he gave up pimping because the girls weren't bringing him enough income—one had stolen some items and had in fact cost him money—and when he returned to Vancouver some time in 1977 Snider resolved to keep straight. For one thing, he was terrified of going to jail. He would kill himself, he once told a girl, before he would go to jail.

But Snider never lost the appraising eye of a pimp. One night early in 1978 he and a friend dropped into an East Vancouver Dairy Queen and there he first took notice of Dorothy Ruth Hoogstraten filling orders behind the counter. She was very tall with the sweet natural looks of a girl, but she moved like a mature woman. Snider turned to his friend and observed, "That girl could make me a lot of money." He got Dorothy's number from another waitress and called her at home. She was eighteen.

Later when she recalled their meeting, Dorothy would feign amused exasperation at Paul's overtures. He was brash, lacking altogether in finesse. But he appealed to her, probably because he was older by nine years and streetwise. He offered to take charge of her and that was nice. Her father, a Dutch immigrant, had left the family when she was very young. Dorothy had floated along like a particle in a solution. There had never been enough money to buy nice things. And now Paul bought her clothes. He gave her a topaz ring set in diamonds. She could escape to his place, a posh apartment with skylights, plants, and deep burgundy furniture. He would buy wine and cook dinner. Afterwards he'd fix hot toddies and play the guitar for her. In public he was an obnoxious braggart; in private he could be a vulnerable, cuddly Jewish boy.

Paul Snider knew that gaping vulnerability of a young girl. Before he came along Dorothy had had only one boyfriend. She had thought of herself as "plain with big hands." At sixteen, her breasts swelled into glorious lobes, but she never really knew what to do about them. She was a shy, comely, undistinguished teenager who wrote sophomoric poetry and had no aspirations other than landing a secretarial job. When Paul told her she was beautiful, she unfolded in the glow of his compliments and was infected by his ambitions for her.

Snider probably never worked Dorothy as a prostitute. He recognized that she was, as one observer put it, "class merchandise" that could be groomed to better advantage. He had tried to promote other girls as playmates, notably a stripper in 1974, but without success. He had often secured recycled playmates or bunnies to work his auto shows and had seen some get burned out on sex and cocaine, languishing because of poor management. Snider dealt gingerly with Dorothy's inexperience and broke her in gradually. After escorting her to her graduation dance—he bought her a ruffled white gown for the occasion—he took her to a German photographer named Uwe Meyer for her first professional portrait. She looked like a flirtatious virgin.

About a month later, Snider called Meyer again, this time to do a nude shooting at Snider's apartment. Meyer arrived with a hairdresser to find Dorothy a little nervous. She clung, as she later recalled, to a scarf or a blouse as a towline to modesty, but she fell quickly into playful postures. She was perfectly pliant.

"She was eager to please," recalls Meyer. "I hesitated to rearrange her breasts thinking it might upset her, but she said, 'Do whatever you like.'"

Meyer hoped to get the $1,000 finder's fee that *Playboy* routinely pays photographers who discover playmates along the byways and backwaters of the continent. But Snider, covering all bets, took Dorothy to another photographer named Ken Honey who had an established track-record with *Playboy*. Honey had at first declined to shoot Dorothy because she was underage and needed a parent's signature on the release. Dorothy, who was reluctant to tell anyone at home about the nude posing, finally broke the news to her mother and persuaded her to sign. Honey sent this set of shots to Los Angeles and was sent a finder's fee. In August 1978, Dorothy flew to Los Angeles for a test shot. It was the first time she had ever been on a plane.

Even to the most cynical sensibilities there is something miraculous to the way Hollywood took to Dorothy Hoogstraten.

In a city overpopulated with beautiful women—most of them soured and disillusioned by twenty-five—Dorothy caught some current fortune and floated steadily upward through the spheres of that indifferent paradise. Her test shots were superb, placing her among the sixteen top contenders for the Twenty-Fifth Anniversary Playmate. And although she lost out to Candy Loving, she was named Playmate of the Month for August 1979. As soon as he learned of her selection, Paul Snider, by Hefner's account at least, flew to Los Angeles and proposed. They did not marry right away but set up housekeeping in a modest apartment in West Los Angeles. It was part of Snider's grand plan that Dorothy should support them both. She was, however, an alien and had no green card. Later, when it appeared her fortunes were on the rise during the fall of 1979, Hefner would personally intervene to secure her a temporary work permit. In the meantime, she was given a job as a bunny at the Century City Playboy Club. The Organization took care of her. It recognized a good thing. While other playmates required cosmetic surgery on breasts or scars, Stratten was nearly perfect. There was a patch of adolescent acne on her forehead and a round birthmark on her hip, but nothing serious. Her most troublesome flaw was a tendency to get plump, but that was controlled through passionate exercise. The only initial change *Playboy* deemed necessary was trimming her shoulder-length blond hair. And the cumbersome "Hoogstraten" became "Stratten."

Playboy photographers had been so impressed by the way Dorothy photographed that a company executive called agent David Wilder of Barr-Wilder Associates. Wilder, who handled the film careers of other playmates, agreed to meet Dorothy for coffee.

"A quality like Dorothy Stratten's comes by once in a lifetime," says Wilder with the solemn exaggeration that comes naturally after a tragedy. "She was exactly what this town likes, a beautiful girl who could act."

More to the point she had at least one trait to meet any need. When Lorimar Productions wanted a "playmate type" for a bit role in *Americathon*, Wilder sent Dorothy. When Columbia wanted a beauty who could skate for *Skatetown*, Wilder sent Dorothy, who could skate like an ace. When the producers of *Buck Rogers* and later *Galaxina* asked simply for a woman who was so beautiful that no one could deny it, Wilder sent Dorothy. And once Dorothy got in the door, it seemed that no one could resist her.

During the spring of 1979, Dorothy was busy modeling or filming. One photographer recalls, "She was green, but took instruction well." From time to time, however, she would have difficulty composing herself on the set. She asked a doctor for a prescription of Valium. It was the adjustments, she explained, and the growing hassles with Paul.

Since coming to LA, Snider had been into some deals of his own, most of them legal but sleazy. He had promoted exotic male dancers at a local disco, a wet underwear contest near Santa Monica, and wet T-shirt contests in the San Fernando Valley. But his chief hopes rested with Dorothy. He reminded her constantly that the two of them had what he called "a lifetime bargain" and he pressed her to marry him. Dorothy was torn by indecision. Friends tried to dissuade her from marrying, saying it could hold back her career, but she replied: "He cares for me so much. He's always there when I need him. I can't ever imagine myself being with any other man but Paul."

They were married in Las Vegas on June 1, 1979, and the following month Dorothy returned to Canada for a promotional tour of the provinces. Paul did not go with her because *Playboy* wanted the marriage kept secret. In Vancouver, Dorothy was greeted like a minor celebrity. The local press, a little caustic but mainly cowed, questioned her obliquely about exploitation. "I see the pictures as nudes, like nude paintings," she said. "They are not made for people to fantasize about." Her family and Paul's family visited her hotel, highly pleased with her success. Her first film was about to be released. The August issue was already on the stands featuring her as a pouting nymph who wrote poetry. (A few plodding iambs were even reprinted.)

And she was going to *star* in a new Canadian film by North American Pictures called *Autumn Born*.

Since the murder, not much has been made of this film, probably because it contained unpleasant overtones of bondage. Dorothy played the lead, a seventeen-year-old rich orphan who is kidnapped and abused by her uncle. Dorothy was excited about the role, although she conceded to a Canadian reporter, "a lot [of it] is watching this girl get beat up."

While Dorothy was being pummeled on the set of *Autumn Born*, Snider busied himself apartment hunting. They were due for a rent raise and were looking to share a place with a doctor friend, a young internist who patronized the Century City Playboy Club. Paul found a two-story Spanish style stucco house near the Santa Monica Freeway in West LA. There was a living room upstairs as well as a bedroom which the doctor claimed. Paul and Dorothy moved into the second bedroom downstairs at the back of the house. Since the doctor spent many nights with his girlfriend, the Sniders had the house much to themselves.

Paul had a growing obsession with Dorothy's destiny. It was, of course, his own. He furnished the house with photographs, and got plates reading "Star-80" for his new Mercedes. He talked about her as the next Playmate of the Year, the next Marilyn Monroe. When he had had a couple of glasses of wine, he would croon, "We're on a rocket ship to the moon." When they hit it big, he said, they would move to Bel-Air Estates where the big producers live.

Dorothy was made uncomfortable by his grandiosity. He was putting her, she confided to friends, in a position where she could not fail without failing them both. But she did not complain to him. They had, after all, a lifetime bargain, and he had brought her a long way.

As her manager he provided the kind of cautionary coaching that starlets rarely receive. He would not let her smoke. He monitored her drinking, which was moderate at any rate. He would have allowed her a little marijuana and cocaine under his supervision, but she showed no interest in drugs, except Valium. Mainly he warned her to be wary of the men she met at the Mansion, men who would promise her things, then use her up. Snider taught her how to finesse a come-on. How to turn a guy down without putting him off. Most important, he discussed with her who she might actually have to sleep with. Hefner, of course, was at the top of the list.

Did Hefner sleep with Dorothy Stratten? Mansion gossips who have provided graphic narratives of Hefner's encounters with other playmates cannot similarly document a tryst with Dorothy. According to bizarre code of the Life—sexual society at the Mansion—fucking Hefner is a strictly voluntary thing. It never hurts a career, but Hefner, with so much sex at his disposal, would consider it unseemly to apply pressure.

Of Stratten, Hefner says, "There was a friendship between us. It wasn't romantic... This was not a very loose lady."

Hefner likes to think of himself as a "father figure" to Stratten who, when she decided to marry, came to tell him about it personally. "She knew I had serious reservations about [Snider]," says Hefner. "I had sufficient reservations... that I had him checked out in terms of a possible police record in Canada... I used the word—and I realized the [risk] I was taking—I said to her that he had a 'pimp-like quality' about him."

Like most playmate husbands, Snider was held at arm's length by the Playboy family. He was only rarely invited to the Mansion, which bothered him, as he would have liked more of an opportunity to cultivate Hefner. And Stratten, who was at the Mansion more frequently to party and roller skate, was never actively into the Life. Indeed, she spoke disdainfully of the "whores" who serviced Hefner's stellar guests. Yet she moved into the circle of Hefner's distinguished favorites when it became apparent that she might have a real future in film.

Playboy, contrary to the perception of aspiring starlets, is not a natural conduit to stardom. Most playmates who go into movies peak with walk-ons and fade away. Those whom Hefner has tried most earnestly to promote in recent years have been abysmal flops. Barbi Benton disintegrated into a jiggling loon and, according to Playboy sources, Hefner's one-time favorite Sondra Theodore went wooden once the camera started to roll.

"Dorothy was important," says one Playboy employee, "because Hefner is regarded by Hollywood as an interloper. They'll come to his parties and play his games. But the won't give him respect. One of the ways he can gain legitimacy is to be a star maker."

There is something poignant about Hefner, master of an empire built on inanimate nudes, but unable to coax these lustrous forms to life on film. His chief preoccupation nowadays is managing the playmates. Yet with all of those beautiful women at his disposal, he has not one Marion Davies to call his own. Dorothy exposed that yearning, that ego weakness, as surely as she revealed the most pathetic side of her husband's nature—his itch for the big score. Hefner simply had more class.

Dorothy's possibilities were made manifest to him during *The Playboy Roller Disco and Pajama Party* taped at the Mansion late in October 1978. Dorothy had a running part and was tremendously appealing.

"Some people have the quality," says Hefner. "I mean... there is something that comes from inside... The camera comes so close that it almost looks beneath the surface and... that magic is there somehow in the eyes... That magic she had. That was a curious combination of sensual appeal and vulnerability."

After the special was aired on television in November, Dorothy's career accelerated rapidly. There was a rush of appearances that left the accumulating impression of stardom. Around the first of December her *Fantasy Island* episode appeared. Later that month, *Buck Rogers in the 25th Century.* But the big news was that Hefner had chosen Dorothy Playmate of the Year for 1980. Although her selection was not announced to the public until April, she began photo sessions with *Playboy* photographer Mario Casilli before the year was out.

Her look was altered markedly from that of sultry minx in the August issue. As Playmate of the Year her image was more defined. No more pouting, soft-focus shots. Stratten was given a burnished high glamour. Her hair fell in the crimped undulating waves of a fifties starlet. Her translucent body was posed against scarlet velour reminiscent of the Monroe classic. One shot of Stratten displaying some of her $200,000 in gifts—a brass bed and a lavender Lore negligee—clearly evoked the platinum ideal of Jean Harlow. Dorothy's apotheosis reached, it seemed, for extremes of innocence and eroticism. In one shot she was draped in black lace and nestled into a couch, buttocks raised in an impish invitation to sodomy. Yet the cover displayed her clad in a chaste little peasant gown, seated in a meadow, head tilted angelically to one side. The dichotomy was an affirmation of her supposed sexual range. She was styled, apparently, as the Complete Goddess for the eighties.

By January 1980—the dawning of her designated decade—Dorothy Stratten was attended by a thickening phalanx of photographers, promoters, duennas, coaches, and managers. Snider, sensing uneasily that she might be moving beyond his reach, became more demanding. He wanted absolute control over her financial affairs and the movie offers she accepted. She argued that he was being unreasonable, that she had an agent and a business manager whose job it was to advise her in those matters. Snider then pressed her to take the $20,000 from Playboy and buy a house. It would be a good investment, he said. He spent a lot of time looking at homes that might suit her, but she always found fault with them. She did not want to commit herself. She suspected, perhaps rightly, that he only wanted to attach another lien on her life.

This domestic squabbling was suspended temporarily in January when it appeared that Dorothy was poised for her big break, a featured role in a comedy called *They All Laughed* starring Audrey Hepburn and Ben Gazzara. It was to be directed by Peter Bogdanovich, whom Dorothy had first met at the roller disco bash in October. According to David Wilder, he and Bogdanovich were partying at the Mansion in January when the director first considered Stratten for the part.

"Jesus Christ," the forty-one-year-old Bogdanovich is supposed to have said. "She's perfect for the girl . . . I don't want her for her tits and ass. I want someone who can act."

Wilder says he took Dorothy to Bogdanovich's house in Bel-Air Estates to read for the role. She went back two or three more times and the director decided she was exactly what he wanted.

Filming was scheduled to begin in late March in New York City. Paul wanted to come along but Dorothy said no. He would get in the way and, at any rate, the set was closed to outsiders. Determined that she should depart Hollywood as a queen, he borrowed their housemate's Rolls Royce and drove her to the airport. He put her on the plane in brash good spirits, then went home to sulk at being left behind.

The affair between Dorothy Stratten and Peter Bogdanovich was conducted in amazing secrecy. In that regard it bore little resemblance to the director's affair with Cybill Shepherd, an escapade that advertised his puerile preference for ingenues. Bogdanovich, doubtless, did not fancy the publicity that might result from a liaison with a twenty-year-old woman married to a hustler. A couple of days before the murder-suicide, he spoke of this to his close friend Hugh Hefner.

"It was the first time I'd seen him in a number of months because he'd been in New York," says Hefner. "He was very, very up. Very excited about her and the film... I don't think that he was playing with this at all. I think it was important to him. I'm talking about the relationship... He was concerned at that point because of what had happened to him and [Cybill]. He was concerned about the publicity related to the relationship because of that. He felt in retrospect, as a matter of fact, that he... that they had kind of caused some of it. And it played havoc with both of their careers for a while."

Stratten, as usual, did not advertise the fact that she was married. When she arrived in New York, she checked quietly into the Wyndham Hotel. The crew knew very little about her except that she showed up on time and seemed very earnest about her small role. She was cordial but kept her distance, spending her time off-camera in a director's chair reading. One day it would be Dickens's *Great Expectations*, the next day a book on dieting. With the help of makeup and hair consultants her looks were rendered chaste and ethereal to defuse her playmate image. "She was a darling little girl," says makeup artist Fern Buckner. "Very beautiful, of course. Whatever you did to her it was all right."

Dorothy had headaches. She was eating very little to keep her weight down and working twelve-hour days because Bogdanovich was pushing the project along at rapid pace. While most of the crew found him a selfish, mean-spirited megalomaniac, the cast by and large found him charming. He was particularly solicitous of Dorothy Stratten. And just as quietly as she had checked into the Wyndham, she moved into his suite at the Plaza. Word spread around the set that Bogdanovich and Stratten were involved but, because they were discreet, they avoided unpleasant gossip. "They weren't hanging all over one another," says one crew member. "It wasn't until the last few weeks when everyone relaxed a bit that they would show up together holding hands." One day Bogdanovich walked over to a couch where Dorothy sat chewing gum. "You shouldn't chew gum," he admonished. "It has sugar in it." She playfully removed the wad from her mouth and deposited it in his palm.

Bogdanovich is less than eager to discuss the affair. His secretary says he will not give interviews until *They All Laughed* is released in April. The director needs a hit badly and who can tell how Stratten's death might affect box office. *Laughed* is, unfortunately, a comedy over which her posthumous performance might throw a pall. Although the plot is being guarded as closely as a national security secret, it goes something like this:

Ben Gazzara is a private detective hired by a wealthy, older man who suspects his spouse, Audrey Hepburn, has a lover. In following her, Gazzara falls in love with her. Meanwhile, Gazzara's sidekick, John Ritter, is hired by another wealthy older man to follow his young bride, Dorothy Stratten. Ritter watches Stratten from afar—through a window as she argues with her husband, as she roller skates at the Roxy. After a few perfunctory conversations, he asks her to marry him. Hepburn and Gazzara make a brief abortive stab at mature love. And Gazzara reverts to dating and mating with teenyboppers.

Within this intricate web of shallow relationships Dorothy, by all accounts, emerges as a shimmering seraph, a vision of perfection clad perennially in white. In one scene she is found sitting in the Algonquin Hotel bathed in a diaphanous light. "It was one of those scene that could make a career," recalls a member of the crew. "People in the screening room rustled when they saw her. She didn't have many lines. She just looked so good." Bogdanovich was so enthusiastic about her that he called Hefner on the West Coast to say he was expanding Dorothy's role—not many more lines, but more exposure.

Paul Snider, meanwhile, was calling the East Coast where he detected a chill in Dorothy's voice. She would be too tired to talk. He would say, "I love you," and she wouldn't answer back. Finally, she began to have her calls screened. Late in April, during a shooting break, she flew to Los Angeles for a flurry of appearances, which included a Playmate of the Year Luncheon and an appearance on *The Johnny Carson Show*. Shortly thereafter, Dorothy left for a grand tour of Canada. She agreed, however, to meet Paul in Vancouver during the second week of May. Her mother was remarrying and she planned to attend the wedding.

The proposed rendezvous worried Dorothy's Playboy traveling companion, Liz Norris. Paul was becoming irascible. He called Dorothy in Toronto and flew into a rage when she suggested that he allow her more freedom. Norris offered to provide her charge with a bodyguard once they arrived in Vancouver, but Dorothy declined. She met Paul and over her objections he checked them into the same hotel. Later, each gave essentially the same account of that encounter. She asked him to loosen his grip. "Let a bird fly," she said. They argued violently, they both sank back into tears. According to Snider, they reconciled and made love. Dorothy never acknowledged that. She later told a friend, however, that she had offered to leave Hollywood and go back to live with him in Vancouver, but he didn't want that. In the end she cut her trip short to get back to shooting.

Snider, by now, realized that his empire was illusory. As her husband he technically had claim to half of her assets, but many of her assets were going into a corporation called Dorothy Stratten Enterprises. He was not one of the officers. When she spoke of financial settlements, she sounded like she was reading a strange script. She was being advised, he suspected, by Bogdanovich's lawyers. (Dorothy's attorney, Wayne Alexander, reportedly represents Bogdanovich too, but Alexander could not be reached for comment.) Late in June, Snider received a letter declaring that he and Dorothy were separated physically and financially. She closed out their joint bank accounts and began advancing him money through her business manager.

Buffeted by forces beyond his control, Snider tried to cut his losses. He could have maintained himself as a promoter or as the manager of a health club. He was an expert craftsman and turned out exercise benches that he sold for $200 a piece. On at least one occasion he had subverted those skills to more dubious ends by building a wooden bondage rack for his private pleasure. But Snider didn't want to be a nobody. His rocket ship had come too close to the moon to leave him content with hang-gliding.

He tried, a little pathetically, to groom another Dorothy Stratten, a seventeen-year-old check-out girl from Riverside who modeled on the side. He had discovered her at an auto show. Patty was of the same statuesque Stratten ilk, and Snider taught her to walk like Dorothy, to dress like Dorothy, and to wear her hair like Dorothy. Eventually she moved into the house that he and Dorothy shared. But she was not another Stratten, and when Snider tried to promote her as a Playmate, Playboy wanted nothing to do with him.

Paul's last hope for a big score was a project begun a month or so before he and Dorothy were married. He had worked out a deal with a couple of photographer friends, Bill and Susan Lachasse, to photograph Dorothy on skates wearing a French-cut skating outfit. From that they would print a poster that they hoped would sell a million copies and net $300,000. After Dorothy's appearance on the Carson show, Snider thought the timing was right. But Dorothy had changed her mind. The Lachasses flew to New York the day after she finished shooting to persuade her to reconsider. They were told by the production office that Dorothy could be found at Bogdanovich's suite at the Plaza.

"It was three or four in the afternoon," says Lachasse. "There had been a cast party the night before. Dorothy answered the door in pajamas and said, 'Oh my God! What are you doing here?' She shut the door and when she came out again she explained 'I can't invite you in. There are people here.' She looked at the photos in the hallway and we could tell by her eyes that she liked them. She took them inside, then came out and said, 'Look how my tits are hanging down.' Somebody in there was telling her what to do. She said, 'Look, I'm confused, have you shown these to Paul?' I said, 'Dorothy, you're divorcing Paul.' And she said, 'I don't know, I just don't know.'"

When Lachasse called the Plaza suite the following week a woman replied, "We don't' know Dorothy Stratten. Stop harassing us."

"Paul felt axed as in every other area," says Lachasse. "That was his last bit of income."

During the anxious spring and early summer, Snider suspected, but could not prove, that Dorothy was having an affair. So as the filming of *They All Laughed* drew to a close in mid-July, he did what, in the comic world of Peter Bogdanovich, many jealous husbands do. He hired a private eye, a twenty-six-year-old freelance detective named Marc Goldstein. The elfish Goldstein, who later claimed to be a friend of both Dorothy and Paul, in fact knew neither of them well. He was retained upon the recommendation of an unidentified third party. He will not say what exactly his mission was, but a Canadian lawyer named Ted Ewachniuk, who represented both Paul and Dorothy in Vancouver, claims that Snider was seeking to document the affair with Bogdanovich in order to sue him for "enticement to breach management contract"—an agreement Snider believed inherent within their marriage contract. That suit was to be filed in British Columbia, thought to be a suitable venue since both Snider and Stratten were still Canadians and, it could be argued, had only gone to Los Angeles for business.

Goldstein began showing up regularly at Snider's apartment. Snider produced poems and love letters from Bogdanovich that he had found among Dorothy's things. He instructed Goldstein to do an asset search on Dorothy and to determine whether or not Bogdanovich was plying her with cocaine.

Even as he squared off for a legal fight, Snider was increasingly despairing. He knew, underneath it all, that he did not have the power or resources to fight Bogdanovich. "Maybe this thing is too big for me," he confided to a friend, and he talked about going back to Vancouver. But the prospect of returning in defeat was too humiliating. He felt Dorothy was now so completely sequestered by attorneys that he would never see her again. Late in July his old machismo gave way to grief. He called Bill Lachasse one night crying because he could not touch Dorothy or even get near her. About the same time, his roommate the doctor returned home one night to find him despondent in the living room. "This is really hard," Paul said, and broke into tears. He wrote fragments of notes to Dorothy that were never sent. One written in red felt-tip marker and later found stuffed into one of his drawers was a rambling plaint on how he couldn't get it together without her. With Ewachniuk's help, he drafted a letter to Bogdanovich telling him to quit influencing Dorothy and that he [Snider] would "forgive" him. But Ewachniuk does not know if the letter was ever posted.

Dorothy, Paul knew, had gone for a holiday in London with Bogdanovich and would be returning to Los Angeles soon. He tortured himself with the scenario of the successful director and his queen showing up at Hefner's Midsummer Night's Dream Party on August 1. He couldn't bear it and blamed Hefner for fostering the affair. He called the Mansion trying to get an invitation to the party and was told he would be welcome only if he came with Dorothy.

But Dorothy did not show up at the party. She was keeping a low profile. She had moved ostensibly into a modest little apartment in Beverly Hills, the address that appeared on her death certificate. The apartment, however, was occupied by an actress who was Bogdanovich's personal assistant. Dorothy had actually moved into Bogdanovich's home in Bel-Air Estates. Where the big producers live.

Several days after her return to Los Angeles, she left for a playmate promotion in Dallas and Houston. There she appeared radiant, apparently reveling in her own success. She had been approached about playing Marilyn Monroe in Larry Schiller's made-for-TV movie, but she had been too busy with the Bogdanovich film. She had been discussed as a candidate for *Charlie's Angels* although Wilder thought she could do better. She was scheduled to meet with independent producer Martin Krofft, who was considering her for his new film, *The Last Desperado*. It all seemed wonderful to her. But Stratten was not so cynical that she could enjoy her good fortune without pangs of regret. She cried in private. Until the end she retained a lingering tenderness for Paul Snider and felt bound to see him taken care of after the divorce. From Houston she gave him a call and agreed to meet him on Friday, August 8, for lunch.

After hearing from her, Snider was as giddy as a con whose sentence has been commuted, for he believed somehow that everything would be all right between them again. The night before their appointed meeting he went out for sandwiches with friends and was his blustering, confident old self. It would be different, he said. He would let her know that he had changed. "I've really got to vacuum the rug," he crowed. "The queen is coming back."

The lunch date, however, was a disaster. The two of them ended up back in the apartment squared off sullenly on the couch. Dorothy confessed at last that she was in love with Bogdanovich and wanted to proceed with some kind of financial settlement. Before leaving she went through her closet and took the clothes she wanted. The rest, she said, he should give to Patty.

Having his hopes raised so high and then dashed again gave Snider a perverse energy. Those who saw him during the five days prior to the murder caught only glimpses of odd behavior. In retrospect they appear to form a pattern of intent. He was preoccupied with guns. Much earlier in the year Snider had borrowed a revolver from a friend named Chip, the consort of one of Dorothy's playmates. Paul never felt easy, he said, without a gun, a holdover from his days on the East End. But Paul had to give the revolver back that Friday afternoon because Chip was leaving town. He looked around for another gun. On Sunday he held a barbecue at his place for a few friends and invited Goldstein. During the afternoon he pulled Goldstein aside and asked the detective to buy a machine gun for him. He needed it, he said, for "home protection." Goldstein talked him out of it.

In the classifieds, Snider found someone in the San Fernando Valley who wanted to sell a 12-gauge Mossberg pump shotgun. He circled the ad and called the owner. On Monday he drove into the Valley to pick up the gun but got lost in the dark. The owner obligingly brought it to a construction site where he showed Snider how to load and fire it.

Dorothy, meanwhile, had promised to call Paul on Sunday but did not ring until Monday, an omission that piqued him. They agreed to meet on Thursday at 11:30 a. m. to discuss the financial settlement. She had been instructed by her advisers to offer him a specified sum. During previous conversations, Paul thought he had heard Dorothy say, "I'll always take care of you," but he could not remember the exact words. Goldstein thought it might be a good idea to wire Snider's body for sound so that they could get a taped account if Dorothy repeated her promise to provide for him. They could not come up with the proper equipment, however, and abandoned the plan.

On Wednesday, the day he picked up the gun, Snider seemed in an excellent mood. He told his roommate that Dorothy would be coming over and that she had agreed to look at a new house that he thought might be a good investment for her. He left the impression that they were on amiable terms. That evening he dropped by Bill Lachasse's studio to look at promotional shots of Patty. There, too, he was relaxed and jovial. In an offhanded way, he told Lachasse that he had bought a gun for protection. He also talked of strange and unrelated things that did not seem menacing in the context of his good spirits. He talked of Claudia Jennings, who had died with a movie in progress. Some playmates get killed, he observed. And when that happens, it causes a lot of chaos.

Bogdanovich had somehow discovered that Dorothy was being trailed by a private eye. He was furious, but Dorothy was apparently not alarmed. She was convinced that she and Paul were on the verge of working out an amicable agreement and she went to meet him as planned. According to the West Los Angeles police, she parked and locked her 1967 Mercury around 11:45 a. m., but the county coroner reports that she arrived later, followed by Goldstein who clocked her into the house at 12:30 p. m. Shortly thereafter, Goldstein called Snider to find out how things were going. Snider replied, in code, that everything was fine. Periodically throughout the afternoon, Goldstein rang Snider with no response. No one entered the house until five when Patty and another of Paul's little girlfriends returned home, noticed Dorothy's car and saw the doors to Snider's room closed. Since they heard no sounds, they assumed he wanted privacy. The two girls left to go skating and returned at 7 p. m. By then the doctor had arrived home and noticed the closed door. He also heard the unanswered ringing on Snider's downstairs phone. Shortly before midnight Goldstein called Patty and asked her to knock at Paul's door. She demurred, so he asked to speak to the doctor. The latter agreed to check but even as he walked downstairs he felt some foreboding. The endless ringing had put him on edge and his German shepherd had been pacing and whining in the yard behind Paul's bedroom. The doctor knocked and when there was no response, he pushed the door open. The scene burnt his senses and he yanked the door shut.

It is impolitic to suggest that Paul Snider loved Dorothy Stratten. Around Hollywood, at least, he is currently limned as brutal and utterly insensitive. If he loved her, it was in the selfish way of one who cannot separate a lover's best interests from one's own. And if he did what he is claimed to have done, he was, as Hugh Hefner would put it, "a very sick guy."

Even now, however, no one can say with certainty that Paul Snider committed either murder or suicide. One of his old confederates claims he bought the gun to "scare" Bogdanovich. The coroner was sufficiently equivocal to deem his death a "questionable suicide/possible homicide." One Los Angeles psychic reportedly attributes the deaths to an unemployed actor involved with Snider in a drug deal. Goldstein, who holds to a theory that both were murdered, is badgering police for results of fingerprintings and paraffin tests, but the police consider Goldstein a meddler and have rebuffed his requests. The West LAPD, which has not yet closed the case, says it cannot determine if it was Snider who fired the shotgun because his hands were coated with too much blood and tissue for tests to be conclusive.

And yet Snider appears to have been following a script of his own choosing. One which would thwart the designs of Playboy and Hollywood. Perhaps he had only meant to frighten Dorothy, to demonstrate to Bogdanovich that he could hold her in thrall at gunpoint. Perhaps he just got carried away with the scene. No one knows exactly how events unfolded after Dorothy entered the house that afternoon. She had apparently spent some time upstairs because her purse was found lying in the middle of the living room floor. In it was a note in Paul's handwriting explaining his financial distress. He had no green card, it said, and he required support. Dorothy's offer, however, fell far short of support. It was a flat settlement of only $7,500 which, she claimed, represented half of her total assets after taxes. "Not enough," said one friend, "to put a nice little sports car in his garage." Perhaps she had brought the first installment to mollify Paul's inevitable disappointment; police found $1,100 in cash among her belongings, another $400 among his. One can only guess at the motives of those two doomed players who, at some point in the afternoon, apparently left the front room and went downstairs.

It is curious that, given the power of the blasts, the little bedroom was not soaked in blood. There was only spattering on the walls, curtains, and television. Perhaps because the room lacked a charnel aspect, the bodies themselves appeared all the more grim. They were nude. Dorothy lay crouched across the bottom corner of a low bed. Both knees were on the carpet and her right shoulder was drooping. Her blond hair hung naturally, oddly unaffected by the violence to her countenance. The shell had entered above her left eye leaving the bones of that seraphic face shattered and displaced in a welter of pulp. Her body, mocking the soft languid poses of her pictorials, was in full rigor.

No one, least of all Hugh Hefner, could have foreseen such a desecration. It was unthinkable that an icon of eroticism presumed by millions of credulous readers to be impervious to the pangs of mortality could be reduced by a pull of a trigger to a corpse, mortally stiff, mortally livid, and crawling with small black ants. For Hefner, in fact, that grotesque alteration must have been particularly bewildering. Within the limits of his understanding, he had done everything right. He had played it clean with Stratten, handling her paternally, providing her with gifts and opportunities and, of course, the affection of the Playboy family. Despite his best efforts, however, she was destroyed. The irony that Hefner does not perceive or at least fails to acknowledge is that Stratten was destroyed by random particulars, but by a germ breeding within the ethic. One of the tacit tenets of Playboy philosophy—that women can be possessed—had found a fervent adherent in Paul Snider. He had bought the dream without qualification, and he thought of himself as perhaps one of Playboy's most honest apostles. He acted out of dark fantasies never intended to be realized. Instead of fondling himself in private, instead of wreaking abstract violence upon a centerfold, he ravaged a playmate in the flesh.

Dorothy had, apparently, been sodomized, though whether this occurred before or after her death is not clear. After the blast, her body was moved and there were what appeared to be bloody handprints on her buttocks and left leg. Near her head was Paul's handmade bondage rack set for rear-entry intercourse. Loops of tape, used and unused, were lying about and strands of long blond hair were discovered clutched in Snider's right hand. He was found face-down lying parallel to the foot of the bed. The muzzle of the Mossberg burnt his right cheek as the shell tore upward through his brain. The blast, instead of driving him backwards, whipped him forward over the length of the gun. He had always said he would rather die than go to jail.

Goldstein arrived before the police and called the Mansion. Hefner, thinking the call a prank, would not come to the phone at first. When he did he asked for the badge number of the officer at the scene. Satisfied that this was no bad joke, Hefner, told his guests in the game house. There were wails of sorrow and disbelief. He then called Bogdanovich. "There was no conversation," Hefner says. "I was afraid that he had gone into shock or something. [When he didn't respond] I called the house under another number. A male friend was there to make sure he was [all right]. He was overcome."

Bogdanovich arranged for Stratten's cremation five days later. Her ashes were placed in an urn and buried in a casket so that he could visit them. Later he would issue his own statement:

> DOROTHY STRATTEN WAS AS GIFTED AND INTELLIGENT AN ACTRESS AS SHE WAS BEAUTIFUL, AND SHE WAS VERY BEAUTIFUL INDEED—IN EVERY WAY IMAGINABLE—MOST PARTICULARLY IN HER HEART. SHE AND I FELL IN LOVE DURING OUR PICTURE AND HAD PLANNED TO BE MARRIED AS SOON AS HER DIVORCE WAS FINAL. THE LOSS TO HER MOTHER AND FATHER, HER SISTER AND BROTHER, TO MY CHILDREN, TO HER FRIENDS AND TO ME IS LARGER THAN WE CAN CALCULATE. BUT THERE IS NO LIFE DOROTHY'S TOUCHED THAT HAS NOT BEEN CHANGED FOR THE BETTER THROUGH KNOWING HER, HOWEVER BRIEFLY. DOROTHY LOOKED AT THE WORLD WITH LOVE, AND BELIEVED THAT ALL PEOPLE WERE GOOD DOWN DEEP. SHE WAS MISTAKEN, BUT IT IS AMONG THE MOST GENEROUS AND NOBLE ERRORS WE CAN MAKE.
>
> PETER BOGDANOVICH

Bogdanovich took the family Hoogstraten in tow. They were stunned, but not apparently embittered by Dorothy's death. "They knew who cared for her," Hefner says. Mother, fathers—both natural and stepfather—sister, and brother flew to Los Angeles for the service and burial at Westwood Memorial Park, the same cemetery, devotees of irony point out, where Marilyn Monroe is buried. Hefner and Bogdanovich were there and after the service the family repaired to Bogdanovich's house for rest and refreshments. It was all quiet and discreet. Dorothy's mother says that she will not talk to the press until the movie comes out. Not until April when Stratten's glimmering ghost will appear on movie screens across the country, bathed in white light and roller skating through a maze of hilarious infidelities.

Playboy, whose corporate cool was shaken by her untimely death, has regained its composure. The December issue features Stratten as one of the "Sex Stars of 1980." At the end of twelve pages of the biggest draws in show business—Bo Derek, Brooke Shields, etc.—she appears topless, one breast draped with a gossamer scarf. A caption laments her death which "cut short what seasoned star watchers predicted was sure to be an outstanding film career."

Hype, of course, often passes for prophecy. Whether or not Dorothy Stratten would have fulfilled her extravagant promise can't be known. Her legacy will not be examined critically because it is really of no consequence. In the end Dorothy Stratten was less memorable for herself than for the yearnings she evoked: in Snider a lust for the score; in Hefner a longing for a star; in Bogdanovich a desire for the eternal ingenue. She was a catalyst for a cycle of ambitions which revealed its players less wicked, perhaps, than pathetic.

As for Paul Snider, his body was returned to Vancouver in permanent exile from Hollywood. It was all too big for him. In that Elysium of dreams and deals, he had reached the limits of his class. His sin, his unforgivable sin, was being small-time.

November 5-11, 1980

Author's Afterword

As a kid I was shy but also very curious. I'd sit in a hutch behind the living room couch and listen to the adults gossip—in this way I learned things that were generally forbidden to children. The world opened up for me in high school when I took my first class in journalism. I realized that a reporter can ask questions others aren't allowed to ask. I no longer had to hide behind the couch to get straight answers.

Since I first took up this work, I've had a note posted on my typewriter—and later my word processor, and later my computer. It reads, simply, "What happened?" Meaning what *really* happened. You have to take away the self-interest, take away the manipulation and spin your interviewees give you, and find out what actually went down. A direct question will keep you, and them, honest. At least it will keep *you* honest. And that's a start.

I can't remember a time in my adult life when I wasn't a journalist. My Midwestern relations observed long ago that I seemed "harder" than I was before I left for New York. I don't know if that was intended as a compliment, but I chose to accept it as one.

I feel extremely fortunate to be able to work from a home office so I could give my son all of the attention and care he needed (with the help of a babysitter)—and still put in at least eight hours a day. Sometimes it meant working later into the night, but I feel I was lucky to have the independence to make those choices. Journalism did that for me.

To be honest, I'm most proud of actually making a living through writing. Did you know that the first American journalist/writer ever to earn his living by solely by writing was Edgar Allan Poe? He was always broke and scrambling. We've come a way since then. Of course the rise in Internet sites and proliferation of news aggregators raises the question of how young journalists coming through the pipeline now will be paid. We've got to work through that. One thing I've learned: Writers find a way to write. They make it happen because they love their craft. I know I did. Hopefully that will be the way in the future as well.

Lane DeGregory

Lane DeGregory is a Pulitzer Prize-winning *Tampa Bay Times* feature writer who prefers writing about people in the shadows. She sweated with a mailman who was mowing strangers' lawns, cried with a mother who was giving up custody of her adopted son, followed a feral child as she tried to fit into a family.

Lane graduated from the University of Virginia, where she was editor in chief of the *Cavalier Daily* student newspaper. Later, she earned a master's degree in rhetoric and communication from the University of Virginia.

For ten years, she wrote news and feature stories for the *Virginian-Pilot*, based in Norfolk, Virginia. In 2000, Lane moved to Florida to write for the *Times*. She's married to a drummer, Dan DeGregory, and they have two teenage sons, Ryland and Tucker; two big, rowdy dogs; and an ornery turtle.

Lane's stories have appeared in the *Best Newspaper Writing* editions of 2000, 2004, 2006, and 2008. She has been a speaker at the Niemen Narrative Conference at Harvard University and in colleges and newsrooms across the country. She has won more than thirty national awards, including the 2009 Pulitzer Prize for feature writing.

To Die For

One teen boy, two teen girls, and homicide

Sarah Ludemann couldn't stop crying.

All through lunch that Tuesday, while the other seniors at Pinellas Park High chattered in the cafeteria, Sarah slumped over a corner table, sobbing.

He did it again, Sarah told her best friend.

Her boyfriend, Josh, kept saying she was the only one. He'd been telling her that the whole time they'd been together. More than a year.

But that day she found out he had been hanging out with his ex—this girl named Rachel.

All morning, while she suffered through school, Rachel was texting Sarah, boasting that Josh was with her. Again.

I'm so over it, Sarah said.

Amber Malinchock didn't know what to say. For months, Sarah's friends had been telling her to forget about Josh. She deserved better.

But when you're eighteen and in love for the first time, you don't listen. Your love becomes your whole life.

Amber tried to get her friend's mind off her problems. She asked Sarah to go to the mall after school, maybe the movies.

No thanks, Sarah said.

She was hoping to see Josh.

About the time Sarah was talking to her best friend, Rachel Wade was at home, talking to hers.

Rachel had the day off from her job at Applebee's. Her friend had come by her apartment to hang out.

He did it again, Rachel said.

Her boyfriend, Josh, had slept over the night before, then bolted. He swore he cared about her, but it didn't feel that way.

Worst of all, she kept finding evidence that he was still seeing his ex—this girl named Sarah.

Sarah posted MySpace photos of herself with Josh at the beach. She bragged that she had been with him in New York over spring break.

I can't trust him, Rachel said.

Egle Nakaite didn't know what to say. For months, Rachel's friends had been telling her to forget about Josh. She could have any guy she wanted.

But when you're nineteen, independent and headstrong, you don't listen. You want to be the one he wants most.

"We didn't know what it was about Josh," Egle would say later. "He just had some kind of hold on her."

That afternoon—April 14, 2009—Egle asked Rachel if she wanted to get together later, maybe hit Starbucks.

Rachel said no.

She was supposed to hang out with Josh.

Rachel and Sarah hated each other, saw each other as competition. But they were more alike than either would have liked to admit.

They were raised in the same modest neighborhood in Pinellas Park. They grew up with both parents, hard-working people who cared about their kids. They went to the same school, walked the same halls. Both girls loved the beach and movies and dogs.

Both were blond, outgoing, with wide eyes and loud laughs. Both had MySpace pages.

Sarah Ludemann was tall and big-boned, a good student who seldom broke her 11 p. m. curfew. A tomboy. A daddy's girl.

Rachel Wade was petite and flirty, the kind of girl boys noticed. Never much of a student, she dropped out of school in tenth grade, got her GED and worked as a waiter, earning enough to rent her own apartment. On her MySpace page, she called herself "Independent Chic."

But the main thing Rachel and Sarah shared was Josh Camacho.

He was "My boo."

"My baby."

"My man."

Two girls' one and only.

Josh had curly hair, the color of coal, spilling across sculpted shoulders. Black eyes, a long nose, wide lips curled into a sneer. His dark jeans hung low on his slim hips. He stood about five feet five, but walked with the swagger of a bigger man.

Josh loved posing for cell phone portraits: flexing his biceps, waving a gun, showing off the tattoo that arcs across his back in inch-high Gothic letters: CAMACHO.

While seeing both Sarah and Rachel, Josh kept up a relationship with a third teenager, a girl he called "my baby mama." They'd had a son together. He spent time with the baby but didn't pay child support.

For a while, in high school, Josh cooked at Chick-fil-A and Pollo Tropical. But after graduation, he didn't go to college, didn't have a steady job or a car.

At nineteen, he stayed with family. Except when he persuaded some girl to let him spend the night.

"A player," police called him.

"A user," girls said.

The battle over this boy started with Silly String, escalated to profane tirades, and ended in tragedy. The story is documented in text and voice mail messages, in cell phone pictures, in Web postings, in reams of documents filed in the inevitable criminal case. The sad, sordid details can be filled in by talking to the girls' friends and devastated parents.

Experts say teenage girls crave approval, that they want to be special, that their feelings are often too intense for them to handle. They don't feel in control of anything, and they yearn for power over their lives.

"So," said Dr. Mitch Spero, a psychologist who specializes in teens, "when they finally feel like they belong to someone, or that someone belongs to them, it comes down to ownership."

A love triangle can turn into a property dispute.

Experts also know this about girls. They almost never kill each other. Girl-on-girl assault has risen, but homicide among females remains the rarest of crimes. According to the Justice Department, there were 6,940 homicides in the United States in 2008. Only two hundred involved women killing women.

Boys tend to kill while committing other crimes, like robbing a store or selling drugs.

For girls, murder is personal.

"Girls are much more likely to kill over relationships: their parents, siblings, boyfriends," said University of South Florida criminology professor Kathleen Heide.

"When a teenage girl feels another girl is intruding on her territory, when she feels someone is disrespecting her, those are the things that upset them most."

Josh Camacho may have understood this. Though he later denied saying it, his girlfriends remember him declaring, "If you love me, you'll fight for me."

On April 14, 2009, Sarah wanted to be with Josh. And Rachel wanted to be with Josh.

By the end of that warm spring night, one of the girls was in jail, facing life in prison.

And the other had bled to death in the street, only a few blocks from home.

Sarah Ludemann lived in the same house her whole life, a single-story lime stucco with a wide porch fringed with wind chimes. Her parents had moved from New York to Florida to live somewhere warm and safe.

They waited sixteen years to have their only child.

Sarah's mom, Gay, is a surgical nurse. Her dad, Charlie, drives a taxi.

Sarah was her dad's sidekick. He took her to karate classes, Lightning games, Keith Urban concerts. She rode beside him in his cab, blaring the radio, singing country songs.

"Sarah loved to sing and dance," said Danielle Eyermann, her friend since preschool. "She was always making up these crazy moves, pretending she was Britney Spears."

By eighth grade at John Hopkins Middle School in St. Petersburg, many of Sarah's friends already had boyfriends. Sarah had crushes on musicians and Rays players, but that was it.

Her friend Amber said, "Sarah never needed a guy to make her happy."

Rachel Wade's mom is an assistant teacher at an elementary school. Her dad drives trucks for a food distributor. Rachel grew up with an older brother in a new brown house with a pool. Her home was a bike ride away from Sarah's, though they didn't know each other as kids.

Rachel was a happy child, her parents said. She loved reading, playing princess, and sketching Disney characters.

"She was always making friends and commanding attention," said her mom, Janet. "All the girls wanted to be like her. All the boys liked her."

Rachel's best friend, Egle, described her as fun, girly. "People sometimes thought she was prissy," Egle said. "But she wasn't, once you got to know her."

Rachel was in elementary school when a new boy joined her class. His family had just moved to Florida. His dad was from New York, mom from the Dominican Republic. He had six brothers and a sister.

And dark curly hair.

Sarah started high school at Tarpon Springs to attend its program in veterinary medicine.

She had to get up in the dark and ride a bus more than an hour to get there. At the end of the day, other girls had guys to walk with them. But at sixteen, Sarah still didn't have a boyfriend. Her dad was always waiting at the bus stop.

The summer after tenth grade, Sarah and Amber spent a lot of time going to the movies and eating at Chick-fil-A. One afternoon, a boy who cooked chicken came out of the back on his break. He smelled like french fries. He waved to Sarah, Amber said. Then he winked.

"She just fell in love with him, right then," Amber said.

He said his name was Josh. Soon, he would be a senior at Pinellas Park High.

Two months later, Sarah told her parents she wasn't sure she still wanted to be a veterinarian.

She didn't know what she wanted to do, really. Except transfer to Pinellas Park.

While Sarah was dancing with her friends and riding in her dad's cab, Rachel was busy with boys. By high school, her parents said, social life had trumped school. She started challenging them, insisting she didn't need their rules.

When Rachel was fifteen, police came to her house because she and her dad were fighting. "She had a 10 p.m. curfew, but she wanted to stay out all night," said her dad, Barry. "I kept telling her nothing good ever happens after midnight."

Rachel ran away all the time, sometimes sneaking out her bedroom window. She slept in strangers' cars, in lounge chairs at apartment pools. She was only fifteen when police caught her in a car, in the school parking lot, with a nineteen-year-old. They charged him with a felony sex offense.

One night, Rachel and her mom were fighting about her boyfriend, according to a police report. Rachel opened a kitchen drawer and pulled out a Pampered Chef knife.

"She didn't point it at me," her mom said later. "She took it with her and ran into the bathroom."

In her sophomore year, Rachel ran away fourteen times and dropped out of school. Her parents took her to counseling, drove her to work at a doggie day care.

At a party, she ran into Josh. It had been years since she'd seen him. He looked good. Not the schoolboy she remembered.

She stopped in to see him at Chick-fil-A.

Josh and Sarah flirted through the summer. But that fall at Pinellas Park High, he would hardly acknowledge her. He would just cut his eyes at her, Amber said, tip his chin.

In November, they finally got together. But even then, "he would never hold her hand or walk with her, claim her in front of other people," Amber said. "When they were alone, he was all over her."

Everyone said Josh was Sarah's first kiss, her first boyfriend, her first everything. He made her feel beautiful, like she mattered.

But her friends were worried. The first sign was when Sarah started wearing pants. Sarah always wore shorts. Even in winter.

"Josh didn't want other guys to see her legs," Amber said. "He started telling her who she could hang out with, who she could talk to."

Sarah started spending all her time with Josh. She was so scared of losing him that she was losing herself.

"She knew he was owning her, but she never thought to leave him," Amber said. If she'd had other boyfriends, she would have known how it feels to break up and get over it.

"But when your first love is at eighteen," Amber said, "things get epic."

Josh saw himself as tough and streetwise. Sarah pretended she was too. On her cell phone, she stored photos of Josh apparently smoking pot, Josh waving a gun. She downloaded hip-hop songs like "Stop Callin' Me" and "Chopped N Skrewed."

She begged her dad for a pit bull. "You gotta be joking!" he remembers saying. He referred to Josh as "the rat." He kept telling her, "That boy is no good."

"But she was in love," Charlie Ludemann said. "You can't do nothing about a teenage girl in love."

He couldn't keep Sarah away from Josh, so he invited Josh over for dinner, took him to ball games. To keep an eye on him.

"Don't let nothing happen to her," he said.

Sarah had never been in any kind of trouble, but now that started to change.

In the first six months she was with Josh, police interviewed her six times, all over public confrontations. She and Josh screamed at each other at intersections. Yelled at Josh's baby mama in the parking lot of the movies. Once, Sarah said Josh had punched her in the face and he admitted it. Her parents wanted her to press charges, but Sarah wouldn't.

The next time her name was in a police report, Rachel's was in it too.

For months, Rachel and Josh were on and off. She knew he had other girls. That's why they kept breaking up.

Rachel's MySpace photo showed her sprawled on her back, her highlighted hair circling her head like a halo. She wrote: "I've heard that I come off as a bitch or intimidating, but trust me, the moment you start to get to know me, you'll realize it's a total misconception."

When she turned eighteen, she got a job at Applebee's and her own apartment. Josh started sleeping over. That changed things between them. He sponged off of her, Rachel's friends said. She got attached.

"She would always tell us how he kept cheating on her," said her friend Egle. "Nobody understood why she liked him."

A few months after Rachel and Josh started dating, she saw a photo on MySpace: Josh with another girl. A tall, big-boned blond beaming as if she owned him. The name tagged on the picture: Sarah Ludemann.

Rachel wrote to Josh in her MySpace blog on June 17, 2008.

"When we first met I was madly in love... but since then things have changed... You called me names, you slept around... I deserve so much better!"

Soon a comment appeared under Rachel's post. It suggested that Josh had "found better."

It was from Sarah.

Somehow Rachel got Sarah's phone number. She left a message on her voice mail. Sarah played it for her friends.

"You're f----- with me when you f--- with Josh," Rachel snarled. "Seriously, ... I'm letting you know now you're either going to get f----- up or something of yours is. Stop being a bitch!"

Sarah wasn't cowed. She and her friends started eating at Applebee's, sitting in Rachel's section. They would harass her, bump into her while she was holding heavy trays.

Rachel left more phone messages for Sarah, called her fat and pathetic. Why would he want you, Rachel chided, when he could have me?

Late one night, a car pulled up next to Rachel at the Taco Bell. Three girls started shooting Silly String at her. One, Rachel told the cops, was Sarah.

Josh and Rachel kept hooking up. But now, instead of just spending the night, he moved in. And he kept seeing Sarah.

Instead of getting angry at him, the girls went after each other.

One time, according to Rachel's friend Egle, Sarah drove past Rachel's apartment and shouted, "Come fight me."

Sarah told police Rachel called her twenty times in two hours, threatening her. When the cops talked to Rachel, she said Sarah sent her nasty e-mails.

Neither girl had thrown a punch or drawn a weapon, so the cops let it go. Sarah's dad thought it would blow over. Rachel's mom told her, "Don't let it get to you."

The parents didn't know how bad things had gotten.

Voice mail from Rachel to Sarah, August 26, 2008: "I'm guaranteeing you I'm going to f------ murder you."

Technology made all this easy, and made things worse.

You can say anything you want in a voice mail or a text message, without having to face the person you're insulting. You can deliver your rant right away. And the recipient can replay it again and again, reopening the wound each time. Sarah did that.

When a feud plays out on the Internet, where everyone can see it, "that only fuels the feelings," said Heide, the USF professor who wrote *Young Killers*.

"The public challenge cannot be shrugged off," she said. "The girl feels compelled to strike back: I'm hurting, so I want her to hurt too."

April 14, 2009.

When Sarah's dad picked her up at school, her eyes were swollen again. She had been crying every day for two weeks.

He tried to hug her, but she pulled away. In the last six months she had lost thirty pounds.

As soon as she got home, Sarah logged onto MySpace and saw Rachel's last login:

Mood: Lovin my boo :)

Was that a taunt? Was he still with her? Sarah texted Josh.

1:06 p. m.: "Whatever Josh, you get so mad at me for everything but you don't give a s--- when she puts something up or says something. You always believe her."

1:08 p. m. "It's like no matter what I do she's always that much better."

1:13 p. m. "All we fight about is her or something that has to do with her, and it sucks. I hate fighting with you . . . I love you so much, but this s--- hurts."

Hours passed. Sarah tried again.

6:36 p. m. "You say you love me, but you don't even have the decency to text me back?"

Finally, at 8:02 p. m., Josh typed, "Bring the movies."

Sarah borrowed her mom's minivan to drive the two blocks to Josh's sister's house. Before she left, she updated her MySpace:

iloveyoubaby.

Across town, Rachel was at her place, waiting to see Josh. She didn't know about Sarah and her movies.

Just about dark, while walking her dog, she heard a car honk. Rachel later told police she saw Sarah cruising by in her mom's minivan. Sarah yelled, "Stay away from my man!"

Rachel said she was scared. She called an old boyfriend, Javier, and told him she didn't want to be alone. Could she come over?

She got her purse, slid open a kitchen drawer and pulled out a steak knife.

Talk to the girls' friends and you start to understand what was going through their minds.

Sarah didn't feel she was worthy of Josh. Without a job or a car, how could she compete? Plus, she told her friends, she still had a curfew!

Rachel is so much prettier, she thought.

But she had already given everything to this guy—her senior year, her heart, her virginity. If he didn't want her anymore, who would?

Rachel was cocky. How could Josh want anyone else? Look at her, she had her own car, her own apartment.

She was so much prettier than Sarah.

Plus, she had known Josh forever. He knew her true self, and she knew him. Of course she was better than that fat loser.

About 11 p. m., the time Sarah was supposed to be home, she and Josh were playing Wii at his sister's house when headlights pierced the windows.

Josh recognized the car: Rachel's red Saturn.

"Now I know why you're not talking to me—because you got her," Rachel texted Josh.

"That's right," typed Josh. It's a wonder he had the dexterity: By then, he later admitted, he had thrown back five vodka shots and smoked seven White Owl blunts of marijuana.

"I don't like you no more. Why are you down this street? Go home."

"No. I'll wait for her to go home," Rachel texted back.

Sarah had already busted curfew. Her dad texted, "When?"

Sarah typed back, "Soon."

Sarah waited until the headlights faded. She watched Rachel drive away.

Just before midnight, Sarah told Josh goodbye. As she was leaving, Josh's sister and her friend asked for a ride to McDonald's. So Sarah loaded them into the minivan.

On the way, Sarah passed a friend at a stop sign. "Guess who I just saw?" her friend said. "Rachel."

She was at a boy named Javier's house, just a few blocks away.

Sarah sped down the two-lane street. Her cell phone rang. She recognized the number and switched to speakerphone.

"I'm going to kill you!" Rachel shrieked. "You and your Mexican boyfriend!"

Sarah saw Rachel outside a white house, leaning against her car, talking to two boys. She slammed to a stop. Left the keys in the ignition, the engine running. Slid out of the driver's seat in her flip-flops. Didn't even close the door. She raced toward Rachel, fists flailing.

Rachel ran into the road. Raised her right hand. With a quick thrust, she jabbed Sarah's shoulder. The next time, the steak knife punctured Sarah's heart.

Clutching her chest, Sarah staggered back to the minivan. By then, Josh's sister had climbed out. "Get back in," Sarah wailed. "We gotta go!"

She collapsed in the driver's seat. Fumbled for her cell. Her hands were sticky with her own blood. She called Josh. "It hurts," she gasped, sliding into the street.

Rachel tossed the knife onto the roof of a neighbor's house. Her phone rang. Josh.

"Where you at?" he demanded. She told him.

He ran the two blocks to Sarah's house, told her dad she had been in a fight. Together, they drove to the street where the minivan was still idling.

Sarah was sprawled by the curb, surrounded by paramedics.

Her dad rushed to her. Cops pulled him back. "I knew she was dead," Charlie Ludemann said later. "I knew there was nothing anyone could do."

He drove Josh to the hospital, but Josh refused to see Sarah. By the time her parents saw her body, Josh was gone.

Back at Javier's house, police found Rachel sitting on a bench, smoking a cigarette, nursing a fat lip. Josh's sister had jumped her, she said, scratched her back and beaten her with a sandal.

Eventually she told them about the knife. Rachel said Sarah had been harassing her for months. She knew she was going to be attacked. She was trying to defend herself.

The questioning continued at the police station. Rachel had seen the ambulance whisk Sarah away. But she didn't know how badly Sarah was hurt. And she didn't seem ready for it when the detective told her.

"Sarah is dead," he said. "You killed her."

Rachel began to sob, and couldn't stop.

Sarah Ludemann's funeral was a month before the high school prom. More than a year later, her parents keep her bedroom a shrine to her. Everything is just as it was, except that her dad destroyed the pictures of Josh.

Rachel Wade has been in the Pinellas County jail for fifteen months. Her trial for second-degree murder is scheduled to begin Tuesday. Rachel's lawyer says she acted in self-defense. She's facing up to life without parole.

If she ever gets out, she wrote to friends, she's going to marry Javier.

As for Josh Camacho, he wasn't allowed at Sarah's funeral. He has never visited Rachel nor written to her.

Police say his parents shipped him off to relatives in New York.

"He don't live here no more," his mom said when called at her Pinellas Park home. She wouldn't say where Josh was.

"Everyone already put his reputation down so bad, told so many lies about my boy," she said. "I don't have nothing to say."

A New York cell is listed in Josh's name. When a reporter called, a young man answered, then hung up. Three times.

In a sworn deposition, Josh said yes, he got around. Yes, he was sleeping with both girls, and with his baby mama. But they were not his girlfriends. "Just friends with benefits," he kept saying.

"Okay," the defense attorney said. "Now, you indicated that you thought that Sarah loved you . . . Did you love her back?"

Josh hesitated, then said softly, "I think I did."

July 20, 2010

Author's Afterword

I grew up in Washington, DC, during the seventies. My dad worked for the government, and my mom was an English teacher. They were big newspaper people. My dad would be reading the *Washington Post* during breakfast, and he would read the stories out loud. I discovered who Bob Woodward and Carl Bernstein were when I was in the second grade, the *Post* reporters who took down a president with their investigative journalism. I thought that was the coolest job ever, that these two young guys could actually do that, bring down a corrupt president.

In elementary school I published a little newspaper. My mom would type it on the typewriter, my dad would Xerox it at the library, and I would give it out to my friends at school. I did the same thing in middle school—we had our own little family paper; my sister took the pictures and I wrote the stories. Then in high school I got really lucky because we had a kickass journalism teacher named Kevin Keegan, and we ended up going to the Gold Crown Awards, sponsored by the Columbia Scholastic Press Association, my sophomore year. So by the time I was sixteen, I was going to Columbia University to be a part of this great journalism experience. I became editor my senior year— and I went back to Columbia. I had this amazing opportunity in high school—a public high school. I probably got the best journalism instruction of my whole career when I was in high school.

For my first journalism job, I typeset car ads. I worked 4 to midnight for the local paper, and I typeset those long classified ads for car dealerships; I also sold ads. I always wanted to do writing, but they weren't going to hire me to be a writer. They basically said, "If you can fill enough pages to meet your salary, then you can write on those pages." The goal was always to be a writer, always, always, always. But it's important to get your foot in the door. You have to do what it takes.

I think the best part of my job is never exactly knowing what I'm going to be doing from one day to the next. I love that every day I learn something new. I love that I get an excuse to talk to everyone from the governor to the guy living under the bridge in a tent. My job allows me to interact with every part of the world, and I think that's such a privilege, to be able to share stories like that—to illuminate people in the shadows. Most folks in the community have no understanding of how hard life can really be.

As a little kid, I wanted to be the one who was sharing the information—I liked to be in the know. What I ended up doing in journalism wasn't what I initially thought. I covered the news for the first ten years of my career, and then I've done feature stories for the last fifteen. So, in those first years, I didn't really see myself as a storyteller. I was much more like, cover the shooting, cover the hurricane, cover the city council meeting. What I do with journalism has definitely changed.

In terms of how it has shaped me? I don't know who I would be if I wasn't a journalist. I'm teaching a class at the University of South Florida right now, and I'm really bad at it, and I don't like it, and I don't see myself as a professor; the role is uncomfortable for me. I'm a writer, you know, I'm a reporter. That's most of who I am.

Journalism has affected me as a mom, not only because it's taken me away from the kids—I missed my son's first date because I had to cover a shooting. But it has also given my kids interesting opportunities to get to know the world in the way most teenagers don't. They've been on a fishing boat and slept in a hurricane shelter with me because I was reporting during a storm. Every time I could get a story that would involve bringing them with me, I would. Every time there was festival or a fair or an opening of a new park, and I felt like I could bring the kids with me, I did. I never knew what my dad did, and I love that they know exactly what I do, for better or for worse.

A lot of young women are being pushed to be editors, so we have more women at the top of the ranks. By the time I was thirty years old, and I realized I really wanted to tell narrative feature stories, my paper in Virginia was saying, "No, we want you to be an editor. We need you here in the newsroom. Go get a team of reporters." But I didn't want to be in a leadership position; I wanted a better writing position.

Because of the tenor in the newsroom and the culture to push women to do that, I know several of my colleagues who got sent down that road rather than continue their writing career. Better money, better hours, I get that. But in the name of gender equality, the women who might have stayed in the ranks of the writers were pushed to get better jobs.

I've always had women in the newsroom to look up to and admire. The editor at the paper in Virginia was a woman, and she was the one who was so keen on bringing other women into leadership roles. My first editor on the narrative team was a woman, and she was also a mother, and she was the best role model for me to figure out how to straddle those worlds. I could ask her anything, from how to get a kid to go to bed at night, to how do I structure the lead of this story, to can I ask this hard question? She used to come over to my place at least once or twice a month with a couple other female reporters who had kids, and we'd have "Mommy night" and order pizza and get a six-pack and let the kids play.

I've won a zillion awards, and that's great, but the thing I love most is when you write a story that has an impact. Once I wrote a story about a fifteen-year-old boy who stood up at church in September and asked someone to adopt him. And ten thousand people from around the world called and wanted to adopt him. And not only that, but there was also a huge increase in the number of adults who inquired about teenagers in foster care, "Can you put me in touch with other teenagers who need homes?" To me, that's the biggest thing. Your stories can lead people to make a difference in their community or make the world better for a kid. If you can write something that gets the public's attention or presents an issue in a different way, to me that's the most gratifying part of all.

Andrea Elliott

Andrea Elliott is a Pulitzer Prize-winning investigative reporter for the *New York Times*. Her 2013 series, "Invisible Child," chronicled the life of an eleven-year-old homeless girl in Brooklyn, winning the George Polk Award, among other honors, and prompting city officials to remove more than four hundred children from substandard shelters.

Before focusing on poverty, Elliott reported extensively on the lives of Muslims in post-9/11 America. Her three-part series, "An Imam in America," was awarded the 2007 Pulitzer Prize in feature writing. She has written about Muslims in the US military, the radicalization of Somali immigrants in Minneapolis and the rise of the anti-sharia movement.

Her cover stories for the *New York Times Magazine* include investigative profiles of a young jihadist from Alabama and a preacher trained at Yale, as well as a ground-breaking report on Moroccan suicide bombers that was a finalist for the 2008 National Magazine Award for Reporting.

In 2014, Elliott received an honorary doctorate from Niagara University, which cited her "courage, perseverance, and a commitment to fairness for those without a public voice rarely demonstrated among writers today."

Her work has been honored by the Overseas Press Club, the American Society of Newspaper Editors, the Society of Professional Journalists and the New York Press Club, and has been featured in the collections *Best Newspaper Writing* and *Islam for Journalists: A Primer on Covering Muslim American Communities in America*.

Elliott came to the *Times* from the *Miami Herald*, where she was a metropolitan reporter. Raised in Washington, DC, by a Chilean mother and an American father, she graduated from Occidental College and earned a master's degree from the Columbia University Graduate School of Journalism, where she was class valedictorian. She lives in New York City.

A Muslim Leader in Brooklyn

A dedicated imam tends his mostly immigrant
Muslim flock in post-9/11 America

Part 1

The imam begins his trek before dawn, his long robe billowing like a ghost through empty streets. In this dark, quiet hour, his thoughts sometimes drift back to the Egyptian farming village where he was born.

But as the sun rises over Bay Ridge, Brooklyn, Sheik Reda Shata's new world comes to life. The R train rattles beneath a littered stretch of sidewalk, where Mexican workers huddle in the cold. An electric Santa dances in a doughnut shop window. Neon signs beckon. Gypsy cabs blare their horns.

The imam slips into a plain brick building, nothing like the golden-domed mosque of his youth. He stops to pray, and then climbs the cracked linoleum steps to his cluttered office. The answering machine blinks frantically, a portent of the endless questions to come.

A teenage girl wants to know: Is it halal, or lawful, to eat a Big Mac? Can alcohol be served, a waiter wonders, if it is prohibited by the Koran? Is it wrong to take out a mortgage, young Muslim professionals ask, when Islam frowns upon monetary interest?

The questions are only a piece of the daily puzzle Mr. Shata must solve as the imam of the Islamic Society of Bay Ridge, a thriving New York mosque where several thousand Muslims worship.

To his congregants, Mr. Shata is far more than the leader of daily prayers and giver of the Friday sermon. Many of them now live in a land without their parents, who typically assist with finding a spouse. There are fewer uncles and cousins to help resolve personal disputes. There is no local House of Fatwa to issue rulings on ethical questions.

Sheik Reda, as he is called, arrived in Brooklyn one year after September 11. Virtually overnight, he became an Islamic judge and nursery school principal, a matchmaker and marriage counselor, a 24-hour hot line on all things Islamic.

Day after day, he must find ways to reconcile Muslim tradition with American life. Little in his rural Egyptian upbringing or years of Islamic scholarship prepared him for the challenge of leading a mosque in America.

The job has worn him down and opened his mind. It has landed him, exhausted, in the hospital and earned him a following far beyond Brooklyn.

"America transformed me from a person of rigidity to flexibility," said Mr. Shata, speaking through an Arabic translator. "I went from a country where a sheik would speak and the people listened to one where the sheik talks and the people talk back."

This is the story of Mr. Shata's journey west: the making of an American imam.

Over the last half-century, the Muslim population in the United States has risen significantly. Immigrants from the Middle East, South Asia and Africa have settled across the country, establishing mosques from Boston to Los Angeles, and turning Islam into one of the nation's fastest growing religions. By some estimates, as many as six million Muslims now live in America.

Leading this flock calls for improvisation. Imams must unify diverse congregations with often-clashing Islamic traditions. They must grapple with the threat of terrorism, answering to law enforcement agents without losing the trust of their fellow Muslims. Sometimes they must set aside conservative beliefs that prevail in the Middle East, the birthplace of Islam.

Islam is a legalistic faith: Muslims believe in a divine law that guides their daily lives, including what they should eat, drink, and wear. In countries where the religion reigns, this is largely the accepted way.

But in the West, what Islamic law prohibits is everywhere. Alcohol fills chocolates. Women jog in sports bras. For many Muslims in America, life is a daily clash between Islamic mores and material temptation. At the center of this clash stands the imam.

In America, imams evoke a simplistic caricature—of robed, bearded clerics issuing fatwas in foreign lands. Hundreds of imams live in the United States, but their portrait remains flatly one-dimensional. Either they are symbols of diversity, breaking the Ramadan fast with smiling politicians, or zealots, hurrying into their storefront mosques.

Mr. Shata, 37, is neither a firebrand nor a ready advocate of progressive Islam. Some of his views would offend conservative Muslims; other beliefs would repel American liberals. He is in many ways a work in progress, mapping his own middle ground between two different worlds.

The imam's cramped, curtained office can hardly contain the dramas that unfold inside. Women cry. Husbands storm off. Friendships end. Every day brings soap opera plots and pitch.

A Moroccan woman falls to her knees near the imam's Hewlett-Packard printer. "Have mercy on me!" she wails to a friend who has accused her of theft. Another day, it is a man whose Lebanese wife has concealed their marriage and newborn son from her strict father. "I will tell him everything!" the husband screams.

Mr. Shata settles dowries, confronts wife abusers, brokers business deals, and tries to arrange marriages. He approaches each problem with an almost scientific certainty that it can be solved. "I try to be more of a doctor than a judge," said Mr. Shata. "A judge sentences. A doctor tries to remedy."

Imams in the United States now serve an estimated twelve hundred mosques. Some of their congregants have lived here for generations, assimilating socially and succeeding professionally. But others are recent immigrants, still struggling to find their place in America. Demographers expect their numbers to rise in the coming decades, possibly surpassing those of American Jews.

Like many of their faithful, most imams in the United States come from abroad. They are recruited primarily for their knowledge of the Koran and the language in which it was revealed, Arabic.

But few are prepared for the test that awaits. Like the parish priests who came generations before, imams are called on to lead a community on the margins of American civic life. They are conduits to and arbiters of an exhilarating, if sometimes hostile world, filled with promise and peril.

More than five thousand miles lie between Brooklyn and Kafr al Battikh, Mr. Shata's birthplace in northeastern Egypt. Situated where the Nile Delta meets the Suez Canal, it was a village of dirt roads and watermelon vines when Mr. Shata was born in 1968.

Egypt was in the throes of change. The country had just suffered a staggering defeat in the Six Day War with Israel, and protests against the government followed. Hoping to counter growing radicalism, a new president, Anwar Sadat, allowed a long-repressed Islamic movement to flourish.

The son of a farmer and fertilizer salesman, Mr. Shata belonged to the lowest rung of Egypt's rural middle class. His house had no electricity. He did not see a television until he was fifteen.

Islam came to him softly, in the rhythms of his grandmother's voice. At bedtime, she would tell him the story of the Prophet Muhammad, the seventh-century founder of Islam. The boy heard much that was familiar. Like the prophet, he had lost his mother at a young age.

"She told me the same story maybe a thousand times," he said.

At the age of five, he began memorizing the Koran. Like thousands of children in the Egyptian countryside, he attended a Sunni religious school subsidized by the government and connected to Al Azhar University, a bastion of Islamic scholarship.

Too poor to buy books, the young Mr. Shata hand-copied from hundreds at the town library. The bound volumes now line the shelves of his Bay Ridge apartment. When he graduated, he enrolled at Al Azhar and headed to Cairo by train. There, he sat on a bench for hours, marveling at the sights.

"I was like a lost child," he said. "Cars. We didn't have them. People of different colors. Foreigners. Women almost naked. It was like an imaginary world."

At eighteen, Mr. Shata thought of becoming a judge. But at his father's urging, he joined the college of imams, the Dawah.

The word means invitation. It refers to the duty of Muslims to invite, or call, others to the faith. Unlike Catholicism or Judaism, Islam has no ordained clergy. The Prophet Muhammad was the religion's first imam, or prayer leader, Islam's closest corollary to a rabbi or priest; schools like the Dawah are its version of a seminary or rabbinate.

After four years, Mr. Shata graduated with honors, seventh in a class of thirty-four hundred.

The next decade brought lessons in adaptation. In need of money, Mr. Shata took a job teaching sharia, or Islamic law, to children in Saudi Arabia, a country guided by Wahhabism, a puritan strain of Sunni Islam. He found his Saudi colleagues' interpretation of the Koran overly literal at times, and the treatment of women, who were not allowed to vote or drive, troubling.

Five years later, he returned to a different form of religious control in Egypt, where most imams are appointed by the government and monitored for signs of radicalism or political dissent.

"They are not allowed to deviate from the curriculum that the government sets for them," said Khaled Abou El Fadl, an Egyptian law professor at the University of California, Los Angeles.

Mr. Shata craved greater independence, and opened a furniture business. But he missed the life of the Dawah and eventually returned to it as the imam of his hometown mosque, which drew four thousand worshipers on Fridays alone.

His duties were clear: he led the five daily prayers and delivered the khutba, or Friday sermon. His mosque, like most in Egypt, was financed and managed by the government. He spent his free time giving lectures, conducting marriage ceremonies and offering occasional religious guidance.

In 2000, Mr. Shata left to work as an imam in the gritty industrial city of Stuttgart, Germany. Europe brought a fresh new freedom. "I saw a wider world," he said. "Anyone with an opinion could express it."

Then came September 11.

Soon after, Mr. Shata's mosque was defiled with graffiti and smeared with feces.

The next summer, Mr. Shata took a call from an imam in Brooklyn. The man, Mohamed Moussa, was leaving his mosque, exhausted by the troubles of his congregants following the terrorist attacks. The mosque was looking for a replacement, and Mr. Shata had come highly recommended by a professor at Al Azhar.

Most imams are recruited to American mosques on the recommendation of other imams or trusted scholars abroad, and are usually offered an annual contract. Some include health benefits and subsidized housing; others are painfully spare. The pay can range from $20,000 to $50,000.

Mr. Shata had heard stories of Muslim hardship in America. The salary at the Islamic Society of Bay Ridge was less than what he was earning in Germany. But foremost on his mind were his wife and three small daughters, whom he had not seen in months. Germany had refused them entry.

He agreed to take the job if he could bring his family to America. In October 2002, the American Embassy in Cairo granted visas to the Shatas and they boarded a plane for New York.

A facade of plain white brick rises up from Fifth Avenue just south of Sixty-Eighth Street in Bay Ridge. Two sets of words, one in Arabic and another in English, announce the mosque's dual identity from a marquee above its gray metal doors.

To the mosque's base—Palestinian, Egyptian, Yemeni, Moroccan, and Algerian immigrants—it is known as Masjid Moussab, named after one of the prophet's companions, Moussab Ibn Omair. To the mosque's English-speaking neighbors, descendants of the Italians, Irish, and Norwegians who once filled the neighborhood, it is the Islamic Society of Bay Ridge.

Mosques across America are commonly named centers or societies, in part because they provide so many services. Some 140 mosques serve New York City, where an estimated six hundred thousand Muslims live, roughly 20 percent of them African American, said Louis Abdellatif Cristillo, an anthropologist at Teachers College who has canvassed the city's mosques.

The Islamic Society of Bay Ridge, like other American mosques, is run by a board of directors, mostly Muslim professionals from the Palestinian territories. What began in 1984 as a small storefront on Bay Ridge Avenue, with no name and no imam, has grown into one of the city's vital Muslim centers, a magnet for new immigrants.

Its four floors pulse with life: a nursery school, an Islamic bookstore, Koran classes, and daily lectures. Some fifteen hundred Muslims worship at the mosque on Fridays, often crouched in prayer on the sidewalk. Albanians, Pakistanis, and others who speak little Arabic listen to live English translations of the sermons through headsets. It is these congregants' crumpled dollar bills, collected in a cardboard box, that enable the mosque to survive.

Among the city's imams, Bay Ridge is seen as a humbling challenge.

"It's the first station for immigrants," said Mr. Moussa, Mr. Shata's predecessor. "And immigrants have a lot of problems."

Mr. Shata landed at Kennedy International Airport wearing a crimson felt hat and a long gray jilbab that fell from his neck to his sandaled toes, the proud dress of an Al Azhar scholar. He spoke no English. But already, he carried some of the West inside. He could quote liberally from Voltaire, Shaw, and Kant. For an Egyptian, he often jokes, he was inexplicably punctual.

The first thing Mr. Shata loved about America, like Germany, was the order.

"In Egypt, if a person passes through a red light, that means he's smart," he said. "In America, he's very disrespected."

Americans stood in line. They tended their yards. One could call the police and hear a rap at the door minutes later. That fact impressed not only Mr. Shata, but also the women of his new mosque.

They had gained a reputation for odd calls to 911. One woman called because a relative abroad had threatened to take her inheritance. "The officers left and didn't write anything," Mr. Shata said, howling with laughter. "There was nothing for them to write."

Another woman called, angry because her husband had agreed to let a daughter from a previous marriage spend the night.

To Mr. Shata, the calls made sense. The women's parents, uncles and brothers—figures of authority in family conflict—were overseas. Instead, they dialed 911, hoping for a local substitute. Soon they would learn to call the imam.

A bearish man with a soft, bearded face, Mr. Shata struck his congregants as an odd blend of things. He was erudite yet funny, authoritative at the mosque's wooden pulpit, and boyishly charming between prayers.

Homemakers, doctors, cabdrivers, and sheiks stopped by to assess the new imam. He regaled them with Dunkin' Donuts coffee, fetched by the Algerian keeper of the mosque, and then told long, poetic stories that left his visitors silent, their coffee cold.

"You just absorb every word he says," said Linda Sarsour, twenty-five, a Muslim activist in Brooklyn.

The imam, too, was taking note. Things worked differently in America, where mosques were run as nonprofit organizations and congregants had a decidedly democratic air. Mr. Shata was shocked when a tone-deaf man insisted on giving the call to prayer. Such a man would be ridiculed in Egypt, where the callers, or muezzinin, have voices so beautiful they sometimes record top-selling CDs.

But in the land of equal opportunity, a man with a mediocre voice could claim discrimination. Mr. Shata relented. He shudders when the voice periodically sounds.

No sooner had Mr. Shata started his new job than all manner of problems arrived at his worn wooden desk: rebellious teenagers, marital strife, confessions of philandering, accusations of theft.

The imam responded creatively. Much of the drama involved hot dog vendors. There was the pair who shared a stand, but could not stand each other. They came to the imam, who helped them divide the business.

The most notorious hot dog seller stood accused of stealing thousands of dollars in donations he had raised for the children of his deceased best friend. But there was no proof. The donations had been in cash. The solution, the imam decided, was to have the man swear an oath on the Koran.

"Whoever lies while taking an oath on the Koran goes blind afterward," said Mr. Shata, stating a belief that has proved useful in cases of theft. A group of men lured the vendor to the mosque, where he confessed to stealing $11,400. His admission was recorded in a waraqa, or document, penned in Arabic and signed by four witnesses. He returned the money in full.

Dozens of waraqas sit in the locked bottom drawer of the imam's desk. In one, a Brooklyn man who burned his wife with an iron vows, in nervous Arabic scrawl, never to do it again. If he fails, he will owe her a $10,000 "disciplinary fine." The police had intervened before, but the woman felt that she needed the imam's help.

For hundreds of Muslims, the Bay Ridge mosque has become a court-house more welcoming than the one downtown, a police precinct more effective than the brick station blocks away. Even the police have used the imam's influence to their advantage, warning disorderly teenagers that they will be taken to the mosque rather than the station.

"They say, 'No, not the imam! He'll tell my parents,'" said Russell Kain, a recently retired officer of the Sixty-Eighth Precinct.

Soon after arriving in Brooklyn, Mr. Shata observed a subtle rift among the women of his mosque. Those who were new to America remained quietly grounded in the traditions of their homelands. But some who had assimilat-ed began to question those strictures. Concepts like shame held less weight. Actions like divorce, abhorred by Mr. Shata, were surprisingly popular.

"The woman who comes from overseas, she's like someone who comes from darkness to a very well-lit place," he said.

In early July, an Egyptian karate teacher shuffled into Mr. Shata's office and sank into a donated couch. He smiled meekly and began to talk. His new wife showed him no affection. She complained about his salary and said he lacked ambition.

The imam urged him to be patient.

Two weeks later, in came the wife. She wanted a divorce.

"We don't understand each other," the woman said. She was thirty-two and had come from Alexandria, Egypt, to work as an Arabic teacher. She had met her husband through a friend in Bay Ridge. Her parents, still in Egypt, had approved cautiously from afar.

"I think you should be patient," said the imam.

"I cannot," she said firmly. "He loves me, but I have to love him, too."

Mr. Shata shifted uncomfortably in his chair. There was nothing he loathed more than granting a divorce.

"It's very hard for me to let him divorce you," he said. "How can I meet God on Judgment Day?"

"It's God's law also to have divorce," she shot back. The debate continued.

Finally, Mr. Shata asked for her parents' phone number in Egypt. Over the speakerphone, they anxiously urged the imam to relent. Their daughter was clearly miserable, and they were too far away to intervene.

With a sigh, Mr. Shata asked his executive secretary, Mohamed, to print a divorce certificate. In the rare instance when the imam agrees to issue one, it is after a couple has filed for divorce with the city.

"Since you're the one demanding divorce, you can never get back together with him," the imam warned. "Ever."

The woman smiled politely.

"What matters for us is the religion," she said later. "Our law is our religion."

The religion's fiqh, or jurisprudence, is built on fourteen centuries of scholarship, but imams in Europe and America often find this body of law insufficient to address life in the West. The quandaries of America were foreign to Mr. Shata.

Pornography was rampant, prompting a question Mr. Shata had never heard in Egypt: is oral sex lawful? Pork and alcohol are forbidden in Islam, raising questions about whether Muslims could sell beer or bacon. Tired of the menacing stares in the subway, women wanted to know if they could remove their headscarves. Muslims were navigating their way through problems Mr. Shata had never fathomed.

For a while, the imam called his fellow sheiks in Egypt with requests for fatwas, or nonbinding legal rulings. But their views carried little relevance to life in America. Some issues, like oral sex, he dared not raise. Over time, he began to find his own answers and became, as he put it, flexible.

Is a Big Mac permissible? Yes, the imam says, but not a bacon cheeseburger.

It is a woman's right, Mr. Shata believes, to remove her hijab if she feels threatened. Muslims can take jobs serving alcohol and pork, he says, but only if other work cannot be found. Oral sex is acceptable, but only between married couples. Mortgages, he says, are necessary to move forward in America.

"Islam is supposed to make a person's life easier, not harder," Mr. Shata explained

In some ways, the imam has resisted change. He has learned little English, and interviews with Mr. Shata over the course of six months required the use of a translator.

Some imams in the United States make a point of shaking hands with women, distancing themselves from the view that such contact is improper. Mr. Shata offers women only a nod.

Daily, he passes the cinema next to his mosque but has never seen a movie in a theater. He says music should be forbidden if it "encourages sexual desire." He won't convert a non-Muslim when it seems more a matter of convenience than true belief.

"Religion is not a piece of clothing that you change," he said after turning away an Ecuadorean immigrant who sought to convert for her Syrian husband. "I don't want someone coming to Islam tonight and leaving it in the morning."

Ten months after he came to America, Mr. Shata collapsed.

It was Friday. The mosque was full. Hundreds of men sat pressed together, their shirts damp with summer. Their wives and daughters huddled in the women's section, one floor below. Word of the imam's sermons had spread, drawing Muslims from Albany and Hartford.

"Praise be to Allah," began Mr. Shata, his voice slowly rising.

Minutes later, the imam recalled, the room began to spin. He fell to the carpet, lost consciousness and spent a week in the hospital, plagued by several symptoms. A social worker and a counselor who treated the imam both said he suffered from exhaustion. The counselor, Ali Gheith, called it "compassion fatigue," an ailment that commonly affects disaster-relief workers.

It was not just the long hours, the new culture and the ceaseless demands that weighed on the imam. Most troubling were the psychological woes of his congregants, which seemed endless.

September 11 had wrought depression and anxiety among Muslims. But unlike many priests or rabbis, imams lacked pastoral training in mental health and knew little about the social services available.

At heart was another complicated truth: imams often approach mental illness from a strictly Islamic perspective. Hardship is viewed as a test of faith, and the answer can be found in tawwakul, trusting in God's plan. The remedy typically suggested by imams is a spiritual one, sought through fasting, prayer, and reflection.

Muslim immigrants also limit themselves to religious solutions because of the stigma surrounding mental illness, said Hamada Hamid, a resident psychiatrist at New York University who founded the *Journal of Muslim Mental Health*. "If somebody says, 'You need this medication,' someone may respond, 'I have tawwakul,'" he said.

Mr. Gheith, a Palestinian immigrant who works in disaster preparedness for the city's health department, began meeting with the imam regularly after his collapse. Mr. Shata needed to learn to disconnect from his congregants, Mr. Gheith said. It was a concept that confounded the imam.

"I did not permit these problems to enter my heart," said Mr. Shata, "nor can I permit them to leave."

The conversations eventually led to a citywide training program for imams, blending Islam with psychology. Mr. Shata learned to identify the symptoms of mental illness and began referring people to treatment.

His congregants often refuse help, blaming black magic or the evil eye for their problems. The evil eye is believed to be a curse driven by envy, confirmed in the bad things that happen to people.

One Palestinian couple in California insisted that their erratic eighteen-year-old son had the evil eye. He was brought to the imam's attention after winding up on the streets of New York, and eventually received a diagnosis of schizophrenia.

Mr. Shata had less success with a man who worshiped at the mosque. He had become paranoid, certain his wife was cursing him with witchcraft. But he refused treatment, insisting divorce was the only cure.

Time and again, Mr. Shata's new country has called for creativity and patience, for a careful negotiation between tradition and modernity.

"Here you don't know what will solve a problem," he said. "It's about looking for a key.'

March 5, 2006

Author's Afterword

I was always a curious kid and I loved to write. But it wasn't until high school that those two things came together in the form of journalism. I started writing for the unfortunately named *Augur Bit,* our school paper, and it just got me excited—the whole process of observing, asking questions and then putting it all into words.

In college, I studied comparative literature, mostly because I didn't have a clue what to study and reading novels sounded like a good way to pass the time. About halfway through college, I took a film course and momentarily fell in love with that medium, taking a brief foray into the documentary world. I have enormous respect for documentary filmmakers. I just prefer a more discrete style of reporting.

I got my first break right out of journalism school when I landed an internship at the *Miami Herald.* I remember asking one of my mentors, Michael Shapiro, for advice and he said, "Don't work as hard as everyone else. Work harder than everyone else." And so that's what I tried to do. I'd work until late at night after coming in early. I came in every weekend. The internship quickly turned into a job covering night cops.

Anytime a story moves people to a new place of understanding, I feel I have done my job.

There is a perception out there that longtime journalists become cynical, hardened people. In my case, I think the opposite may have happened. The more time that passes, the more struck I am by the unpredictability of the human heart and by the capacity of people to question the world around them and to change.

I don't believe gender should play a role in how we understand our abilities in any particular field. But as in most professions today, I stand on the shoulders of the women who fought their way in decades earlier. Hopefully, many years from now, this long line of sisters will have brought about the things we still lack today, like pay equity.

Amy Harmon

Amy Harmon is a reporter for the *New York Times* who seeks to illuminate the intersection of science and society through narrative storytelling. She has won two Pulitzer Prizes, one in 2008 for her series, "The DNA Age," the other as part of a team for the series "How Race is Lived in America" in 2001. Her "Target Cancer" series received the 2011 National Academies of Science award for print journalism. In 2012, her article about a young man with autism coming of age won the Casey Medal for meritorious reporting. She is also the author of a Kindle single, "Asperger Love," based on her reporting about a young couple both on the autism spectrum. A story from her recent series about the clash between scientific consensus and popular perceptions of genetically engineered food is included in the 2014 anthology *Best American Science and Nature Writing*. Harmon is the recipient of a Guggenheim fellowship in science writing. She lives in New York City with her husband and ten-year-old daughter.

Facing Life With a Lethal Gene

A young woman's decision to discover her genetic destiny
leads to life-altering changes

The test, the counselor said, had come back positive.

Katharine Moser inhaled sharply. She thought she was as ready as anyone could be to face her genetic destiny. She had attended a genetic counseling
session and visited a psychiatrist, as required by the clinic. She had undergone
the recommended neurological exam. And yet, she realized in that moment,
she had never expected to hear those words.

"What do I do now?" Ms. Moser asked.

"What do you want to do?" the counselor replied.

"Cry," she said quietly.

Her best friend, Colleen Elio, seated next to her, had already begun.

Ms. Moser was twenty-three. It had taken her months to convince the
clinic at New York-Presbyterian Hospital/Columbia University Medical Center
in Manhattan that she wanted, at such a young age, to find out whether she
carried the gene for Huntington's disease.

Huntington's, the incurable brain disorder that possessed her grandfather's body and ravaged his mind for three decades, typically strikes in middle
age. But most young adults who know the disease runs in their family have
avoided the DNA test that can tell whether they will get it, preferring the torture—and hope—of not knowing.

Ms. Moser is part of a vanguard of people at risk for Huntington's who are
choosing to learn early what their future holds. Facing their genetic heritage,
they say, will help them decide how to live their lives.

Yet even as a raft of new DNA tests are revealing predispositions to all kinds of conditions, including breast cancer, depression, and dementia, little is known about what it is like to live with such knowledge.

"What runs in your own family, and would you want to know?" said Nancy Wexler, a neuropsychologist at Columbia and the president of the Hereditary Disease Foundation, which has pioneered Huntington's research. "Soon everyone is going to have an option like this. You make the decision to test, you have to live with the consequences."

On that drizzly spring morning two years ago, Ms. Moser was feeling her way, with perhaps the most definitive and disturbing verdict genetic testing has to offer. Anyone who carries the gene will inevitably develop Huntington's.

She fought her tears. She tried for humor.

Don't let yourself get too thin, said the clinic's social worker. Not a problem, Ms. Moser responded, gesturing to her curvy frame. No more than two drinks at a time. Perhaps, Ms. Moser suggested to Ms. Elio, she meant one in each hand.

Then came anger.

"Why me?" she remembers thinking, in a refrain she found hard to shake in the coming months. "I'm the good one. It's not like I'm sick because I have emphysema from smoking or I did something dangerous."

The gene that will kill Ms. Moser sits on the short arm of everyone's fourth chromosome, where the letters of the genetic alphabet normally repeat C-A-G as many as thirty-five times in a row. In people who develop Huntington's, however, there are more than thirty-five repeats.

No one quite knows why this DNA hiccup causes cell death in the brain, leading Huntington's patients to jerk and twitch uncontrollably and rendering them progressively unable to walk, talk, think, and swallow. But the greater the number of repeats, the earlier symptoms tend to appear and the faster they progress.

Ms. Moser's "CAG number" was forty-five, the counselor said. She had more repeats than her grandfather, whose first symptoms—loss of short-term memory, mood swings, and a constant ticking noise he made with his mouth—surfaced when he turned fifty. But it was another year before Ms. Moser would realize that she could have less than twelve years until she showed symptoms.

Immediately after getting her results, Ms. Moser was too busy making plans.

"I'm going to become super-strong and super-balanced," she vowed over lunch with Ms. Elio, her straight brown hair pulled into a determined bun. "So when I start to lose it I'll be a little closer to normal."

In the tumultuous months that followed, Ms. Moser often found herself unable to remember what normal had once been. She forced herself to renounce the crush she had long nursed on a certain firefighter, sure that marriage was no longer an option for her. She threw herself into fund-raising in the hopes that someone would find a cure. Sometimes, she raged.

She never, she said, regretted being tested. But at night, crying herself to sleep in the dark of her lavender bedroom, she would go over and over it. She was the same, but she was also different. And there was nothing she could do.

Ms. Moser grew up in Connecticut, part of a large Irish Catholic family. Like many families affected by Huntington's, Ms. Moser's regarded the disease as a curse, not to be mentioned even as it dominated their lives in the form of her grandfather's writhing body and unpredictable rages.

Once, staying in Ms. Moser's room on a visit, he broke her trundle bed with his violent, involuntary jerking. Another time, he came into the kitchen naked, his underpants on his head. When the children giggled, Ms. Moser's mother defended her father: "If you don't like it, get out of my house and go."

But no one explained what had happened to their grandfather, Thomas Dowd, a former New York City police officer who once had dreams of retiring to Florida.

In 1990, Mr. Dowd's older brother, living in a veteran's hospital in an advanced stage of the disease, was strangled in his own restraints. But a year or so later, when Ms. Moser wanted to do her sixth-grade science project on Huntington's, her mother recoiled.

"Why," she demanded, "would you want to do it on this disease that is killing your grandfather?"

Ms. Moser was left to confirm for herself, through library books and a CD-ROM encyclopedia, that she and her brothers, her mother, her aunts, an uncle, and cousins could all face the same fate.

Any child who has a parent with Huntington's has a 50 percent chance of having inherited the gene that causes it, Ms. Moser learned.

Her mother, who asked not to be identified by name for fear of discrimination, had not always been so guarded. At one point, she drove around with a "Cure HD" sign in the window of her van. She told people that her father had "Woody Guthrie's disease," invoking the folk icon who died of Huntington's in 1967.

But her efforts to raise awareness soon foundered. Huntington's is a rare genetic disease, affecting about thirty thousand people in the United States, with about two hundred and fifty thousand more at risk. Few people know what it is. Strangers assumed her father's unsteady walk, a frequent early symptom, meant he was drunk.

"Nobody has compassion," Ms. Moser's mother concluded. "People look at you like you're strange, and 'What's wrong with you?'"

Shortly after a simple DNA test became available for Huntington's in 1993, one of Ms. Moser's aunts tested positive. Another, driven to find out if her own medical problems were related to Huntington's, tested negative. But when Ms. Moser announced as a teenager that she wanted to get tested one day, her mother insisted that she should not. If her daughter carried the gene, that meant she did, too. And she did not want to know.

"You don't want to know stuff like that," Ms. Moser's mother said in an interview. "You want to enjoy life."

Ms. Moser's father, who met and married his wife six years before Ms. Moser's grandfather received his Huntington's diagnosis, said he had managed not to think much about her at-risk status.

"So she was at risk," he said. "Everyone's at risk for everything."

The test, Ms. Moser remembers her mother suggesting, would cost thousands of dollars. Still, in college, Ms. Moser often trolled the Web for information about it. Mostly, she imagined how sweet it would be to know she did not have the gene. But increasingly she was haunted, too, by the suspicion that her mother did.

As awful as it was, she admitted to Ms. Elio, her freshman-year neighbor at Elizabethtown College in Pennsylvania, she almost hoped it was true. It would explain her mother's strokes of meanness, her unpredictable flashes of anger.

Ms. Moser's mother said she had never considered the conflicts with her daughter out of the ordinary. "All my friends who had daughters said that was all normal, and when she's twenty-five she'll be your best friend," she said. "I was waiting for that to happen, but I guess it's not happening."

When Ms. Moser graduated in 2003 with a degree in occupational therapy, their relationship, never peaceful, was getting worse. She moved to Queens without giving her mother her new address.

Out of school, Ms. Moser soon spotted a listing for a job at Terence Cardinal Cooke Health Care Center, a nursing home on the Upper East Side of Manhattan. She knew it was meant for her.

Her grandfather had died there in 2002 after living for a decade at the home, one of only a handful in the country with a unit devoted entirely to Huntington's.

"I hated visiting him growing up," Ms. Moser said. "It was scary."

Now, though, she was drawn to see the disease up close.

On breaks from her duties elsewhere, she visited her cousin James Dowd, the son of her grandfather's brother who had come to live in the Huntington's unit several years earlier. It was there, in a conversation with another staff member, that she learned she could be tested for only a few hundred dollars at the Columbia clinic across town. She scheduled an appointment for the next week.

The staff at Columbia urged Ms. Moser to consider the downside of genetic testing. Some people battle depression after they test positive. And the information, she was cautioned, could make it harder for her to get a job or health insurance.

But Ms. Moser bristled at the idea that she should have to remain ignorant about her genetic status to avoid discrimination. "I didn't do anything wrong," she said. "It's not like telling people I'm a drug addict."

She also recalls rejecting a counselor's suggestion that she might have asked to be tested as a way of crying for help.

"I'm like, 'No,'" Ms. Moser recalls replying. "'I've come to be tested because I want to know.'"

No one routinely collects demographic information about who gets tested for Huntington's. At the Huntington's Disease Center at Columbia, staff members say they have seen few young people taking the test.

Ms. Moser is still part of a distinct minority. But some researchers say her attitude is increasingly common among young people who know they may develop Huntington's.

More informed about the genetics of the disease than any previous generation, they are convinced that they would rather know how many healthy years they have left than wake up one day to find the illness upon them. They are confident that new reproductive technologies can allow them to have children without transmitting the disease and are eager to be first in line should a treatment become available.

"We're seeing a shift," said Dr. Michael Hayden, a professor of human genetics at the University of British Columbia in Vancouver who has been providing various tests for Huntington's for twenty years. "Younger people are coming for testing now, people in their twenties and early thirties; before, that was very rare. I've counseled some of them. They feel it is part of their heritage and that it is possible to lead a life that's not defined by this gene."

Before the test, Ms. Moser made two lists of life goals. Under "if negative," she wrote married, children and Ireland. Under "if positive" was exercise, vitamins and ballroom dancing. Balance, in that case, would be important. Opening a bed-and-breakfast, a goal since childhood, made both lists.

In the weeks before getting the test results, Ms. Moser gave Ms. Elio explicit instructions about acceptable responses. If she was negative, flowers were OK. If positive, they were not. In either case, drinking was acceptable. Crying was not.

But it was Ms. Elio's husband, Chris Elio, who first broached the subject of taking care of Ms. Moser, whom their young children called "my Katie," as in "this is my mom, this is my dad, this is my Katie." They should address it before the results were in, Mr. Elio told his wife, so that she would not feel, later, that they had done it out of a sense of obligation.

The next day, in an e-mail note that was unusually formal for friends who sent text messages constantly and watched "Desperate Housewives" while on the phone together, Ms. Elio told Ms. Moser that she and her husband wanted her to move in with them if she got sick. Ms. Moser set the note aside. She did not expect to need it.

The results had come a week early, and Ms. Moser assured her friends that the "Sex and the City" trivia party she had planned for that night was still on. After all, she was not sick, not dying. And she had already made the dips.

"I'm the same person I've always been," she insisted that night as her guests gamely dipped strawberries in her chocolate fountain. "It's been in me from the beginning."

But when she went to work the next day, she lingered outside the door of the occupational therapy gym, not wanting to face her colleagues. She avoided the Huntington's floor entirely, choosing to attend to patients ailing of just about anything else. "It's too hard to look at them," she told her friends.

In those first months, Ms. Moser summoned all her strength to pretend that nothing cataclysmic had happened. At times, it seemed easy enough. In the mirror, the same green eyes looked back at her. She was still tall, a devoted Julia Roberts fan, a prolific baker.

She dropped the news of her genetic status into some conversations like small talk, but kept it from her family. She made light of her newfound fate, though often friends were not sure how to take the jokes.

"That's my Huntington's kicking in," she told Rachel Markan, a coworker, after knocking a patient's folder on the floor.

Other times, Ms. Moser abruptly dropped any pretense of routine banter. On a trip to Florida, she and Ms. Elio saw a man in a wheelchair being tube-fed, a method often used to keep Huntington's patients alive for years after they can no longer swallow.

"I don't want a feeding tube," she announced flatly.

In those early days, she calculated that she had at least until fifty before symptoms set in. That was enough time to open a bed-and-breakfast, if she acted fast. Enough time to repay $70,000 in student loans under her thirty-year term.

Doing the math on the loans, though, could send her into a tailspin.

"I'll be repaying them and then I'll start getting sick," she said. "I mean, there's no time in there."

At the end of the summer, as the weather grew colder, Ms. Moser forced herself to return to the Huntington's unit.

In each patient, she saw her future: the biophysicist slumped in his wheelchair, the refrigerator repairman inert in his bed, the onetime professional tennis player who floated through the common room, arms undulating in the startlingly graceful movements that had earned the disease its original name, "Huntington's chorea," from the Greek "to dance."

Then there was her cousin Jimmy, who had wrapped papers for the *New York Post* for nineteen years until suddenly he could no longer tie the knots. When she greeted him, his bright blue eyes darted to her face, then away. If he knew her, it was impossible to tell.

She did what she could for them. She customized their wheelchairs with padding to fit each one's unique tics. She doled out special silverware, oversized or bent in just the right angles to prolong their ability to feed themselves.

Fending off despair, Ms. Moser was also filled with new purpose. Someone, somewhere, she told friends, had to find a cure.

It has been over a century since the disease was identified by George Huntington, a doctor in Amagansett, NY, and over a decade since researchers first found the gene responsible for it.

To raise money for research, Ms. Moser volunteered for walks and dinners and golf outings sponsored by the Huntington's Disease Society of America. She organized a Hula-Hoop-a-thon on the roof of Cardinal Cooke, then a bowl-a-thon at the Port Authority. But at many of the events, attendance was sparse.

It is hard to get people to turn out for Huntington's benefits, she learned from the society's professional fund-raisers. Even families affected by the disease, the most obvious constituents, often will not help publicize events.

"They don't want people to know they're connected to Huntington's," Ms. Moser said, with a mix of anger and recognition. "It's like in my family—it's not a good thing."

Her first session with a therapist brought a chilling glimpse of how the disorder is viewed even by some who know plenty about it. "She told me it was my moral and ethical obligation not to have children," Ms. Moser told Ms. Elio by cell phone as soon as she left the office, her voice breaking.

In lulls between fund-raisers, Ms. Moser raced to educate her own world about Huntington's. She added links about the disease to her MySpace page. She plastered her desk at work with "Cure HD" stickers and starred in a video about the Huntington's unit for her union's website.

Ms. Moser gave blood for one study and spoke into a microphone for researchers trying to detect subtle speech differences in people who have extra CAG repeats before more noticeable disease symptoms emerge.

When researchers found a way to cure mice bred to replicate features of the disease in humans, Ms. Moser sent the news to friends and acquaintances.

But it was hard to celebrate. "Thank God," the joke went around on the Huntington's National Youth Alliance e-mail list Ms. Moser subscribed to, "at least there won't be any more poor mice wandering around with Huntington's disease."

In October, one of Ms. Moser's aunts lost her balance while walking and broke her nose. It was the latest in a series of falls. "The cure needs to be soon for me," Ms. Moser said. "Sooner for everybody else."

In the waiting room of the Dutchess County family courthouse on a crisp morning in the fall of 2005, Ms. Moser approached her mother, who turned away.

"I need to tell her something important," Ms. Moser told a family member who had accompanied her mother to the hearing.

He conveyed the message and brought one in return: Unless she was dying, her mother did not have anything to say to her.

That Ms. Moser had tested positive meant that her mother would develop Huntington's, if she had not already. A year earlier, Ms. Moser's mother had convinced a judge that her sister, Nora Maldonado, was neglecting her daughter. She was given guardianship of the daughter, four-year-old Jillian.

Ms. Moser had been skeptical of her mother's accusations that Ms. Maldonado was not feeding or bathing Jillian properly, and she wondered whether her effort to claim Jillian had been induced by the psychological symptoms of the disease.

Her testimony about her mother's genetic status, Ms. Moser knew, could help persuade the judge to return Jillian. Ms. Maldonado had found out years earlier that she did not have the Huntington's gene.

Ms. Moser did not believe that someone in the early stages of Huntington's should automatically be disqualified from taking care of a child. But her own rocky childhood had convinced her that Jillian would be better off with Ms. Maldonado.

She told her aunt's lawyer about her test results and agreed to testify.

In the courtroom, Ms. Moser took the witness stand. Her mother's lawyer jumped up as soon as the topic of Huntington's arose. It was irrelevant, he said. But by the time the judge had sustained his objections, Ms. Moser's mother, stricken, had understood.

The next day, in the bathroom, Ms. Maldonado approached Ms. Moser's mother.

"I'm sorry," she said. Ms. Moser's mother said nothing.

The court has continued to let Ms. Moser's mother retain guardianship of Jillian. But she has not spoken to her daughter again.

"It's a horrible illness," Ms. Moser's mother said, months later, gesturing to her husband. "Now he has a wife who has it. Did she think of him? Did she think of me? Who's going to marry her?"

Before the test, it was as if Ms. Moser had been balanced between parallel universes, one in which she would never get the disease and one in which she would. The test had made her whole.

She began to prepare the Elio children and Jillian for her illness, determined that they would not be scared, as she had been with her grandfather. When Jillian wanted to know how people got Huntington's disease "in their pants," Ms. Moser wrote the text of a children's book that explained what these other kinds of "genes" were and why they would make her sick.

But over the winter, Ms. Elio complained gently that her friend had become "Ms. H. D." And an impromptu note that arrived for the children in the early spring convinced her that Ms. Moser was dwelling too much on her own death.

"You all make me so happy, and I am so proud of who you are and who you will be," read the note, on rainbow scratch-and-write paper. "I will always remember the fun things we do together."

Taking matters into her own hands, Ms. Elio created a profile for Ms. Moser on an online dating service. Ms. Moser was skeptical but supplied a picture. Dating, she said, was the worst thing about knowing she had the

Huntington's gene. It was hard to imagine someone falling enough in love with her to take on Huntington's knowingly, or asking it of someone she loved. At the same time, she said, knowing her status could help her find the right person, if he was out there.

"Either way, I was going to get sick," she said. "And I'd want someone who could handle it. If, by some twist of fate, I do get married and have children, at least we know what we're getting into."

After much debate, the friends settled on the third date as the right time to mention Huntington's. But when the first date came, Ms. Moser wished she could just blurt it out.

"It kind of just lingers there," she said. "I really just want to be able to tell people, 'Someday, I'm going to have Huntington's disease.'"

Last May 6, a year to the day after she had received her test results, the subject line "CAG Count" caught Ms. Moser's attention as she was scrolling through the online discussion forums of the Huntington's Disease Advocacy Center. She knew she had forty-five CAG repeats, but she had never investigated it further.

She clicked on the message.

"My mother's CAG was forty-three," it read. "She started forgetting the punch line to jokes at thirty-nine/forty." Another woman whose husband's CAG count was forty-seven had just sold his car. "He's thirty-nine years old," she wrote. "It was time for him to quit driving."

Quickly, Ms. Moser scanned a chart that accompanied the messages for her number, forty-five. The median age of onset to which it corresponded was thirty-seven.

Ms. Elio got drunk with her husband the night Ms. Moser finally told her.

"That's twelve years away," Ms. Moser said.

The statistic, they knew, meant that half of those with her CAG number started showing symptoms after age thirty-seven. But it also meant that the other half started showing symptoms earlier.

Ms. Moser, meanwhile, flew to the annual convention of the Huntington's Disease Society, which she had decided at the last minute to attend.

"Mother or father?" one woman, twenty-three, from Chicago, asked a few minutes after meeting Ms. Moser in the elevator of the Milwaukee Hilton. "Have you tested? What's your CAG?"

She was close to getting herself tested, the woman confided. How did it feel to know?

"It's hard to think the other way anymore of not knowing," Ms. Moser replied. "It's become a part of my life."

After years of trying to wring conversation from her family about Huntington's, Ms. Moser suddenly found herself bathing in it. But for the first time in a long time, her mind was on other things. At a youth support group meeting in the hotel hallway, she took her place in the misshapen circle. Later, on the dance floor, the spasms of the symptomatic seemed as natural as the gyrations of the normal.

"I'm not alone in this," Ms. Moser remembers thinking. "This affects other people, too, and we all just have to live our lives."

July 15, the day of Ms. Moser's twenty-fifth birthday party, was sunny, with a hint of moisture in the air. At her aunt's house in Long Beach, NY, Ms. Moser wore a dress with pictures of cocktails on it. It was, she and Ms. Elio told anyone who would listen, her "cocktail dress." They drew the quotation marks in the air.

A bowl of "Cure HD" pins sat on the table. Over burgers from the barbecue, Ms. Moser mentioned to family members from her father's side that she had tested positive for the Huntington's gene.

"What's that?" one cousin asked.

"It will affect my ability to walk, talk, and think," Ms. Moser said. "Sometime before I'm fifty."

"That's soon," an uncle said matter-of-factly.

"So do you have to take medication?" her cousin asked.

"There's nothing really to take," Ms. Moser said.

She and the Elios put on bathing suits, loaded the children in a wagon and walked to the beach.

More than anything now, Ms. Moser said, she is filled with a sense of urgency.

"I have a lot to do," she said. "And I don't have a lot of time."

Over the next months, Ms. Moser took tennis lessons every Sunday morning and went to church in the evening.

When a planned vacation with the Elio family fell through at the last minute, she went anyway, packing Disney World, Universal Studios, Wet 'n Wild and Sea World into thirty-six hours with a high school friend who lives in Orlando. She was honored at a dinner by the New York chapter of the Huntington's society for her outreach efforts and managed a brief thank-you speech despite her discomfort with public speaking.

Having made a New Year's resolution to learn to ride a unicycle, she bought a used one. "My legs are tired, my arms are tired, and I definitely need protection," she reported to Ms. Elio. On Super Bowl Sunday, she waded into the freezing Atlantic Ocean for a Polar Bear swim to raise money for the Make-a-Wish Foundation.

Ms. Elio complained that she hardly got to see her friend. But one recent weekend, they packed up the Elio children and drove to the house the Elios were renovating in eastern Pennsylvania. The kitchen floor needed grouting, and, rejecting the home improvement gospel that calls for a special tool designed for the purpose, Ms. Moser and Ms. Elio had decided to use pastry bags.

As they turned into the driveway, Ms. Moser studied the semi-attached house next door. Maybe she would move in one day, as the Elios had proposed. Then, when she could no longer care for herself, they could put in a door.

First, though, she wanted to travel. She had heard of a job that would place her in different occupational therapy positions across the country every few months and was planning to apply.

"I'm thinking Hawaii first," she said.

March 18, 2007

Author's Afterword

I didn't really start out like a lot of people in this industry. They start out wanting to be professional journalists, but that wasn't actually my goal. I more wanted to be involved in political activism on campus, through the student newspaper.

When I graduated, I needed a job. At that time, you were able to just call up the local newspapers and ask if they would let you do some freelance work—that's how I got my clips. Then after that, a fellow *Michigan Daily* alum introduced me to the *Los Angeles Times*'s bureau chief in Detroit—and I got a job, essentially an intern in the Detroit bureau of the *LA Times*. The bureau chief wanted me to cover the basic auto industry beat, but he let me do other types of stories, too. He taught me how to write news and feature stories, and then the *Times* liked what I was doing enough that they wanted to bring me to Los Angeles. When I went to Los Angeles, I was still an intern. They had a job slot called a "two-year temporary reporter." You were *not* to assume you would get a permanent job after that, but it turned out I had this early interest in the Internet, and a rather exotic skill at the time—I knew how to send e-mail. I had a personal interest in staying in touch with my college friends through the Internet, but before I knew it, I kind of used that interest to delve into broader social issues and create a beat that I ended up calling "the sociology of technology." I wrote about that for the *LA Times*; later I went to the *New York Times* and did the same thing.

All you have to do to be a good journalist is be able to listen to people and tell their stories I don't think that women as a group are better suited or that men or any group of people are better suited than another group. I've met so many people and become involved pretty intimately in the lives of so many different people than I would have had I not had the excuse of being a nosy journalist. I value those relationships. Often my stories take a year or more to report; I get to know the subject well. Afterward, I stay in touch with them. They're not in my inner circle of friends, but some of them have become real friends, not just sources. I feel as if I personally benefit from delving inside other people's heads. It actually helps give me a better perspective of my own life. That's what I really try to do in my stories. If they work, they transport you into the head and life of another person, and that kind of experience benefits you as a person as well as just giving you information.

The best part of my job is the reporting. I like going out to wherever I have to be and observing people and talking to people and asking endless questions and gathering all the information. The hardest part is the writing . . . I think that there's actually a part before the writing that is the hardest part. I kind of started out thinking I knew what the story was, but then I'm like, "Why did I think this was a story? Why did I spend months reporting on this subject?" And there's like a moment of *panic*. Or it could be more than a moment; it could be *weeks* of panic, when I'm trying to figure out exactly how to tell a story. But once I finish a first draft, it gets better after that. Reporting is definitely my favorite, but my favorite is publishing. You can't get to the publishing without the writing, so . . .

Diana B. Henriques

Diana B. Henriques, the author of the *New York Times* bestseller *The Wizard of Lies: Bernie Madoff and the Death of Trust*, has been a writer for the *New York Times* since 1989. She was previously a staff writer for *Barron's*, a Wall Street correspondent for the *Philadelphia Inquirer*, and an investigative reporter for the *Trenton Times*.

In 2005, Henriques was a finalist for a Pulitzer Prize and won a George Polk Award, the Worth Bingham Prize for Investigative Reporting and Harvard's Goldsmith Prize for her 2004 series exposing insurance and investment rip-offs of young military consumers. She was also a member of the *New York Times* team that was a Pulitzer finalist for its coverage of the 2008 financial crisis.

In May 2011, HBO optioned *The Wizard of Lies* and engaged Henriques as a consultant to help develop the book into a film.

Henriques is also the author of three previous books: *The Machinery of Greed*, *Fidelity's World* and *The White Sharks of Wall Street*. She and her husband Larry live in Hoboken, NJ.

Military Insurance Scams

Insurance sales practices mislead
soldiers and violate Pentagon rules

Part 1

Nicholas Stachler was nineteen years old when he reported for basic training
with the Army at Fort Benning, GA, before shipping out for eleven months to
Iraq.

A gentle, trusting man, he had only weeks earlier graduated from high
school with a handful of trophies in hockey and soccer, middling grades and
hardly a clue about how to handle his money. He had held only casual jobs
babysitting and mowing lawns and had never opened a checking account. The
bus trip to boot camp, from the foothills of the Appalachians in southern Ohio
to the kudzu-covered fields of western Georgia, took him farther from home
than he had ever been.

About six weeks into his training—six weeks of combat drills and
drummed-in lessons in Army ways—he tasted one of the less-honorable traditions of military life: a compulsory classroom briefing on personal finance
that was a life insurance sales pitch in disguise.

As he remembers the class and as base investigative records show, two
insurance agents quick-stepped him and his classmates through a stack of
paperwork, pointing out where they should sign their names, where they
should scribble their initials. They were given no time to read the documents
and no copies to keep.

Specialist Stachler says he thought he had arranged to have $100 a month
deducted from his pay for some sort of Army-endorsed savings plan or mutual
fund. When he returned from Iraq, he found that he had not been saving the

money at all. He had been paying $100 a month in premiums for an insurance policy that promised him some cash value far down the road and a death benefit that was almost certainly less than $44,000, a small amount compared with the $250,000 in life insurance he had through a military-sponsored plan that cost him $16.25 a month.

"I asked him what this money was coming out of his paycheck for, and he didn't even know," said his mother, Pamela M. Stachler of Athens, Ohio.

Specialist Stachler's experience is not uncommon. A six-month examination by the *New York Times*, drawing on military and court records and interviews with dozens of industry executives and servicemen and women, has found that several financial services companies or their agents are using questionable tactics on military bases to sell insurance and investments that may not fit the needs of people in uniform.

Insurance agents have made misleading pitches to "captive" audiences like the ones at Fort Benning. They have posed as counselors on veterans benefits and independent financial advisers. And they have solicited soldiers in their barracks or while they were on duty, violations of Defense Department regulations.

The Pentagon has been aware of practices like these since the Vietnam War; investigations have even cited specific companies and agents. But because of industry lobbying, congressional pressure, weak enforcement, and the Pentagon's ineffective oversight, almost no action has been taken to sanction those responsible or to better protect those who are vulnerable, the *Times* has found.

And the problem has only intensified since the beginning of the Iraq war, say military employees who monitor insurance agents. With the death toll rising in Iraq, interest in insurance among the troops has surged, making the war a selling opportunity for many agents, they said.

The military market includes hundreds of thousands of men and women, many of them young and financially unsophisticated, all of them trained to trust leadership, obey orders, and show loyalty to comrades.

To reach the buyers, many companies have used their military connections to lend credibility to their sales efforts, recruiting heavily from among retired or former military people for their corporate boards and sales forces. The advisory board at one company, First Command Financial Planning in Fort Worth, includes Gen. Anthony C. Zinni, the retired commander in chief of the US Central Command.

Many financial experts say the products sold are often ill-suited for the military people who buy them. Like Specialist Stachler, almost all service members purchase low-cost insurance through the military, and, like him, 94 percent carry the maximum coverage of $250,000, the Defense Department says. But agents are nevertheless selling these men and women policies that have steep premiums for relatively small amounts of coverage.

A young marine at Camp Pendleton, Calif., for example, was sold a twenty-year insurance policy last fall that gave him a death benefit of just under $28,000, plus some cash value far in the future, in exchange for $6,600 in premiums paid in the first seven years. That was more than fourteen times what the same death benefit would have cost him under his military-sponsored plan.

Another product heavily promoted to military people is a type of mutual fund in which 50 percent of the first-year contributions are consumed as fees, a deal considered so expensive that such funds all but disappeared from the civilian market almost twenty years ago.

The insurance industry's leadership says rogue agents are to blame for the problems. The companies say that they have never knowingly tolerated these agents and that they dismiss the ones who are caught. A vast majority of their military customers, the companies say, are satisfied and loyal.

The industry's leaders also argue that existing Defense Department rules covering financial sales on military bases, if properly enforced, would be more than adequate to protect service members from the occasional episodes of abuse without cutting them off from legitimate information about insurance and investments.

Industry executives defend their products as appropriate and say they employ veterans as agents and advisers because they better understand the financial and personal pressures of military life. But many military leaders worry that the approach exploits, for private profit, the obedience, trust, and loyalty that they work to instill in troops.

If a soldier or a sailor winds up feeling cheated or misled, the blame is as likely to go to the military as to the offending sales agents and companies, said John M. Molino, who, as the deputy undersecretary of defense for military community and family policy, is responsible for Pentagon policy on these issues. That can damage morale, inhibit recruitment, and discourage reenlistment, he said.

"When we allow a person on an installation," Mr. Molino said, "there is at least the implication that we have sanctioned your presence."

But barring sales agents from bases is not the solution, said Frank Keating, the former governor of Oklahoma, who is president of the American Council of Life Insurers, a lobbying group.

"Anything that is unethical or inappropriate should not exist, period," Mr. Keating said. But "someone who is mature enough to fight and quite possibly die for their country," he added, "should be freely able to decide how much and what kind of life insurance they should have."

That argument does not satisfy people like Capt. James A. Shaw, commander of the Second Battalion's 325th Airborne Infantry Regiment at Fort Bragg, NC. In his experience, he said, the training that produces competent soldiers may make them vulnerable to a disguised pitch from a friendly agent in the classroom who is a veteran.

"It's an environment where you do what you're told," Captain Shaw said. "They are learning stuff that will save their lives in combat. Those classes are the law."

When the topic switches from weapons maintenance to personal finance, he said, "there's no real reason to suspect otherwise."

Specialist Stachler and four other soldiers who were in the room remember well the day in late summer 2002 when they unwittingly bought an insurance policy at Fort Benning from two men they had never seen before.

The sales pitch, they said, came during a compulsory "briefing" on personal finance held in a classroom on the first floor of the soldiers' sprawling three-story barracks in a wooded corner of the Sand Hill training area. About two hundred recruits were present. The two men seemed to be on friendly terms with several of the sergeants, according to the soldiers, each of whom was interviewed in person or by phone.

The visiting insurance agents talked to the recruits about savings and investment.

"There was not a word about life insurance," said one soldier, Specialist Brandon Conger, a tall, intense twenty-year-old from Butler, MO, a small town near Kansas City.

But there was plenty of paperwork to fill out. Specialist Stachler said it was the agents who did that. "We had to sign things," he said, including the critical "allotment form," which authorizes the Army to deduct money from a soldier's paycheck, in this case to be paid to the insurance company.

What they said they experienced that day violated several provisions of Defense Department Directive 1344.7, which prohibits agents from soliciting "recruits, trainees and transient personnel in a 'mass' or 'captive' audience" on bases, soliciting on-duty personnel, using deceptive methods or possessing the allotment forms.

And what the soldiers signed up for was not what they had thought.

One soldier, Specialist Michael Fresenburg, twenty, who recently became engaged to his high school sweetheart back home in Columbia, MO, said he thought he had agreed to participate in "a sort of savings fund."

"I understood that there would be two accounts," he said, "one I could draw from at any time, and the other I couldn't touch for seven years."

The accounts were in fact a complex form of insurance, one that indeed allowed the soldiers to contribute to a savings fund at competitive interest rates. But there was a catch: they could participate only if they bought an expensive twenty-year life insurance policy, one with premiums that would eat up all of their monthly payments in the first year and three-fourths of their payments over the next six years.

Insurance experts say the policies are intended for knowledgeable long-term investors who have savings to spare. They are almost never suitable for modest-income people as young and financially inexperienced as Specialist Stachler and his fellow soldiers.

"A young, single person with no dependents and no debts probably doesn't need life insurance at all," said Professor James M. Carson, an insurance expert at Florida State University. Service members with families probably do need insurance and might want more than the $250,000 offered through the military's low-cost plan, but cash-accumulation policies like these, he said, are an expensive way to obtain that additional coverage.

Moreover, the penalties for early withdrawals and the slow-growing cash value in most of the policies make them a terrible vehicle for short-term savings and a poor method for long-term investment, Professor Carson said. "If they just put their money into a money market fund," he said, "they would be outearning the rate of return on most cash-value life insurance policies like these." The companies that sell the policies say they help military people save while providing some supplemental insurance coverage. But whether this was the right type of life insurance for the five men, now at Fort Bragg, is almost moot: none of them realized they were buying life insurance. The only paperwork they received, they say, is a one-page statement on the status of their accumulation fund; it says nothing about any insurance benefits.

In Ohio, Ms. Stachler, a forty-eight-year-old employee of the US Forest Service and a single mother, paid such close attention to her son's finances while he was in Iraq that she once noticed bills for a modest shopping spree at the post exchange at Baghdad International Airport and teased him about it in their next phone call. She is adamant that no life insurance policy arrived in the mail for her son at his home in Ohio, his address of record.

"From the day he left Athens, Ohio, for the military, anything that came in with his name on it, I opened," she said. "There was no policy."

Specialist Stachler canceled the policy when he discovered what it was. Of the $1,800 deducted from his paychecks while he was at war, his mother said, he received $500 back. The rest had been eaten up by the premiums he did not know he was paying. "I was really bummed," he said.

Specialist Conger and Specialist Fresenburg emerged from Iraq still holding onto the grimy, dog-eared business cards they had collected at Fort Benning. Both cards bear the name of an insurance agency in Columbus, GA, the city nearest the base. On one card, someone had penciled in the name Ron Thurman.

Ron Thurman is identified in Fort Benning records as one of several local representatives of the American Amicable Life Insurance Company of Waco, TX, a prominent player in the military insurance market.

Now living in Bamberg, Germany, Mr. Thurman did not respond to a registered letter or to numerous telephone messages left at his office over the last month. But in a letter he sent to legal officers at Fort Benning, he said he had thought that the briefings had been approved by the sergeants in charge, although he acknowledged that agents are not allowed to solicit the trainees at Sand Hill at Fort Benning. "We promise this wouldn't happen again," he wrote. "We are very sorry."

The authorities at Fort Benning first learned about the improper briefings early last year; a young private told them when he came to them for help in canceling his policy. After an investigation, they barred Mr. Thurman from the base last October, along with another man from the same nearby agency. A third man affiliated with the agency received a warning letter, said Lt. Col. Ralph J. Tremaglio III, the deputy staff judge advocate at Fort Benning.

Colonel Tremaglio said his office received a call from the agency's owner in December. "He said he had been contacted by the vice president of American Amicable about Mr. Thurman," the colonel said. According to his file, the caller wanted to confirm that Mr. Thurman was barred only from Fort Benning, not from all military bases.

American Amicable disputes that. In a written statement, it said it did not learn about the Fort Benning incident until a few months ago, when a reporter asked about it. "The situation is currently under investigation," the company said, and it "will respond with the appropriate actions once the facts are known."

It also insisted that the policies sold at Fort Benning had been mailed to the soldiers' homes. It would not say how much coverage the $100-a-month policies offered, but the average death benefit it has paid in the Iraq conflict is less than $44,000. When three marines who bought similar policies last year were killed recently, the company paid out $87,155, or about $29,000 a marine.

Second Lt. Craig Cunningham, a feisty West Point graduate serving at Fort Bliss in El Paso, remembers a reception for officers in training that he attended at the base officers club last fall.

"There were one hundred lieutenants or so, a pretty big group," Lieutenant Cunningham said. "They had a bar and a reception area, with finger food on one side. Everyone's mingling."

At one point the chitchat stopped as someone made a pitch encouraging the group to join the officers club and a nonprofit military fraternal organization, the Association of the United States Army.

Conversation resumed. Sometime later someone called for another halt, "to talk about First Command," Lieutenant Cunningham said.

"There were several agents there, mingling and handing out business cards," he said. He recalled that the agents were retired military officers.

The companies selling financial services in the military market try to recruit former military people to be their agents, people who can fit smoothly into receptions like the one at Fort Bliss.

"They're buying access," said Robert R. Sparks, a lawyer in Covington, KY, who has handled cases for military consumers. "That's all they're getting. But that's all they need, because their customers are used to going along with authority."

Few companies have more fervently embraced this form of salesmanship, called affinity marketing, than First Command, a forty-six-year-old financial services company originally known by the gawky name USPA and IRA. The company said all of the three hundred thousand families that it serves are headed by former or active-duty commissioned officers or higher-ranking noncommissioned officers; it does not serve lower-ranking service people. And almost all of its 1,007 agents have served in the military or "have military connections." None, it says, have been cited for rule violations.

First Command's paid advisory board, trumpeted on its website, includes several retired military luminaries, among them General Zinni, who calls himself an enthusiastic customer. "I even advised my son, who is a marine, to join" the company, he said in a recent interview. He said he was comfortable with the use the company had made of his affiliation. "It just lets their clients know that this is the type of people they have on their board," he said.

The board also includes several other prominent military retirees, including the former Coast Guard Commandant Robert E. Kramek; Gen. Lloyd

W. Newton, the Air Force pilot known as Fig Newton who flew with the Thunderbirds flying team; and Vice Adm. John R. Ryan, a former superintendent of the Naval Academy.

What First Command does "is affinity marketing, but I don't think there's anything wrong with that," said Lamar C. Smith, the chief executive, a former Air Force captain who was a pilot in the Vietnam War. As veterans, he said, his agents "speak the language" of the military and know, perhaps better than civilians, how life on a base can put pressure on a family's finances. Families move often and on short notice, Mr. Smith said, making it difficult for a spouse to hold a job; debt levels are higher than in civilian life. But where First Command sees a sales force attuned to the needs of its market niche, some of its critics see agents whose ties to senior officers and retired brass can unduly influence the financial decisions of junior officers.

"They go after these young, young lieutenants with an agent who is, say, a retired colonel," said Sandra Benintende, a military spouse at Fort Knox, KY, who worked briefly for a First Command office. She recalled that one young customer waiting for a meeting with his agent once asked her, "Should I call him 'Sir'?"

The company says it relies only on word-of-mouth referrals to cultivate customers. Interviews with a score of young officers and their spouses, however, produced an equal number of anecdotes about other ways that First Command sought out prospects.

One remembered a "sailor of the year" reception that the company sponsored in Norfolk, VA, at which agents passed out business cards. Families at Fort Knox know that First Command provides a free "happy hour" buffet on Fridays at a bar near the base, Mrs. Benintende said.

From their first meeting with a company agent, clients are encouraged to provide the names of other prospects and to invite friends and coworkers to the free dinners. The presence of senior officers among the satisfied customers at such events was cited by many young military people as something that persuaded them to sign up with First Command.

And there is no doubt that First Command has tens of thousands of satisfied customers. Among them are Lt. Col. Rande and Karen Read of Weatherford, TX, west of Fort Worth. Retired from the Air Force, Colonel Read is a pilot for American Airlines; Mrs. Read is a former Air Force nurse.

Mr. Read's first agent, he recalled, was a former Air Force captain a few years older than him. "I was taking a shotgun approach, continually dabbling," he said. With coaching from his agent, he said, he started a regular savings and investment plan in 1982.

But the free dinners and hand-holding make a sales effort like this expensive and time-consuming. Only financial products that generate high front-end commissions can compensate agents for the amount of work required, financial experts said.

Insurance agents who want to sell policies on base at Camp Pendleton, north of San Diego, must first pass a written test on their mastery of military rules. One question asks: "When may an insurance agent give classes for the sole purpose of informing service members of their VA benefits?"

The correct answer is "Never."

That prohibition did not stop several agents for Pioneer American Insurance Company, a sister company of American Amicable, from arranging "veterans benefits" classes last summer for marines at Camp Pendleton's training school, camp lawyers said. Posing as instructors, the agents had actually come to sell insurance, the lawyers said.

The ruse may have gone undetected by the camp authorities had not a retired master gunnery sergeant called the school last August to complain about a policy that his twenty-three-year-old son, one of the trainees, had just purchased. (The Marines declined to disclose the names of the sergeant or his son.) An investigation was begun and passed to Capt. Jonathan Strasburg, who is head of research and civil law in the staff judge advocate's office at Camp Pendleton.

At one point an undercover investigator was assigned to attend a "veterans benefits" briefing. The investigator reported that the agents would talk about benefits "anytime anyone in authority was in the room," Captain Strasburg said.

"But when the troop handler would leave the room," he said, "the VA talk would stop, almost midsentence, and they would roll into their investment pitch."

In his report, Captain Strasburg wrote that the officer in charge did not realize that the volunteer instructors were insurance agents and, in any case, was unfamiliar with the rules that barred agents from holding such classes, a chronic problem on bases, military lawyers say.

In affidavits, many of the marines that Captain Strasburg interviewed said the agents had instructed them to sign and initial stacks of unread documents, including both the allotment forms that set up payroll deductions and the company's "Statement of Understanding" forms. These certify that each marine had requested the sales appointment, was off duty at the time and had understood the details of the insurance being purchased.

The policy that the retired sergeant's son and presumably other train-ees bought provided a death benefit of just under $28,000 for twenty years in exchange for premiums that totaled $6,600 over the first seven years, includ-ing $1,200 in the first year. After the twentieth year, the policy would expire with some cash value, most of which would have accumulated in its final years. Under the military's program, the same amount of coverage would cost just $468, the Strasburg report said.

Like the Pentagon's code, the camp's rules forbid soliciting business from new recruits or trainees. The reason is simple, Captain Strasburg said, these young marines "are taught to question nothing."

Captain Strasburg ultimately identified 345 marines who had bought insurance through the improper briefings. Of the dozens he interviewed, he said in his report, all "felt they were obligated to sign up."

"They all believed the plan was endorsed by the Marine Corps," he concluded.

The Marines found no indication that Pioneer American had known about these improper activities, and the company agreed to offer refunds. It also dismissed the agents, the company said, under a "zero tolerance" policy it had put in place in October 2000.

The earlier improper briefings at Fort Benning had a different aftermath. Barred from the base last October, Mr. Thurman began working for American Amicable on military bases in Europe almost immediately. According to Millie Waters, a public affairs officer in Europe, the company requested a permit for Mr. Thurman on November 6; the permit was approved on December 11.

Army authorities in Europe knew he had been barred from Fort Benning, Ms. Waters said, but they issued the permit, because the exclusion had been limited to Fort Benning and because an American Amicable executive in Europe had vouched for him.

But company executives in Texas said they had not known about the action against Mr. Thurman when he moved to Germany and would not have approved his transfer if they had. The company said it cut its ties to Mr. Thurman in June and is investigating how his transfer was approved.

Since October 2000, the company has made a considerable effort to make sure that its agents "understand the moral issues involved in insurance sales," the company said in its statement.

"The examples cited here of personnel who have violated the company's trust do not reflect a lack of commitment" by the company, it said. Overall, it considers its compliance record to be very good, given that it has more than three hundred agents working as independent contractors around the world.

When Captain Jennifer Jusseaume was a junior at the Air Force Academy in Colorado Springs in 1998, she took advantage of lenient loan terms that financial companies have traditionally offered to third-year students at the military academies. She borrowed $19,000, at 1.5 percent interest.

She knew she would use some of the money to pay off her credit card debt. But while she was deciding what to do with the rest, her commanding officer arranged a financial briefing for his cadets in their squadron's common area. The briefing was given by the commander's investment adviser, a retired officer who was an agent with First Command

"It was about investing," said Captain Jusseaume, now twenty-five and married to Capt. Brian Jusseaume, who returned from duty in the Persian Gulf in time for the arrival of their first child this month. "If you were interested, you signed your name." She did, ultimately investing in two mutual funds that First Command sells as an agent for several large mutual fund families.

Both funds, the Fidelity Destiny Fund II and the Pioneer Independence Fund, consumed half of the first year's investment in sales charges, a drag on her future returns from which she will never recover.

The type of mutual fund that First Command sells to virtually all its customers is traditionally called a contractual plan. Under this plan, fund shares are purchased in monthly installments over fifteen or twenty years.

The plans have been around since the 1930s but all but vanished from the civilian market in the early 1980s after decades of sales abuses and regulatory crackdowns. Their biggest drawback, fund experts say, is the impact that the loss of 50 percent of the first year's investment has on future earnings. Even a faithful investor never recovers from that burden, regardless of how well the fund does over time. And investors who do not go the distance—historically a high percentage—wind up paying a substantial percentage of their total investment in sales charges.

The Securities and Exchange Commission urged Congress in 1966 to abolish contractual plans. Instead, bowing to industry pressure, Congress only modified the rules governing them. It now allowed investors to withdraw from new plans within forty-five days with a full refund and within eighteen months with an 85 percent refund.

The amendments made contractual plans less attractive. Indeed, they have become so obscure that the Investment Company Institute, the fund industry's trade group, has not kept statistics on them since 1985.

In contrast to the enormous variety of mutual funds available in today's market, only a handful are still sold as contractual plans; First Command offers five, managed by Fidelity, AIM/Invesco, Pioneer, and Franklin Templeton.

First Command and the fund companies that sell the plans fully disclose those first-year fees. In their defense, they say that contractual plans help discipline investors by keeping them from making costly shifts in and out of the market. And, they say, the plans compensate agents for the labor-intensive work of turning young military couples into savers and investors.

Among First Command's satisfied customers are First Sgt. Mike Boardman and his wife, Terry. Sergeant Boardman, who has been in the Army for twenty years, is a big, powerfully built man with firm opinions, a forceful personality, and a fierce devotion to his troops. "I led sixty-one men into Iraq and led sixty-one out," he said. "I consider myself a good soldier. But I don't know anything about mutual funds and I don't want to know. I don't want to have to read the business pages. I barely have time to read the sports pages."

In an interview arranged by First Command, Sergeant Boardman said the up-front fees had curbed any temptation to stop making the monthly contributions. "Also, I felt I'd paid them to do a job for me over time," he said, "and I'm going to make them do that job."

Mr. Smith, the chief executive of First Command and himself a longtime investor in contractual plans, argues that the choice for most young officers is not between a contractual plan and a low-cost, more flexible mutual fund. "The choice," he said, "is between saving money through investments in a contractual plan or spending it and winding up with nothing."

But less happy customers say that the front-end fees have sapped the earning power of their hard-earned investments and locked them into disappointing or inconsistently managed funds.

Lt. Cmdr. Dale Folsom, now the senior controller for the Coast Guard's search and rescue center in New Orleans, began his career as an enlisted man. In less than a dozen years he rose to the rank of chief petty officer and, in 1993, graduated from the Coast Guard's officer candidate school in Yorktown, VA.

Two years later, Commander Folsom signed up with First Command and was steered out of his simple portfolio of savings bonds into the Fidelity Destiny II Fund, a contractual plan.

"I was a little surprised that, in addition to the 50 percent load and annual management fees, there is also a monthly 'sales and creation charge' and custodian fees," he said. After fees ate up half of his $300 monthly investment in the first year of the plan, the smaller continuing fees reduced it to $293.97.

"I just wish I had realized that what they were selling at such a high price was discipline and I already had that," Commander Folsom said.

Several longtime executives of the mutual fund industry said they were amazed that these archaic plans are still a staple of the military market.

"Would I ever recommend that an investor buy contractual plans? No, I would not," said John C. Bogle, the founder of the Vanguard Group, the mutual fund management company, and an advocate of low-cost mutual fund investing.

But Commander Folsom said his disgust with First Command is based not just on his experience with contractual plans, but also on the advice the company gave to a young, single Coast Guard officer he knows.

The young man, who is in his mid-twenties and confesses to having haphazard financial habits, takes home slightly more than $3,900 a month, thanks to a $600-a-month raise last year. But precisely $600 is being deducted automatically from his paycheck under the financial plan designed for him last fall by First Command.

He is putting $300 a month into contractual plans, although after the upfront fees are paid, only half of that is actually being invested on his behalf. Another $150 is going into a money market fund at First Command Bank, the company's online savings institution. And $142.69 is being deducted for $250,000 in life insurance, duplicating the $250,000 in coverage he is already buying through the military for $16.25 a month, one-eighth as much. (The higher-priced First Command policy has some slow-growing cash value and a clause that guarantees that he can get coverage when he leaves the service.)

But the punch line for Commander Folsom is that the money the young man is steering toward First Command could be helping to pay off his ever-deepening debt. The young man, who agreed to be interviewed on the condition of anonymity, confirmed that his debts total almost $51,000. Of that, almost $16,000 is credit card debt, of which more than $5,700 is incurring interest charges of 25 percent.

First Command said it could not comment on a client's affairs but defended the advice reflected in the man's plan, noting that it is important for young officers to save and invest even as they pay their debts.

Gerald Cannizzaro, a financial planner in suburban Washington and a member of the National Association of Personal Financial Advisors, was one of several financial planners who were stunned at the advice the young officer was getting.

"If you were talking to a bunch of NAPFA people, they'd be in a coma by now," Mr. Cannizzaro said. "This is so bad. Why is he investing money when he has all that credit card debt? It makes no sense except to generate commissions for someone."

High up-front fees are not the only disadvantage of many products sold in the military market, financial experts say.

About half the people who buy cash-value insurance policies drop them within the first seven years, academic experts say, barely the break-even point for most policyholders. The dropout rate is higher for military policies than for those in the civilian market, industry analysts said. As for contractual plans like those Captain Jusseaume owns, studies show, roughly half the investors who have bought them dropped out early.

First Command says its dropout rates are much lower, for insurance and investments. Its analysis shows that one of every four plans it has sold since 1980, more than one hundred and fifty-six thousand plans, were dropped before completion, and that one out of ten was dropped after customers had paid into them for at least five years.

The figures, critics said, raise doubts about whether the high front-end fees actually accomplish what First Command says they will: instilling discipline and providing the personal attention that helps inexperienced investors stay the course.

But the young Coast Guard officer seemed content with the advice he was getting from his First Command agent, a retired military officer.

Captain Jusseaume, the Air Force officer, expressed some regret about her reliance on First Command's advice. "Looking back on it," she said, "I know I could have done something better with the money."

So why had she decided, as a cadet, to rely on First Command? "Our commander made it clear that he was with First Command and he had been very happy," she said. "I was really swayed by that."

Lt. Wayne V. Hildreth, retired, of Jacksonville, FL, conducted one of the Navy's most extensive investigations of the improper sale of financial products on military bases. The experience, he says, taught him two troubling lessons.

First, he learned that the problems extended far beyond one company or one branch of the military. Second, he learned that the Pentagon was capable of ignoring the problems, even for decades.

His discouraging education came in 1997. He was looking into complaints about agents of Academy Life Insurance Company, at the time a prominent player in the military market. Among other things, the agents were accused of improperly using their relationship with the Non-Commissioned Officers Association, a military fraternal group, to sell policies.

The Pentagon, he discovered, already knew about many of the problems he was investigating. It had known at least since the Vietnam War, in fact, thanks to the reporting of Richard C. Barnard in the *Army Times* in 1974.

When Lieutenant Hildreth first encountered the newspaper's work months into his 1997 investigation, he said, it nearly broke his heart.

"The sales methods and practices described in this article mirror those sales methods and practices I have uncovered," he wrote in his report. It was evident, he went on, that Defense Department officials knew of the practices involving Academy Life "yet appear to have done nothing."

His report, submitted in 1997, appealed for Pentagon-level action to address the structural problems he had identified. The Pentagon's response was to order more studies and, a year later, to bar Academy Life temporarily from the military market. The company denied any wrongdoing. It was the first and only department-level action against an insurer.

That response was not nearly strong enough, Lieutenant Hildreth said. "The fact that you are still finding these incidents on base today proves that," he said in a recent interview.

The first Pentagon study ordered was by its inspector general, who looked at life insurance sales on eleven military bases around the country selected at random. The final report, released with little fanfare in March 1999 and eliciting little congressional interest, found improper practices at all eleven bases.

It detailed them: "misleading sales presentations, presentations by unauthorized personnel, presentations to captive audiences, soliciting during duty hours, and soliciting in the barracks."

The report recommended stricter penalties and better communication with state insurance regulators. It also urged that a task force be set up to consider either enforcing existing rules more vigorously or banning agents from military bases entirely.

The Pentagon then ordered another study, this one by Brig. Gen. Thomas R. Cuthbert, retired, a Harvard-educated lawyer and the former chief judge of the Army's Court of Criminal Appeals.

His seventy-page report, delivered in May 2000, was an indictment of the status quo at the Defense Department. Its policies, he wrote, "have been routinely violated" for thirty years. His recommendation echoed the inspector general's: "Either devote substantial additional resources to the regulation of insurance sales on military installations or flatly prohibit the on-base solicitation of life insurance products."

The report also detailed how agents from several specific companies, including American Amicable, Pioneer American, and First Command, had been the targets of complaints at individual bases over the years. The study drew a flurry of media attention and a fierce reaction in the insurance industry.

The Pentagon responded by setting up the Insurance Solicitation Oversight Working Group to examine the issue further.

The group's draft report, an undated copy of which was obtained by the *New York Times*, noted that the group had been told that banning agents from military bases "was not an option." Instead it recommended better personal finance training for the troops and stricter enforcement of the rules. It also urged that the Pentagon work more closely with state insurance commissioners.

Last summer the Pentagon signaled that it was ready to propose concrete steps to address the problems documented in its own studies. This set off a fresh round of industry opposition. So far, no proposal has been announced, although Mr. Molino, the Defense Department official responsible for the policy, said he hoped to act this summer.

Long before General Cuthbert issued his report, Lieutenant Hildreth had retired from the Navy, disillusioned about the Pentagon's willingness to address the problems he had uncovered in 1997.

"I sensed that nobody was going to do anything," he said in an interview this spring. "I lost confidence in a system that I had once had a lot of confidence in."

July 20, 2004

Author's Afterword

When I was about thirteen or fourteen, I participated—through my high school in Roanoke, VA—in a work-experience program called Junior Achievement. Because a friend did, I signed up for the Junior Achievement unit at the local newspaper, the *Roanoke Times and World News*. That was my first taste of journalism and I simply fell head over heels in love with it—it seemed to me back then that newsrooms were the most exciting places on the planet, filled with the most interesting people in the universe. I still feel that way.

I sort of stumbled into investigative reporting while working at the Trenton *Times* in the late 1970s. I got a tip about some shady activities at a big government housing finance agency and was encouraged by a wonderful editor to pursue it. I found I had a knack for the document-intensive, detail-driven, delayed-gratification work that was needed for investigative journalism; after that I looked for more opportunities to pursue similar projects. Even though I love investigative work, I have spent a lot of time doing breaking news and news-driven features, as well. I believe these basics need to be mastered before you go on to the big stuff. The truth is, there were only a few years during my career at the *New York Times* when I was doing large-scale investigative projects exclusively. But in the end, my general approach to reporting of all types is to apply many of the tools of investigative reporting to whatever form of writing I'm doing—from week-long features to years-long books.

Not to be immodest, but one reason you get hooked on this kind of work is the opportunity to actually do something. There have been a few stories I've worked on where in a small way I felt I really changed the world. An investigative series on sub-par medical care for state prisoners in New Jersey led to the creation of a prison medical wing to treat prisoners with chronic illnesses, like diabetes or asthma, that had too often been death sentences in their old cell blocks. An examination of deceptive and unsuitable financial products being sold to unsophisticated military personnel led to a host of important and lasting legislative and policy reforms and cash refunds for the soldiers affected.

I'm also proud of stretching myself to produce four books while working at the newspaper full-time, a discipline that has enabled me, now, to devote myself full-time to book number five. From a personal standpoint, I am very proud of my concerted effort to improve my writing skills over the years. I am not yet satisfied, but I've certainly made progress.

Thirty years ago, I'd have said my favorite part of journalism is, without a doubt, reporting. Solving the puzzle, collecting clues, tracking down leads—those have always been such enormous fun for me. But over time, I became aware that great reporting is wasted if you cannot get people to read the results, and I started really working on improving my writing. The process of writing is not yet my favorite. But it is a lot more satisfying than it used to be.

There's not much I'd change in my own job, beyond the obvious subtraction of the remaining sexism that rears its ugly head now and then. The best part? It's a tough call. I'd probably say there are two things tied for first place: 1) The opportunity to be constantly learning, extending my horizons and stretching my mental muscles, and 2) The wonderful people—colleagues and sources—I get to hang out with.

Beginning with Nellie Bly and Ida Tarbell, women have long been making journalistic history with their courageous reporting work. Women columnists like Sylvia Porter, Flora Lewis, and Dorothy Thompson certainly shaped history with their opinions and insights from the earliest decades of the twentieth century. But women were generally not able to advance in the roles that guided and shaped journalism as an industry. Women as editors and publishers were virtually nonexistent—or, at least, almost invisible—when I was first starting out in journalism. Kay Graham at the *Washington Post* was an inspiration, but a rarity.

Journalism has given me more courage than I would otherwise have ever had—courage to confront bullies, dispute errors, challenge conventional wisdom. And, of course, journalism has given me a passport to a world of fascinating people, intriguing problems, and extraordinary places that have all left their mark on who I am and how I think.

Anne Hull

Anne Hull is a reporter on the national staff of the *Washington Post*. She has written about race, class, immigration, the attacks on 9/11 and Hurricane Katrina. Hull's reporting on the treatment of wounded soldiers at Walter Reed Army Medical Center, along with *Post* reporter Dana Priest and photographer Michel du Cille, resulted in sweeping reform to the nation's care of wounded veterans. For this work, the *Post* was awarded the 2008 Pulitzer Prize for Public Service.

Hull started as a reporter at the *St. Petersburg Times* in Florida. She is a recipient of a Nieman Fellowship at Harvard University (1995) and the Berlin Prize at the American Academy in Berlin (2010.) She was a visiting professor of journalism at Princeton University. She serves as a trustee for the Poynter Institute for Media Studies and lives in Washington.

A Better Life

Women from a small village in Mexico
travel to America for a greater opportunity

Part 1

It was early afternoon when the girl stepped into the shade of Señor Herrera's small store. She unfolded her mother's shopping list and set it on the wooden counter. A hot wind blew outside.

Señor Herrera was cutting down a rope of chorizo for her when the telephone rang. "Ay," he said, wiping his knife.

Señor Herrera owned the only telephone in Palomas. When news came, he would step outside and shout the bulletin through cupped hands, knowing it would be passed from house to house. The priest is delayed. The medicine for the sick horse is coming.

But this time, he leaned on the counter and spoke to the young girl.

Ve dile a las señoras que ya es hora.

Go tell the ladies it is time.

The girl ran into the daylight, past the mesquite fences and the burro braying in the dusty street. She stopped at a blue iron gate, where a woman was pinning laundry to a clothesline.

The girl called out. *Señora, señora, teléfono.*

Juana Cedillo stood in her patio, blown with the powdery shale of the desert highlands. She'd been expecting the message. Now it had arrived. There would be no more waiting with the empty suitcase under the bed.

She went inside and gave her daughter the news.

Ya es hora de irnos.

The hour has come for us to go.

More than twenty-six hundred miles away, on the upper coast of North Carolina, a man slurped down his cereal at the kitchen counter and walked out his back door. By the time he poured a quart of oil into his smoking Johnson outboard, it was 5:30 and already hot.

At fifty, Mickey Daniels Jr. was sandy-haired and muscular, with pale blue eyes reddened by the sun. He guided his twenty-one-foot boat out of the harbor.

Along the grassy banks were the rusted-out hulks of trawlers that history had washed aside. Six mornings a week, Mickey Junior passed through the tunnel of dead ships.

He had 140 crab pots sunk in the shallow waters of Roanoke Sound, each marked by a green and white buoy with the name DANIELS. Most seafood operators wore tan slacks to the office. The owner of Daniels Seafood still idled from buoy to buoy himself.

"I s'pose I'm the last of it," he said, without nostalgia.

By midmorning, he'd hauled in five hundred pounds of blue crabs. Drenched in sweat, Mickey Junior opened up the throttle and aimed for home. The fishing village of Wanchese lay before him, on the south end of Roanoke Island, just in from North Carolina's Outer Banks.

Unworldly and sheltered, Roanoke Island had been isolated for so long that natives like Mickey Daniels Jr. spoke with a dialect from the English settlers of the 1600s. "I sat down" sounded like "I set doon."

But Mickey Junior was thoroughly modern in one regard.

In early 1998, he telephoned the North Carolina Growers Association and placed an order for twelve women from Mexico. He needed them for the May start of the 1998 blue crab season. They cost $130 apiece.

As a boy in the 1950s, Mickey Junior saw the old school buses drive past his house each morning carrying black women. They would unload at the doors of the crab houses. Inside, the women took their places at iced metal tables piled with hundreds of pounds of cooked blue crabs.

Using their bare hands and short steel knives, they extracted the precious tablespoons of meat.

At the end of the day, the women were loaded back on the buses and returned to their tilting porches along Good Luck Street in Manteo, on the other end of Roanoke Island.

The pickers had a saying: "Lord, you don't retire. You just die."

Which is what began to happen in the early 1990s. As Mickey Daniels Jr. said, "The blacks was dyin' off and we didn't have no replacements."

Crab picking was a job that Americans on the eve of the twenty-first century considered too low-paying and foul.

The saviors were across the border.

In 1998, almost three thousand Mexican women were allowed into the United States as "guest workers" for the annual blue crab season.

Mickey Daniels Jr.'s workers came from a place called Palomas. The details of their lives mattered little to him; it was their speed at the crab-picking table that counted. The women raced against the clock like no one he'd ever seen.

They were human capital, ordered like product and shipped in for a season of labor.

When the women of Palomas set out on the back roads of the new global economy, they placed their lives with whoever had bought the rights to their work.

They had a name for the United States. *La tortilla grande*, they called it, for its spectacular moneymaking opportunities.

They begged and bribed their way into jobs in the crab houses.

With a Greyhound bus ticket and a $145 work visa, a pipeline was laid between a buzzardy ranch in central Mexico and a three-hundred-year-old fishing village off the coast of North Carolina.

In the end, the women from Palomas were what allowed the eighth-generation fisherman to keep his world from dying off.

"With the Mexicans, you can get all you want, when you want," Mickey Daniels Jr. said.

But the bargain worked both ways, something Mickey Junior didn't yet understand as he leaned on his dock, calculating the arrival of the women from Palomas.

If America was going to take a piece of them, they were going to take a piece of it.

In the high plains of central Mexico, in the state of San Luis Potosí, Highway 80 is abandoned for a dirt road. Palomas is reached by hitching a ride in the back of a sagging truck and climbing nine miles through steep hills.

No one passes through Palomas. One road leads in. Still, a bright sign welcomes visitors: ¡Bienvenido!

On the town square, the evening game of soccer was played with a deflated old ball, amid shouts of "Uncle!" or "Professor!" The field was a swirl of white powder, and the shirtless young men looked as if they had been rolled in flour.

The game was presided over by a bronze statue of Saturnino Cedillo, the rebel general who in the early nineteen hundreds established Palomas as an *ejido*, a peasant landholding cooperative. The general built a *hacienda* with mahogany doors and a vista of the hills. Legend says his wife wanted the house painted white, so it was called *Palomas*, the Spanish word for doves.

The house was now crumbling, the general's bullring overgrown with weeds, his body entombed. But stretching out beneath the old hacienda was a grid of concrete block homes and a few leaning adobes, where twenty-one hundred residents fought the dust and the desolation.

The ranch was camouflaged in brown and gray: the unpainted concrete, the tin roofs, the choke of grit, the mesquite sticks bundled for fences, the wandering packs of burros. Color was saved for the insides of houses. A bowl of limes in a turquoise kitchen. Pomegranates cut open on yellow tile.

There was no government in Palomas. Law and order were upheld by watchful grandmothers and household statues of the Virgin Mary. Wedding parties took place beneath a string of light bulbs on the empty basketball court near Señor Herrera's store.

Economically, Palomas spun on its own forgotten axis. The daily wage for picking corn or tomatoes was thirty-five pesos, the equivalent of about four dollars.

In 1992, a woman drove up to Palomas and knocked on the gates of several houses. Her skin was fair, not the burnished copper of the ranchers, and her chestnut hair was fashionably trimmed at the shoulders. She worked for a Texas labor recruiter named Jorge del Alamo.

Close to 20 percent of the men in Palomas were already leaving each spring for agricultural work in the southeastern United States, many brokered through del Alamo.

But the job recruiter who visited Palomas that day wasn't interested in men. She asked for women.

And when she had their attention—when they'd stopped drying their hands on their aprons and offering their visitor a glass of sweet rice milk—she made an astonishing pitch.

Any woman willing to leave home for six months could earn $6,000 working in a US crab house.

The idea—and the sum of money—were impossible to grasp. Women were the backbone of domestic life. And now suddenly, a wife or daughter could earn ten times what the men earned in the fields around Palomas.

A small group left that first year for seafood processing plants in North Carolina, Virginia, or Maryland.

The women proved to be excellent savers. The Western Union money orders flowed back to Palomas. Señor Herrera began stocking his shelves with pumpkin bread, sardines, Pantene shampoo.

The warriors returned after six months. Grandmothers held their ears against the high-pitched whir of new electric blenders. Children begged their mothers for TVs to watch Los Simpsons.

The women paid for new roofs on their houses, replacing tin and mud with beams and concrete. The new capitalists carried gold-clasp purses and walked the unpaved streets of Palomas like urban sophisticates.

But the money brought trouble. Husbands and wives may have squabbled in the past, they may have sulked in separate beds, but divorce was unheard of. Men began to complain that financial independence was ruining the women.

When one woman came home from North Carolina wearing pants, her husband stormed out of the house, returning with a new dress.

"Here," he said, demanding she revert to the wife he knew.

In a place that still used roosters for alarm clocks, the feminist revolution had arrived.

By the spring of 1998, nearly fifty women—one in fifteen—were leaving for the start of the blue crab season.

Daughters were begging their mothers for permission to go. Some young women would never come home when the crab season ended.

The United States was a thief. It stole. It always had. But it had never taken the women of Palomas before.

Among the last to leave were the twelve bound for Daniels Seafood in North Carolina.

Juana Cedillo woke early and braided her hair. In the kitchen, she lit a breakfast fire. Then the tortillas, slap, slap, slap, the morning music drifting from every open shutter in Palomas. Juana made a stack of sixty and stirred a cup of Sanka.

She was thirty-five, barely five feet tall in her sandals. Her pans of tamales had gradually found their way to her hips. For a mother of eight, she was unusually mild-mannered. A hen would fall asleep in her hand as she drew the hatchet back to chop its neck.

Juana Cedillo was the fastest crab picker Daniels Seafood had ever seen. But in the weeks leading up to her departure, her stomach churned. It would be her third season. She began drinking Maalox.

Her L-shaped house in Palomas—the concrete was still wet from the expansion—was a shrine built by crab money. A new toilet gleamed in the outhouse in the yard. Silver faucets sparkled in the kitchen sink.

"What else do we need?" Juana's husband had asked.

"You never know when the US doesn't want you anymore," Juana said. "We must go while we can."

Construction on the new Catholic church in Palomas had stalled. One more season at Daniels Seafood, Juana reasoned, could finance finishing the church, buying new Bibles and most of all, sending a daughter to high school in a nearby city.

That morning, Alejandro, eight, and Eduardo, six, slept like fragile soldiers in the bed they shared. Juana implored them with a wake-up call from the kitchen. "Get up, it's time for school," she ordered, as Eduardo covered his head with the sheet.

She never watched them, but she watched them now from the doorway. She would not see them for six months. Did they understand why she was doing this?

The boys pulled on their wrinkled clothes from a pile and stumbled to the small kitchen table. Eduardo pouted over the plate of scrambled eggs and tortillas Juana placed before him. He wanted cornflakes.

"Eat," Juana said.

After breakfast, he sat at the edge of Juana's bed, watching her pack. "Where are my vitamins?" Juana asked. "I must be strong." She wrapped her Bible in plastic, and bundled her passport and identification papers in a rubber band.

The house was emptying out. The children would go next door to Juana's mother. Her husband and oldest son had already left for their $6.50-an-hour spring jobs in Virginia hanging tobacco.

In the bedroom next to Juana's, the last family member to pack her suitcase was Ana Rosa. Juana's nineteen-year-old daughter was following her mother to Daniels Seafood.

Ana Rosa gathered her nail polish and holy cards. Carefully, she wiped the dust of Palomas from her good leather shoes and wrapped them in plastic so they would arrive in North Carolina clean.

Ana Rosa had studied accounting for eighteen months in Mexico City. When her parents could no longer afford the tuition, she returned to Palomas, taking her place at the wash basin. The accounting student finally convinced her parents that an American crab house held more of a future than Palomas.

They agreed to let her work at Daniels Seafood, only because Juana would also be there.

Ana Rosa was pious, shy, and beautiful. Carved lips and skin like dark honey. Dutifully, she wrapped her sister's warm lunch in an embroidered cloth and delivered it to the school each noon. She swept and mopped and cooked. Her hazel eyes filled with tears when she prayed.

But Ana Rosa was nineteen years old. She packed her best blue jeans for the trip to America.

On her last day, Ana Rosa looked around Palomas and felt not a scrap of regret for wanting to leave.

When electricity came to Palomas in the late 1970s, Ana Rosa's generation was the first to have television. The reception was snowy, and the dented aluminum antennas had to be pointing in the right direction. But what she saw was enough.

Ana Rosa imagined what $6,000 could buy.

She conspired with her twenty-year-old cousin, Delia Tovar, who was also going to Daniels Seafood.

On the afternoon before her departure, Delia was in the kitchen, her fingers stained with jalapeno. Delia chopped and fried, sidestepping her sisters in a synchronized ballet over the bare concrete floor. Her older brother, Luis, came in through the screen door and washed his hands in a bucket in the sink. He sat at the table, waiting for his plate. He objected to his sisters' going to work in the States.

"The distance is very hard on families," he said, his wife standing behind his chair while he ate. "When they come back, the families are not as close. Life is not the same. The women come home with ideas."

Delia said nothing.

She had liquid black eyes, watchful and cautious. When she pulled back her hair, lifting it from her delicate neck in the heat, a small gold elephant rode on each of her earlobes. The earrings should have been a warning. Delia Tovar was no pushover.

She had worked at Daniels Seafood the previous year, along with her mother. But this year, she was going with her younger sister, Cecilia.

Ceci, as she was known, was eighteen, fearless and sharp-witted. But Delia wondered how she could prepare her young sister for what awaited them. Ceci had never even seen a crab before, let alone thousands piled on tabletops.

On their last night, the Tovar sisters took their evening baths, and rifled through their closets for pleated skirts and silk blouses. They combed out their hair and arranged plastic patio chairs on the sidewalk. Young men on bicycles positioned themselves outside Señor Herrera's store across the street to watch them. Delia barely glanced their way.

When darkness fell, their mother signaled them inside. Unmarried women on the streets after dark invited gossip.

Just when Delia and Ceci thought they would escape Palomas without a farewell lecture, their mother came into their pink bedroom.

"It's easy to fall in love," Delia's mother said, "but the ground needs to be firm beneath your feet."

Then she put it more bluntly: "I trust you and God that you won't get pregnant and stay in the US."

The job recruiter had left specific instructions for the women going to Daniels Seafood: Be at the bus station in Ciudad del Maíz by 6 p. m. on Friday.

Juana spent her last hours baking corn bread in her outdoor kiln. Ana Rosa wrapped warm gorditas in a plastic garbage bag. It would be a long bus ride to North Carolina, and they did not want to go hungry.

Juana's youngest sons, ages six and eight, played soccer in the sandy courtyard, unable to bear the sight of their mother's suitcase near the door.

At 4:30, Juana called the children inside. Her long hair was still wet from her shower. The van was due. She asked everyone to kneel.

Ana Rosa knelt on the bare concrete floor and joined hands with her brothers and sisters. The children's voices were high and metallic, but it was Juana who could be heard above all. She asked one favor of God.

"I leave them with you, Lord," she cried, her eyes closed. *"Gracias, Señor Jesus, gracias. Gracias, mi padre."*

Tears rolled down Ana Rosa's smooth cheeks. The eleven-year-old, Claudia, brushed her eyes. Eduardo looked at his bare feet.

When the van honked outside, Juana was the first to stand.

The oldest boy loaded the suitcases. At the patio gate, near her rosebush, Juana hugged the children goodbye, saying each of their names aloud.

"Alejandro."

"Claudia."

"Maria de los Angeles."

"Tomás."

"Lorena."

"Eduardo."

Instinctively, Juana hugged her youngest child once more. As she boarded the van and pulled the door closed, Eduardo's screams shook her. *"Mami, mami!"* he cried. A burro at the gate began braying, and Eduardo flailed at the animal before throwing himself on the ground, sobbing.

"Hurry!" Juana begged the driver. Juana's shoulders heaved. Someone reached for the roll of toilet paper jammed into the dusty dashboard. Ana Rosa passed it to her mother, but first wiped away her own tears. The van pushed through the streets of Palomas.

Three suitcases were waiting in front of a house across from Señor Herrera's store. As the driver honked, the door opened, and eight family members spilled out into the street in a jumble of hugs and goodbyes. Delia and Ceci Tovar were in the middle.

Their mother hung back. "The rich need the poor and the poor need the rich," she often said, justifying why Mexicans were always saying goodbye in the name of a better life. But she whispered no great words of wisdom into her daughters' ears now. When she held them tightly one last time, tears streamed down her cheeks.

The van sagged with the weight of eighteen passengers. Suitcases were shoved in corners and piled to the ceiling. Just lifting a hand to wipe a brow was impossible. Sweat trickled between breasts. The air was thick and sweet from body odor, hard to breathe.

The dashboard radio was nothing more than a rusted shell of antique parts, but the driver leaned forward and twisted the knobs, desperate to break the silence. No one spoke as the van picked up speed. An accordion *canción* played. Delia turned around once, to look back, but Palomas was gone.

In 1998, more than two hundred Mexicans died trying to sneak across the 1,951-mile US border. They suffocated in car trunks or died in the desert trying to evade immigration control laws.

But the women from Palomas were golden.

They were "guest workers."

Migrant farmworkers had been coming to the States for years under a program called H2A.

The H2B program allowed US employers to hire foreigners for nonagricultural seasonal jobs if Americans were unavailable.

These "guest workers" cleaned motel rooms in South Carolina or processed crawfish in Louisiana. Most were Mexican. When their season of labor ended, they were expected to return home or risk deportation.

In 1992, the US Department of Labor allowed roughly 8,000 H2Bs into the country. By 1997, the number had tripled to 25,250.

Most of the jobs were low-paying, greasy, bloody, grimy and tedious, sometimes hazardous.

In a boom economy, Americans weren't rushing to pluck feathers from electrocuted chickens for six dollars an hour.

Poor Mexicans were. For many, one man held the keys: a Texas labor recruiter named Jorge del Alamo.

Del Alamo built a lucrative empire funneling Mexicans to legal contract work in the United States. One of his biggest customers was the North Carolina Growers Association, which brokered labor out to farms, fields, and seafood processing plants.

Del Alamo charged each Mexican eighty-five dollars in recruiting fees. His local recruiters—del Alamo had twelve satellite offices scattered across rural Mexico—charged an additional thirty-five dollars. No small sum to a Mexican whose daily average income was four dollars.

Cuban-born and courtly, del Alamo looked like a white-haired grandfather as he drove his Volvo to work each morning, on the fifth floor of a bank building with a marble lobby in San Antonio, Texas.

Lawyers at Texas Rural Legal Aid estimated del Alamo moved more than eighteen thousand Mexicans across the border in 1998, pulling in more than $1.6 million.

Paying del Alamo was just the first cash outlay for the women from Palomas. For work visas, bus tickets and customs fees, they ended up paying close to $400 for one season of work at Daniels Seafood.

Smugglers were charging up to $1,000 to get Mexicans across the tightened US border.

At $400, del Alamo was a bargain.

All they needed was the visa.

After leaving Palomas, the women waited for several hours in Ciudad del Maíz before catching the 11 p. m. bus to the industrial city of Monterrey.

"Sleep every chance you can," Delia warned her sister, arranging her pillow.

Ana Rosa rested against Juana. The *gorditas* she'd baked in her kiln in Palomas gave off a floury aroma, the last traces of home.

They arrived at the sprawling Monterrey bus terminal at 6:15 a. m., stiff and dazed from the all-night ride.

When their eyes adjusted to the fluorescent glare, they could see there were hundreds of others like them: exhausted travelers from the interior of Mexico, slumped next to worn suitcases and plastic water jugs.

Jorge del Alamo's labor pipeline was calibrated for efficiency and volume. He could orchestrate the border crossing of a thousand workers in a night. His company, Del Al Associates, kept an office at the Monterrey bus terminal.

Small and windowless, no larger than eight by fourteen feet, the office was a formidable processing center. Visa applications and Mexican passports were stacked on desks.

The process was simple. The US consulate was three miles from the bus station. A del Alamo associate would hand-carry the visa applications to the consulate for processing. A few hours later, the associate returned to the bus terminal with a box of visas. The workers would then board buses for the border, 147 miles to the north.

The women from Palomas knew what to do. They found the office, at the end of an underground hallway. Juana was resigned. Her goodbyes had been said. Her Maalox bottle was tucked in her purse. In six months, she would return to Palomas with enough money to finish the church.

The del Alamo representative appeared at the door. In her sleek, beige blazer and heels, she towered over the women from Palomas, whose dark clothes had been washed on a stone. Her tone was curt. Something was wrong. She pointed to names on a list.

"You must come back Tuesday for an interview at the consulate," she said.

Juana, Ana Rosa, and three other women from Palomas were told to return for a face-to-face interview at the consulate Tuesday.

It was Saturday morning. They had barely slept. They had traveled all night to reach Monterrey. They had no money for a hotel. But they accepted the news without protest, with a deep familiarity of accepting someone else's plans.

Juana slumped. She could not endure another round of goodbyes with her children. And yet the church was counting on her money.

Ana Rosa sat down. Without the visa, she faced a long summer in Palomas.

Two visas had been granted. "Who, who?" the women asked.

They went to Delia and Ceci Tovar.

The Tovar sisters grabbed their suitcases. The bus to the border was waiting. Delia called back to Ana Rosa. "You'll make it in a few days, cousin."

Three hours later, Delia and Ceci reached the Mexican border town of Nuevo Laredo. Delia could see Border Patrol vehicles cruising the fence line in the shimmering bands of heat. Why hadn't the others been granted visas, she wondered. A US helicopter whooshed overhead.

They were dropped off at an old colonial plaza, joined by two other women, both del Alamo recruits also being sent to Daniels Seafood.

Except for Delia, all were first-timers, and the fear showed.

"*Andale,*" Delia said, leading the charge. It was 97 degrees. The streets burned through their shoes. They would cross into Texas by walking across the Rio Grande on International Bridge 1.

Nuevo Laredo was a crush of Americans carrying *piñatas* and clanking bottles of duty-free tequila. "These Mexicans get you coming and going, don't they?" said a tourist, dropping thirty-five cents into the turnstiles of the bridge.

Delia and Ceci followed, lugging their suitcases. They were on the bridge. Delia could see the brown bathwater of the Rio Grande rushing below the grates of the steel span. US Border Patrol guards were straight ahead, waiting at the end of the bridge.

At customs, drug-sniffing dogs pulled at short leashes. Ceci's eyes flashed nervously as she dug for her passport. Car trunks were searched as the undersides of vehicles were swept with mirrors. In 1998, US Border Patrol agents apprehended 103,441 illegal migrants in the Laredo sector alone.

Delia gave her younger sister a look. Don't worry, she seemed to say, we have the paperwork.

They crossed.

On the Texas side, they found the Laredo Greyhound station, five blocks from the Rio Grande. They had a seven-hour wait for their bus, passing the time on metal chairs in the glow of the candy machines.

With their ninety-nine dollar tickets to Elizabeth City, N.C., they left on the 11 p. m. coach.

Time becomes liquid on a two-thousand-mile bus ride. Fevered hallucinations jolt the body awake in trembling fits. Just as deep sleep seems possible, the mighty hydraulic brakes of the Greyhound gasp, and the overhead lights blast on for a 3 a. m. bus transfer.

Before dawn, the Greyhound peeled by Waco and its prefab prairie wood structures. The bus was dark and cold as it flew along the interstate like a low bird. To stay warm, Ceci and Delia curled around each other, breathing softly as they slept, folded into the years of familiarity.

In the leaden sky of daybreak, the winged evangelical churches of Dallas appeared like spaceships that had landed along the Texas interstate.

From the window, Ceci noticed a Chevrolet dealership. It was larger than Palomas. "*Grande,*" she whispered.

The bus driver's voice crept into the silence, like a lonely night-shift disc jockey. "It's not even right about 7 o'clock, what with the light traffic of Sunday morning, we should be early into Dallas," he announced.

From Interstate 20, Louisiana and its oil refineries rolled past. The road made a tunnel through the green. The noon church bells of downtown Shreveport chimed in the muggy Sunday air.

On the back roads, Vidalia onion stands along the bayous were tended by old men at rickety card tables. The bus tore past them and their forgotten regions.

Somewhere in Mississippi, a man in the fifteenth row opened a brown paper sack, filling the bus with a smoky-orange smell, the way mesquite smelled when it burned in Palomas. The scent was so familiar that Ceci turned around, only to see a man in a straw hat eating barbecued ribs.

She closed her eyes.

And dreamt. On her last night in Palomas, a young man had called her on the phone at Señor Herrera's store. Goodbye for the summer, Ceci had told him, blowing a kiss into the receiver. They met at high school. Graduation. The diploma. Her parents watching. Her white dress. Sleep. Her bed. The rising noise of the animals each morning: the roosters dropping down from the branches of the mesquite trees, the quarreling burros, the horses that nickered to each other across fences. The smell of the breakfast fire. The sound of cartoons. Her nephew.

Ceci awakened. A sign outside the window said Spartanburg. The bus was gliding through a chute of trees.

Sitting behind her were three Mexican men bound for the tobacco fields of North Carolina. They were fantasizing about food, using tones reserved for a beautiful woman.

Eggs with chorizo, one of the men said, speaking in Spanish.

My mother's tortillas, said another.

Ah, said the third friend, tamales with green sauce.

Delia and Ceci listened, their mouths watering.

As the miles rolled by, the men kept topping each other, until their imaginary banquet in Mexico was spilling over. Then there was silence.

On the third day, they crossed into North Carolina.

Inside the crab picking room at Daniels Seafood, an announcement was made:

"The Spanish ladies are coming."

Mary Tillett's plastic apron was splattered with bits of crab and shell. She'd been expecting the news.

In the spring of 1998, four black women still worked as crab pickers for Daniels Seafood. They were all that remained of the original thirteen. The youngest was sixty-three.

They sat around a silver-topped table heaped with steamed blue crabs, trading gossip or supermarket prices, pushing their eyeglasses back up their noses with their wrists.

Sometimes, they sang. *Highway to Heaven* was a favorite.

"It sounds like church in there," a tourist from Michigan said one day, stopping in Daniels Seafood to buy a pound of crab meat. "May I take their picture?"

At eighty-four, Mary Tillett was the oldest. Her hair was the color of metal filings, pressed the old-fashioned way, with an iron she heated on her stove. Her skin was as smooth as pecan shells. Her hands were large and strong.

She started working in a crab house in 1929.

"I'm doing fairly, by and by," she'd say, her tongue engraved with the relic dialect spoken by natives of Roanoke Island.

But lately, her head would drop and her crab knife would go slack in her hand. She'd doze off.

The arrival of the Mexicans brought pressure. The black women stopped taking a lunch break. Instead, they nibbled corn bread or potted meat they brought from home, wrapped in paper towels in their patent leather pocketbooks. Mary Tillett wasn't even sure where Mexico was, only that it was far.

"Lord knows, they must need it mighty bad to come all this way," she said.

The crab house had been her pitiful domain for so long it never occurred to her that someone else would want it.

May 9, 1999

Author's Afterword

My parents both wrote for their college newspaper, and for a short time my mother wrote a column for a small town newspaper. None of this was really spoken of and neither were professional journalists, but they communicated best by writing—notes, letters, journals. Truly, I never considered becoming a journalist. And then, right after high school, I got a job as a "copy kid" at the *St. Petersburg Times*. Once inside that newsroom, it just felt familiar, something like home. After that I took whatever job in the newsroom that was open: It wasn't a classroom that taught me the role of the newspaper in society, it was answering phones on the city desk. For the neglected, the cheated, and the invisible, the newspaper was their last hope.

A lack of formal training or college degree would've probably been obstacles at other newspapers; luckily not at the *St. Petersburg Times*. The paper's most fierce reporter, Lucy Morgan, lacked similar qualifications; nevertheless, her work as a journalist brought down a corrupt sheriff and exposed drug rings. In general she was the most feared journalist in Florida. In 1985 she became the first woman to win the Pulitzer Prize for investigative reporting. Lucy Morgan reminded our editors that to hire conventionally or by pedigree was a bad idea.

As with any profession, the longer you stick with it the more you might develop a faint arrogance—that you know how a story will turn out, that you see how the system always favors the powerful, and that things that get fixed often go back to being broken. The redundancy of journalism can dim the curiosity over time, and it's this skepticism one has to fight against. Personally, journalism gave me a place to belong. All the stories and the people in them allowed an up-close nearness with the peak emotions in life. This can't help but change you as a person.

The best part of the job is to see something or hear something or wonder about something and then to chase down the "why." To shine a flashlight into dark and hidden corners, and see if good can come of it. To be riding on the back of a truck in the desert highlands of Mexico and have it considered work.

Regrets rain down after every story, when the weak spots and missed opportunities seem glaring; there's not a single story I wouldn't request a do-over on. But these are just a writer's worries. I wish more than anything I could protect the very people I lay open—the everyday people who suffer along in obscurity until a reporter appears, asking them to share their frailties and insecurities and misdeeds. The subject agrees to trade away his or her privacy in hopes that a story might bring some greater good. This feels like a corrupt contract. Even more so in the age of social media, which can act as a platform for cowards to heap on their uninformed cruelties.

Writing is hard and 95 percent of it is painstaking. The last 5 percent can be like flying.

Julia Keller

Julia Keller, winner of the Pulitzer Prize, is the author of *Summer of the Dead* (Minotaur), the third novel in her popular and critically acclaimed mystery series set in Appalachia. The first book in the series, *A Killing in the Hills* (2012), received starred reviews from *Library Journal*, *Booklist*, *Kirkus Reviews* and *Publishers Weekly*; the latter named it a Pick of the Week. It also won the Barry Award for Best First Novel. *Bitter River* (2013), the second novel in the series, has "an elegiac force to it that is powerful and gripping," according to bestselling author Michael Connelly.

Keller was born and raised in West Virginia. She graduated from Marshall University and earned a doctoral degree in English Literature at Ohio State University; her dissertation explored literary biographies of Virginia Woolf. She was awarded a Nieman Fellowship at Harvard University, and later served as McGraw Professor of Writing at Princeton University. She has also taught at The University of Notre Dame and The University of Chicago, and has served four times as a juror for the Pulitzer Prizes.

Keller won the 2005 Pulitzer Prize for her three-part series on a deadly tornado that swept through Utica, IL, in 2004. The series ran in the *Chicago Tribune*, the newspaper for which she worked for twelve years, before resigning in 2012 to devote herself full time to fiction.

A Wicked Wind Takes Aim

It took only ten seconds for a tornado to decimate
the entire community of Utica, IL.

Part 1

Ten seconds. Count it: One. Two. Three. Four. Five. Six. Seven. Eight. Nine. Ten. Ten seconds was roughly how long it lasted. Nobody had a stopwatch, nothing can be proven definitively, but that's the consensus. The tornado that swooped through Utica at 6:09 p. m. April 20 took some ten seconds to do what it did. Ten seconds is barely a flicker. It's a long, deep breath. It's no time at all. It's an eternity.

If the sky could hold a grudge, it would look the way the sky looked over northern Illinois that day. Low, gray clouds stretched to the edges in a thin veneer of menace. Rain came and went, came and went, came and went.

The technical name for what gathered up there was stratiform cloud cover, but Albert Pietrycha had a better way to describe it: "murk." It was a Gothic-sounding word for a Gothic-looking sky. A sky that, in its own oblique way, was sending a message.

Pietrycha is a meteorologist in the Chicago forecast office of the National Weather Service, a tidy, buttoned-down building in Romeoville, about twenty-five miles southwest of Chicago. It's a setting that seems a bit too ordinary for its role, too bland for the place where the first act of a tragedy already was being recorded. Where the sky's bad intentions were just becoming visible, simmering in the low-slung clouds.

A short distance away, disparate elements—air, water, and old sandstone blocks—soon would slam into each other like cars in a freeway pileup, ending eight lives and changing other lives forever.

The survivors would henceforth be haunted by the oldest, most vexing question of all: whether there is a destiny that shapes our fates or whether it is simply a matter of chance, of luck, of the way the wind blows.

It was a busy day for Pietrycha and his colleagues. The classic ingredients for a tornado—warm air to the south, cooler air north and a hint of wind shear—had seemed imminent most of the morning. Spring and early summer are boom times for tornadoes, the most violent storms on Earth.

What bothered Pietrycha was a warm front that loitered ominously across southern Illinois. If the front's moist, humid air moved north too quickly in the daylight hours, clashing with cooler air, the instability could create thunderstorms liable to split off into tornadoes.

But by early afternoon, it seemed that maybe, just maybe, northern Illinois would escape. If the front waited until after sunset to arrive, its impact would be negligible because the air near the ground—with no sunshine to warm it—would cool off. Nope, a relieved Pietrycha said to himself. Probably not today.

It was only a hunch. Meteorologists know a lot about tornadoes, but with all they know, they still can't say why some thunderstorms generate tornadoes and some don't. Or why tornadoes, once unleashed, do what they do and go where they go.

That's why forecasting is as much art as science. Too many warnings not followed by actual tornadoes make people skeptical and careless. Too many warnings can be as dangerous as too few. And while meteorologists can spot an approaching hurricane days in advance, the average warning time for a tornado is eleven minutes.

What she was thinking was, *Gotta beat that rain.*

Frowning up at a sky as flat and gray as a cookie sheet, Shelba Bimm, sixty-five, figured she just might be able to outrun the next downpour. Worth a try, anyway.

Bimm was standing in the driveway of her house at 238 W. Church St. in Utica, population 977, just outside Starved Rock State Park.

It was precisely 5:15 p. m. She had her schedule figured down to the minute. Busy people do that. But this ornery rain—will it or won't it, and if it starts up again, how long will it last?—was irksome.

She was due in Oglesby at 6 p. m. for the weekly class she was taking for her certification as an EMT Intermediate, the next level up from EMT, a rank Bimm had held since 1980, answering the frequent summons from the Utica volunteer fire department. Folks in town were accustomed to the sight of the white-haired Bimm in the driver's seat of her black Honda CRV, yanking on the wheel with one hand and gripping her dispatch radio with the other.

Shelba Bimm had been a first-grade teacher for forty-two years. She was retired now—if that's what you want to call it, even though she was at least as busy these days as she'd ever been when running a classroom, what with her EMT work and the dollhouse business she operated out of the front room of her home. And now she and Dave Edgcomb, Utica's fire chief, were taking classes to upgrade their credentials.

Oglesby is a fifteen-minute drive from Utica, so normally Bimm didn't hit the road until 5:30 p. m. But then again, she thought, *Just look at that sky.*

If she left now, she might be able to get there and dash from the parking lot at Illinois Valley Community College and into class without getting soaked. *It's gonna be one hell of a storm,* she thought.

So she scooted into her car—the one with the can't-miss-it license plate BIMM 2—and took off, backing out of her driveway and heading east on Church Street.

At the four-way stop a few yards from her house she turned south on Mill Street. Near the corner was a bar called Milestone. A block later, at the corner of Mill and Canal Street, she passed Duffy's Tavern.

Bimm turned west on Illinois Highway 71 and then headed on into Oglesby, pulling into the campus parking lot at 5:30 p. m. The western sky was getting blacker and blacker, as if something had been spilled on the other side of it and was seeping through.

All told, it took her less than a minute to cross Utica. Had she happened to lift her pale blue eyes to the rear view mirror as she left the city limits, she would have seen, poised there like a tableau in a snow globe just before it's shaken up, her last intact view of the little town she loved.

Pietrycha and his colleagues work in a big square room with a central ring of linked desks and a computer monitor perched on just about every flat surface.

Across Pietrycha's work station, six computer screens glowed with radar information that told him, through tiny pixels of perky green and hot red and bold yellow, about hail and rain, about wind rotation and velocity.

To check the screens, Pietrycha, a slender man with short sandy hair and the preoccupied air of someone who's always working out a math problem in his head, quickly rolled his chair back and forth, back and forth, screen to screen to screen, taking frequent swigs from a Coke can.

As 4 p.m. approached, the end of his shift, the warm front was still daw-dling in southern Illinois. Looking good. So Pietrycha got ready to go. He lives in Oswego, some thirteen miles northwest of Romeoville.

To Mark Ratzer, a fellow meteorologist with a neat blond crew cut who was in charge of the office that day, Pietrycha said, "Hey, if things get out of hand, call me."

The specials at Duffy's Tavern that night, according to the green felt-tip letter-ing on the white board above the bar, were: "All You Can Eat Spaghetti w/garlic breadsticks, $4.99" and "Cajun NY Strip w/onions and peppers and potato sal-ad, $16.99" and "2 stuffed walleye, $13.99." The soup was cheesy broccoli.

Lisle Elsbury, fifty-six, had bought Duffy's a year ago. Buying it meant leaving behind the life he knew as a heating and air conditioning repairman in Lyons, and slapping down all his chips right here in Utica.

Elsbury was a compact man with a nervous energy that seemed to oscillate just beneath his skin. His small gray mustache dipped at either end, curling around his upper lip like a parenthesis.

He liked to stand behind the long bar, its rich brown wood so ancient and polished by innumerable elbows that it looked sumptuous, almost liquid. It shimmered in the light.

If he'd glanced out the big front window just then, he might have seen Bimm's black Honda going south on Mill as she headed to class. But Elsbury was too busy to be gazing out windows. When you owned a bar and grill, there was always something to do. Always a ledger to balance, a glass to rinse, a burger to turn.

After a rocky start—Utica is a tough town to break into, with friendships stretching back decades—Elsbury was feeling pretty good. Things were look-ing up, even though there were four other taverns in town—Skoog's Pub, Joy & Ed's, Canal Port, and Milestone—all within a stone's throw.

Duffy's and Milestone were the new kids on the block. Not literally— the buildings were each more than a century old, two-story structures that anchored either end of Utica's roughly one-block business district. The pro-prietors, not the properties, were new. Elsbury and his wife, Pat, had bought Duffy's; Larry Ventrice and his wife, Marian, were running Milestone.

They were alike in a lot of ways, the Elsburys and the Ventrices. They were two couples trying to make a go of it in a new business in a new town. Money was tight. Hours were long. You worked as hard as you could work, and you still weren't sure sometimes if you were going to survive.

At this time of day, though, with the sun going down and the room filling up, Elsbury was reminded of the reasons he loved running a bar. Toughest work he'd ever done, but Lord, he just loved the feel of the place. The laughter. The talk. The scrape of chair legs on the red-painted plywood floor. A kind of benign, peppy chaos.

Two TV sets were angled on small platforms extending from the wall at both ends of the bar, their screens busy with maps sprouting wavy lines and harsh-looking arrows. Bartender Chris Rochelle, twenty-three, a skinny, good-looking kid with spiky black hair, had changed both sets from ESPN to the Weather Channel.

The sky, he told anybody who asked, just didn't look right to him. Didn't look right at all.

By the time Pietrycha walked back into the weather service office at about 5:45 p. m., everything had changed. It was as if an orchestra conductor, with a simple flick of the baton, had abruptly altered the room's tempo. What had been casual was suddenly intense. Phones rang, people scurried back and forth, frowning meteorologists hunched over computer screens.

That lackadaisical warm front suddenly had come to life, moving north much faster than any of the forecasters thought it would, initiating the fatal tangle of warm and cold air. Tornadoes darted across the Midwest, making jailbreaks from the thunderstorms.

At 5:32 p. m., Pietrycha's colleague, radar operator Rich Brumer, had issued a tornado warning for north-central Illinois. Typically, a watch—which alerts people to be on their guard—precedes a warning, but the warm front had risen so fast that Brumer went straight to the warning.

Now it was a matter of what meteorologists call interrogating the storm: keeping an eye on the screens as the data pours in, supplied by the Doppler radar tower that rises just behind the Romeoville office. In one sense, Pietrycha and his colleagues are immensely powerful as they compile fact after fact after fact about the atmosphere. They know just about everything there is to know about the air, the clouds, the wind, the rain.

But in another sense, they're utterly helpless. They don't know the "ground truth": the meteorological term for what's actually happening to real people, people who don't just record and measure the weather but must live through it.

That night, the weather service would tally fifty-three tornadoes in the Midwest. Fourteen whipsawed across north-central and northeastern Illinois.

One of those—born about two miles southwest of Granville and cutting a fifteen-and-a-half-mile, two-hundred-yard-wide notch from Granville to Utica—seemed to make a beeline for a venerable two-story tavern. It would arrive at 6:09 p. m.

At 5:55 p. m. the phone rang in Beverly Wood's mobile home in Utica. It was her daughter, Dena Mallie, a vivacious forty-four-year-old who lives in Peru, just west of Utica.

"We're having really bad hail," Mallie told her mother.

Wood, sixty-seven, was in the middle of dinner with Wayne Ball, sixty-three, whom she'd dated for years and who lived in a mobile home right across the road, and Helen Studebaker Mahnke, eighty-one, another friend who lived in the same trailer park just east of the downtown business district.

Wood and Ball were an easy, comfortable couple, with an affection that ran deep and true. When Ball's hands were severely frostbitten during his work with the railroad several years ago, and had to be bandaged and immobile for many months, it was Wood who fed him, who lit and held his cigarettes for him.

Wood had heated up a frozen pizza and mixed a few drinks. Mallie could hear music in the background; the three old friends had settled in for the evening. But Wood deeply feared storms.

"We're going to scoot," she told Mallie. "We're going uptown."

Trailers, as everybody knew, were notoriously vulnerable in bad weather. It made sense for Wood, Mahnke, and Ball to hunker down in one of the Utica taverns, one of those big, reliable old buildings that could shrug off a storm like it had been shrugging them off for decades.

Leaving the pizza—minus the three slices they'd just eaten—on the table with the drinks, because they'd be back in a jiffy, Wood, Mahnke, and Ball hurried outside and climbed into Wood's car, a taupe Buick Century.

It couldn't have taken Wood more than a minute to drive them to the bar, even pausing for the single stop sign on East Church, even heeding the posted speed limit of twenty mph.

She parked across the street, and they quickly walked in through Milestone's double doors. Wood was in such a hurry she didn't lock the car; for her, an unheard-of lapse. It was just after 6 p. m.

Relief. They were, they thought, safe now.

For several minutes before the three arrived, Milestone's lights flickered.

Larry Ventrice, forty-nine, was getting irritated. On or off, he didn't care. Just wished they'd make up their mind, on or off, on or off. It climbed a person's nerves, real quick.

He was a restless, impatient man, a man with a finger-snap temper but a good heart. He hailed from Bridgeport, a South Side Chicago neighborhood, and was proud of it, and he was proud as well of what he'd done with the tavern: filled it with funky antiques such as a roulette wheel and fake "WANTED" posters that gave the place a toe-tapping, down-home feel. The atmosphere started at the threshold, where a couple of horseshoes served as door pulls, and continued on around to the building's southern exterior, where a big, colorful mural, a rollicking pioneer scene with wagon trains and sod-busters, had been painted on the sandstone blocks.

Larry Ventrice knew about the bad weather heading their way. On the big TV set over the bar he'd heard the stations yakking about tornadoes and seeking shelter and all the rest of it, but he wasn't worried. Why should he be? Milestone, with its thick sandstone walls, flat concrete roof and slate foundation, was as solid as a vault. It was 117 years old, but just as hard times strengthened a person's character, surely rough weather over the years toughened up a building, didn't it? Showed its true mettle. Milestone was a survivor. You'd bet your life on it.

Larry knew just about everybody who was there that night, and they knew him. His cousin Jim Ventrice, seventy, was sitting at a table finishing up a bowl of chicken noodle soup while waiting for his second course, a pork chop sandwich he'd ordered from Marian Ventrice, fifty, Larry's wife. Everybody called Jim Ventrice "Cousin Junior" or just Junior.

Junior, a slight man who wore his shirt tucked in and his hair combed neatly back from his forehead, had gotten to Milestone at about 5:40 p. m. that night. He stopped in at least once a day because he liked the bar's cozy, nobody's-a-stranger ambience.

He'd taken a seat, spotted Jay Vezain at the bar, and called out, "Hey, Jay, how're you?"

Vezain, forty-seven, who worked at the Utica grain elevator just south of Duffy's, was nursing a bottle of beer. "I'm OK, Junior, how're you?"

He had a good sense of humor, Vezain did, and the kind of smile to go with it: quick, mischievous-looking. A lot of folks saved their best jokes for Vezain, just to see that smile.

Over in the corner, Carol Schultheis, forty—Wayne Ball's daughter—was playing the video poker game, shoving in coins and waiting for luck, and taking occasional drags on a Marlboro Light. She'd been diagnosed with multiple sclerosis a few years ago, but so far it hadn't slowed her down; she was a day-shift cook at Joy & Ed's, and everybody in Utica knew her and she knew everybody right back, and if you passed her on the street you'd get a smile and a wave and maybe a naughty joke or two.

Rich Little, thirty-seven, a truck driver from nearby Troy Grove, was sitting at the bar, drinking a bottle of Bud Light. He was supposed to meet his girlfriend here at 6:30 p. m.

Back in the kitchen, Debbie Miller, forty-four, pushed a pork chop around on the grill for Junior's sandwich.

The lights flickered again. The door opened, and Wood, Mahnke, and Ball came in.

Just after that, Debbie Miller's family spilled in through the back door, a pinwheeling mass of kids that must have quickly overwhelmed the small hallway and kitchen, a living scribble of elbows and long legs and sneakers and stick-thin arms, talking and pushing.

There was Debbie's husband, Mike, forty-nine, lanky and bushy-haired; sons Mike Jr., eighteen, Gregg, fourteen, and Christopher, eight; and daughters Ashley, sixteen, and Jennifer, twelve; along with Gregg's best friend Jarad Stillwell, thirteen.

Mike Miller's lean, lined, mournful face seemed to carry all the family's woes in its crevices. They'd had a lot of hard luck over the years. Money was tight, and Mike's salary from the Illinois Central Railroad never seemed quite able to stretch from one payday to the next, not with all those skinny tow-headed kids to take care of. Debbie Miller had signed on as a cook at Milestone about a year and a half ago, and Ashley and Mike Jr. sometimes came along, too, to wait tables or sweep up, netting a few bucks from Larry.

So when Mike Miller, back in the family's little blue house a half-mile south on Washington Street, had gotten spooked by those increasingly agitated TV weather reports, he thought of Milestone. Milestone was a second home. And Milestone, he figured, would be safer. It was big and thick-walled and had a stone-floored basement that was reassuring just to think about.

Milestone, anybody would tell you, was as sturdy as a preacher's promise.

Mike had just pulled a frozen pizza out of the oven for the kids' dinner, but to heck with it: They could eat when they got back home in a few minutes, after the storm passed.

So Mike ran down the crumbling steps with his children right behind him, and everybody scrambled into the family's Ford LTD.

By the time he and the kids got to the bar—two minutes later, tops—Debbie Miller was shutting down the grill, just like Larry had told her to.

"Everybody in the basement," Marian Ventrice said. "Kids first. Get the kids." She was a nervous, fretful, excitable woman, and you could hear the anxiety spiking in her voice.

The basement door was toward the front of the bar, under the stairs leading to the second floor. It was an old-fashioned cellar door, flush with the wooden floor, and you pulled up on a metal handle then flipped the door over.

Jarad and Gregg trooped down the wooden stairs, followed by Jennifer, Christopher, Ashley, and Mike Jr., and then the adults. They moved quickly, efficiently, but without panic, because they were heading to safety; the basement was a haven, the basement was exactly where you'd want to be at that moment. Thick stone floor, low ceiling. Like a cave.

"Stick together, everybody stick together," Marian said, and she and Larry went to the center of the basement. So did the older people—Wood, Ball, and Mahnke—and the Miller family piled up against the north wall, just beyond the bottom of the stairs. Gregg and Jarad headed to the south wall, next to the walk-in cooler.

Everybody was still talking, still speculating about the storm, and Mahnke asked Ashley and Jennifer their names. Marian was agitated, jittery, but everybody else was relaxed and casual, so casual, in fact, that Junior and Little had brought their beers with them. They set them on top of the chest-high freezer against which they stood, waiting for somebody to tell them it was OK to go back upstairs. No big deal.

At 5:58 p. m., Dena Mallie saw it from her driveway in Peru.

As it blossomed darkly, a huge batwing erasing the sky around it, a Utica contractor named Buck Bierbom saw it from his backyard.

Rona Burrows saw it. She leaned out the front door at Mill Street Market, where she worked as a cashier, and looked up at the sky.

Lisle Elsbury saw it from the alley behind Duffy's.

It was a great black mass, a swirling coil some two hundred yards wide at the ground—it was wider in the sky—heading northeast at about thirty mph. They looked up and saw it but they thought: No. Couldn't be. Could it?

There was a wild beauty to it, a fiercely knotted loveliness that was like nothing they'd ever seen. They could see debris swirling in it, pulled in and out and sucked up and around, frenzied sticks of wood, trees, dirt, other things, everything.

The ones who watched it come, watched it fill more and more of the blue-green sky like the canvas of a finicky painter who decides to slather the whole thing in black and start over, felt almost hypnotized at first, rooted to the earth but looking up, up, up. "Awesome" is the word that came instantly to Mallie. And not the way teenagers meant it. Awesome as in something that fills you up with awe.

Steve Maltas, twenty-three, a Utica volunteer firefighter with a trim goatee and a distinct aversion to small talk, was at the car wash in Utica's south end. He heard the report from the LaSalle Fire Department on his dispatch radio: A tornado was bearing down on them.

Maltas gunned his pickup toward the fire station, just up on Mill across from Milestone. He knew where the switch was to activate the tornado siren, the mechanical wail that would give his friends and neighbors a fighting chance.

He braked in front of the yellow-brick firehouse, cut the engine, raced inside and ran smack into a dilemma: He had no authority. Only the chief was supposed to give the OK to sound the warning. Another firefighter, quiet, blond Shane Burrows, twenty-three—Rona Burrows' son—was there too. He had tried to reach Edgcomb, but the chief's cell phone was turned off—a requirement for the EMT class.

The two men had seconds to decide and what they decided was:

Screw the rules.

Flip the switch. A moment later they were joined in the firehouse by Steve Maltas' mother, Gloria, who'd hustled there when she heard about the storm. She, too, worked at the firehouse in her spare time.

But even with the siren, the townspeople weren't paying attention. When Gloria Maltas looked outside, she saw them standing in the street, watching the sky. Maybe they thought the siren was just a precaution, or maybe they were trusting old Utican wisdom: A tornado won't go in a valley. A tornado won't cross water. Both were false.

So Gloria, ordinarily a shy, reticent woman who deeply disliked anything that could be remotely construed as making a spectacle of herself, who usually spoke in a soft, whispery voice that made listeners lean in a little to catch her words, did something wholly uncharacteristic: She directed Steve to one side of Mill Street and she took the other, and they began running and yelling at people who stood in the doorways, telling them to get inside, take cover, for God's sake go back in.

Gloria kept running. She ran faster than she'd ever run before, and she didn't realize how fast she was running. A day or so later, her legs ached and she couldn't figure out why, and then she remembered the running, running up and down Mill Street, screaming at people who must've wondered what on earth had gotten into sweet little Gloria Maltas.

Steve Maltas made it back to the fire station, where his last warning was issued to a few folks who stood in the doorway of the bar across the street. "Get in! Get back in!" he hollered, and he saw that one of them was Jay Vezain, who did as he was told, and then the others who'd been standing behind Vezain went back in, too.

Because the fire station didn't have a basement, Maltas and Burrows and the other firefighters who had gathered there headed for the boiler room. They heaved the door shut behind them, and then they waited, having done all they could do, for whatever the next flurry of seconds would bring.

Gloria Maltas, whose last warning was to the people standing outside Duffy's, wasn't going to make it back to the fire station. It was only a block away, and she had started back, thinking she could do it, but then she glanced over her shoulder and Oh my God saw the tornado gaining on her, spreading out behind her.

She was running toward the station, running and running, but there wasn't time, there wasn't time. The big black triangle was rising right behind her, capturing more and more of the sky.

At Mill Street Market, the tiny grocery store in the middle of the block, Gloria halted at the glass door—the one with the "We appreciate our customers" sign—and pounded on it. Closed, locked. Nobody stirred inside. Gloria had done her job too well. They were all in the back, she guessed, having fled into the big walk-in freezer.

Still Gloria pounded and hollered, because there was nothing else to do, no other option. She had to get inside somewhere, anywhere, and then she saw Rona Burrows running toward the door, jiggling the key in the lock, twisting it, that lock was always stubborn.

"Hurry up!" cried Burrows, pulling her inside. "If I have to see you flying through the air, I'll kill you!" she added, half-laughing, half-sobbing, and then they got to the back of the store, past the meat display case and into the freezer where the others—Mary Jo and Bruce Conner, the couple who managed the market, and a woman Gloria didn't know—were huddled.

They waited that final minute, not knowing if they were really safe, not knowing if the walls would hold, not knowing if these were the last seconds of their lives, and they embraced, and then—at 6:09 p. m.—there was a sound like hundreds of cars being dumped on the roof, and they knew that it was, unmistakably, upon them.

December 5, 2004

Author's Afterword

I stumbled into journalism. I was an English major all the way—undergrad through my doctoral degree—and never had a journalism course. I talked my way into my first newspaper job by brandishing clips from Isaac Asimov's *Science Fiction Magazine*; I had sold a couple of science-fiction limericks to that publication, for a dollar a line. My first editor happened to love limericks. He took a chance on me.

At the risk of sounding shrill and self-pitying and all of those things that a woman's not supposed to sound like (just ask Hillary Clinton), ambitious female writers still have a difficult time being taken seriously in the work world. If you're a young woman writer with passion, you're often treated like a cute pet, given a pat on the head and told to calm down; if you're a middle-aged woman writer, your passion is dismissed as hormonally motivated.

I think all women writers face the same obstacle: the daunting challenge of making sure one's work is respected.

One female editor I worked with recalled that when she was first hired by the *Columbus Dispatch* as a reporter in the 1960s, a male editor opposed her hiring because, as he later told her, "We've already got a woman." Feature sections were once called "women's pages."

These days, you'd be hard-pressed to find a position at any newspaper— from publisher to cop-shop reporter—that a woman has not occupied. Progress definitely has occurred.

All marginalized groups—women, ethnic or racial or religious minorities, the disabled—bring unique qualities to journalism, much more so than do members of the majority culture, simply because those on the outside, look- ing in, always see more clearly, and see differently, and are better motivated to probe and to push. That's what people miss about the need for diversity in newsrooms, I think: It's not about quotas. It's not just a nice idea about inclu- siveness. It makes for a richer, fuller product. I used to drive my managers at the *Chicago Tribune* crazy when they'd have "diversity talks" among the staff; they wanted to talk only about race, and I'd say, "How many Appalachians do we have in the newsroom? How many Muslims? How many Baptists? How many people on Medicare and Social Security? How many are receiving kid- ney dialysis?" Diversity doesn't just mean race or sex or ethnicity.

I suppose I'm expected to say I'm most proud of receiving a Pulitzer Prize, but in truth, I'm most proud of the simple fact that I have earned my living by my pen for most of my adult life. Writers are craftspeople, and we earn our bread day by day, as we go; we don't get tenure and there's no civil service protection. Nothing is guaranteed. We're only as good as our last story or our most recent book. There's a restless, dogged, dynamic quality to being a writer, in addition to the creative aspect. We are always, in effect, singing for our supper.

My Utica tornado story wasn't supposed to be a "seven-month process." It was supposed to be a single story, finished in a few days. Once I had visited Utica, walked around and talked to some of the people, however, I sensed the possibility for a more substantive and overtly literary narrative approach, after which it was a matter of persuading my editors to forgo a quick and dirty, one-shot story on the recovery efforts after the tornado, and to let me spend a bit of time there.

While I was doing the research and writing, I still had to do my regular job of book reviewing and column writing. Most of the reporting for the Utica story, in fact, was done on my own time, on nights and weekends. Once I settled down to write, I was guided by the example of the late Jim Bishop, a wonderful journalist who wrote a book called *The Day Kennedy Was Shot*. (He also wrote about the days Lincoln was shot and Christ was crucified, but the Kennedy book is the one I most revere.) Bishop had a three-ring binder, and he filled it with a second-by-second analysis of the day in question. His reporting was thorough and meticulous. From the massive amount of information in the binder, he distilled a beautiful, moving, and nuanced narrative of that tragic event. I tried to do a similar thing with the Utica tornado: trace its progression, second by second, through the experiences of the people who were affected by it.

The reporting effort was enormous and arduous; instead of just doing one or two interviews with the main characters in the story and then putting those quotes in the story, I practically moved in with them, going back again and again and again, until I could tell the story from their perspective.

I've recently transitioned into fiction writing. I feel that fiction, more than nonfiction, is the only lasting way to tell the world's story. Nonfiction is a good place to start—facts, heaven knows, are crucial—but in the end, fiction is the medium that gives us the true feel of an event, a personality, an epoch. For instance, there are many excellent journalistic accounts of the Great Depression, but when we desire to know what it really felt like to be broke and hopeless, we turn to John Steinbeck's *The Grapes of Wrath*. There are many masterful nonfiction books about politics, but none surpass Robert Penn Warren's *All the King's Men* as a portrait of the ruthless accumulation of political power in this country.

I wanted to be a novelist long before I became a journalist, but I benefited immensely from my work for newspapers. The opening scene in *Bitter River*, my second novel, came from an event I covered as a young reporter. And the catastrophe in the middle of *Bitter River*—I can say no more, in deference to spoiler alerts—was informed by my coverage of similar emergencies as a general assignment reporter.

My work as a journalist definitely made me a keener observer of life. It also inculcated a rigor and efficiency, and an ability to manage my time. On the negative side, I believe journalism makes its practitioners more cynical and skeptical. You learn, of necessity, to reduce people and their motivations to bite-sized, homogenous chunks—which is often distorting, and always dispiriting. But you also learn to remember that life is way more complicated than the sum of its parts.

Athelia Knight

Athelia Knight, a thirty-three-year veteran of the *Washington Post*, is an adjunct professor in the Department of English at Georgetown University. She has been a lecturer in the Council of the Humanities and Ferris Professor of Journalism at Princeton University. She also has been a professor-in-residence at Hampton University. A former Nieman Fellow at Harvard University, Knight was a staff reporter in various departments at the *Washington Post*, including metro, sports, and investigative news. She is an award-winning reporter and Pulitzer finalist.

Knight's last eight years at the *Post* were spent working with students interested in journalism careers. She was assistant director and later director of the *Post's* Young Journalists Development Program, which the newspaper created in 1997 to help train the next generation of journalists.

A Year at McKinley High School

A year in the life of McKinley High School in Washington, DC

Part 1

There was the usual chaos last December 19 when the students of McKinley High School in Northeast Washington gathered in the gymnasium for the annual Christmas assembly. They talked loudly among themselves, paying little attention to the McKinley choir's gospel performance. But when Dwayne Hall stood at center court to read the names of the honor roll students, the crowd quieted enough so that his voice could be heard.

"Please come forward as I call your names," said Hall, who had been invited to the special ceremony as McKinley's top graduate from the previous year. "Valerie Allen. Lisa Anderson. Tracie Andrews. Monica Barnhill..."

No one came forward. "Are these people here?" Hall asked. A few students snickered. He continued reading from the list. Still, no one stood up. School principal Bettye W. Topps took the microphone. "I want those people whose names have been called to come forward," she said, almost barking a command. "Front and center, now!" Several students began coming down from the bleachers. When Hall finished reading the names, fifty-three in all, about twenty students stood at center court.

As the assembly ended, Topps glowered as she surveyed the thousand or so students in the gym, occasionally adjusting the maroon scarf on her gray dress. A minute went by. The crowd grew silent. Topps, a forty-three-year-old Alabama native whose childhood dream was to become a teacher, scolded them for being "the poorest audience I have ever been a part of" and said:

"There is something strange... when people who have obtained excellence are embarrassed to come forward. I don't understand why you would rather be mediocre than excellent. I don't understand how those of you who have worked to be excellent can let some of you manage to make people feel bad . . . You should not be the exception. You should be the rule."

What Topps saw that day was a dramatic example of how academic values have been turned upside down at McKinley. Somehow, an environment has emerged that discourages excellence and encourages mediocrity, that inhibits creativity and fosters complacency. McKinley has its share of smart and energetic students, but they are not the strongest force in the school.

It is common to walk into a classroom and find that a majority of the students have come to class unprepared, neglecting to bring with them the most basic tools of learning—textbook or pencil or paper or homework. Frequently, the teachers chastise them; often, the students return to class unprepared, as if nothing had been said. Teachers seem to accept that many students have a nonchalant attitude toward learning, turning their attention instead to those who show an interest in doing well.

To be smart at McKinley, to do well, is to be different. To be different is to stand out. And standing out, calling attention to oneself, is not cool. "They want to do well," Topps said of her honor roll students. "But they don't want to be identified as people who do well."

Being cool is being able to skate by, to pass with a minimum of effort. "Nobody cares if I'm smart," said eleventh grader Irvin Kenny, an honor roll student whose friends call him "undercover smart" because he camouflages his academic talents. "I hang with people who are not smart. People see me in the hall a lot. I'm loud in class . . . I make a lot of noise. But I still get my work done."

This is not the McKinley of the 1960s, when some of the best young students in the District competed for admission to the school's pre-engineering, science, and music programs. Its graduates from that period include men and women, nearly all of them black, who went on to distinguish themselves as doctors, lawyers, nurses, research scientists, educators, corporate executives, and government officials. To attend "Tech," as it was known in those days, was considered an opportunity, a first step to a bright future.

That legacy is hardly in evidence now. McKinley's curriculum still includes pre-engineering and science courses that are not available at most DC high schools, but the best students go elsewhere, to Wilson High School or Banneker High School (a special academic school created six years ago) or the Duke Ellington School of the Arts, bypassing the imposing Georgian brick building on the hill that overlooks Second and T streets NE.

Among the District's fourteen high schools, McKinley is neither the best nor the worst; it falls squarely in the middle on test scores and on the percentage of graduates who go on to college. Like many other urban schools, its enrollment has declined dramatically; in 1967, it had 2,442 students, twice as many as it had when the new school year began last week.

And, according to several experts who have studied urban schools, it shares many of the characteristics—and problems—usually found in an urban high school. It is part of a school system in which the majority of students come from poorer families than most of those who attend public school in Washington's more affluent suburbs, the result of several decades of migration from cities to the suburbs.

Although a significant number of black and white families with higher incomes have remained in the District, many have chosen to send their children to private or parochial schools. About 15 percent of school-age DC children attended nonpublic schools last year, according to DC government statistics. Several years ago, the DC school system took steps to recapture those families, implementing special programs at the elementary school level and creating Banneker.

I spent nearly all of the 1986–87 school year at McKinley, attempting to answer some basic questions about today's urban high school: How do teachers motivate their students? How do the students cope with the pressures they face? Is the school helping the students to learn—or standing in their way?

The answers came from learning about incidents such as this: One day last fall, teacher Beulah Smith told her first-period senior English class that she was disappointed because more than half of the thirty seniors had done poorly on a writing assignment. She decided to read aloud the best paper, bringing groans from the class. "I know you're going to read Kenny's first," one student said, a reference to Kenneth Jackson, whose work was regularly praised by Smith.

After class, Kenneth stopped by Smith's desk and asked her not to read his papers aloud again. She tried to dissuade him, but Kenneth insisted. For the remainder of the year, she tacked his best papers on her green-covered bulletin board near her desk, but she did not read them to the class.

In an interview later, Kenneth said it wasn't the teasing that bothered him, it was that he saw no reason for the teacher to read his work to his classmates. "It wasn't of interest to them," he said.

On Friday morning, October 10, my second full day at the school, Topps took me on a tour of the fifty-nine-year-old building, which was undergoing its first major renovation. She stepped around a dusty plastic sheet hanging from a ceiling in a first-floor corridor and complained: "You won't be seeing a typical school year."

As we made our way past several closed-off areas, including some marked "Asbestos Dust Hazard," Topps pointed out some problems: The auditorium, which was supposed to be finished soon after school opened, was nowhere near completion. The public address system still wasn't working. The main office was closed and its occupants, including Topps and her four assistant principals, were working out of temporary quarters on separate floors. Fifteen classrooms were unavailable and the heating system wasn't working properly.

Nonetheless, Topps said, she was pushing ahead with her goals for the year. She felt that the school was at a critical stage. The faculty, which had been badly splintered when she took over as principal in 1982, finally seemed to have some momentum. They even had a slogan for the year, a theme that seemed to sum up Topps' hopes: "Renewing the Legacy—Listening to the Past, Working for the Future."

The tour was a mixture of grandeur and griminess. The school was designed to fit with the rest of monumental Washington: It has a Greek revival façade, including six thirty-foot columns and a balcony with a spectacular view of downtown Washington. Inside the main entrance is a marble foyer, which opens onto corridors with terrazzo floors made of polished marble chips set in cement. There is a greenhouse and a dramatic oval skylight in the library, and most of the classrooms have hardwood floors.

But the greenhouse hasn't been used in years and is now filled with debris. The library's skylight is intact, but a fifty-year-old mural featuring scenes from American history was removed and replaced with wallpaper during the summer renovation. In some classrooms, the windowpanes were so dirty—or had been replaced with plywood or a brownish-looking opaque plastic—that teachers showed films without drawing the shades.

On the second floor, Topps ran into music teacher Beatrice Gilkes. In the days when McKinley attracted top-notch music students, Gilkes had more than forty students; with the decline in the school's enrollment and the scaling back of the music program, she now has eighteen. Inside her classroom are three pianos—two baby grands and a concert grand—that were once used freely by her students. She now keeps them locked unless a student asks to use them.

Gilkes has seen the school change dramatically since she joined the faculty in 1954, the same year that the US Supreme Court issued its *Brown v. Board of Education of Topeka* ruling, ordering an end to the segregated school systems that existed in Washington and throughout the nation. Within a few years, as white families began leaving the neighborhood or sending their children to private school, the all-white school became nearly all black. She saw the introduction of the "track system" in 1956, which grouped students by academic ability, and the demise of that system in 1967 when a federal judge banned such groupings as discriminatory against poor blacks.

McKinley's students come primarily from a wide area of Northeast Washington that encompasses several poor and middle-class neighborhoods, from public housing on Montana Avenue and Edgewood Terrace, from well-appointed town houses in Fort Lincoln near the Maryland border, from shingled and brick homes in Woodridge and Brookland. After school, many students head off to work; more than half of last year's senior class had half-day schedules so they could work part time.

Several times during the tour, Topps stopped to handle a disciplinary problem. She corralled two boys who were in the hall without permission and ordered them to class. She caught two "outsiders"—two boys who were not McKinley students—peeking into a second-floor classroom.

Later, she played down the significance of the incidents, saying it was easy to make too much of disciplinary issues. It was more important, she said, to establish a certain decorum and make clear to students that you expect them to behave appropriately. When she first came to the school, she was so disgusted with student behavior at assemblies that she held practice sessions on the proper ways to sit, to applaud, to enter and leave.

The key to a good school, she said, is good teaching. The best teachers—the ones who can motivate the least interested students—are the ones who are knowledgeable, well-prepared, and creative. "Doing the same thing, the same way, will not make it," she said.

At the same time, she said, a good school could be hurt by a bad image. In the spring of 1986, she said, McKinley was unfairly branded as a drug school after seven McKinley students were charged with selling drugs to a police officer posing as a student. (Another undercover officer posed as a student last year, too, I learned at the end of the year. No arrests, however, were made at any time during the year.) Topps blamed the media for the way the issue was covered.

The tour was over and we were back at her office. She said, almost coldly, that if I wanted to write about "bad" teachers and "bad" students, she could give me names and save me time. Was I willing to look at the total picture?

I told her that I wanted to learn all about the school, but I particularly wanted to find out what was happening inside the classroom. "Fine," she said. Then she reminded me again: "The whole picture."

The heating system wasn't working again and room 107, where Anne Harding's senior English class met, was chilly. Although it was October 14, some students were bundled up in sweaters and coats.

Harding, a slender, dark-haired woman who has taught at McKinley for twenty years, was irritated. The school year was six weeks old and the class hadn't finished a refresher section on grammar. She couldn't seem to get anyone to do the work, even though the class was a requirement for graduation. "It might be elementary and boring," she told them, "but you need to learn it. You should have learned it in the fifth grade."

Leaning against her desk, in front of a "Renewing the Legacy" sign tacked above the blackboard, Harding asked the class for an example of a sentence with a subordinate clause. No one responded. "I'm waiting for the sentence," she said, tapping one of her black pumps on the hardwood floor. Unable to get anyone to volunteer, Harding had to call on someone before she could get an answer. Later she said, "Part of the reason you don't understand is your attention span is too short. You are waiting for the commercial."

She hoped that the literature part of the course would stimulate their interest. As a first step, she assigned them to write a brief paper about a "hero"—anyone they admired. The paper was due Wednesday, October 22.

But in class that day, only twenty-five of the course's thirty-eight students were there and only eight said they had written a paper. Harding was annoyed. She turned to Katrice Barnes, who usually did her homework, and told her to read her paper aloud.

"Are you ready?" Harding asked.

Katrice pulled her paper out of her notebook. "Don't you all laugh," she said, turning to her classmates.

"Don't worry about the laughing," Harding said, picking up her pen and indicating that she planned to make a note in her grade book of anyone who teased Katrice. "I got that covered."

Katrice twisted around in her seat and started to read. Her hero, she said, was Sylvester Stallone. A couple of boys put their hands over their mouths to muffle their laughter; Harding looked at them in disgust.

No one said anything as Katrice described how she admired Stallone because he played tough and macho characters in his movies. Although it was not the classic definition of a hero, Harding praised Katrice, saying she had tried to identify certain heroic traits and had done the assignment as required.

After four other students read their papers—their heroes were members of their families—Harding closed her grade book and addressed the students who had not done the homework.

"I can't conduct my class if you don't do what you're supposed to do," she said. "You will need more than a high school education if you're going to succeed in life. You will need more than what I have and what your parents have . . . I don't like my class unprepared. I want you to learn something in this class."

On a wet and gloomy Thursday morning, December 18, teacher David M. Messman peeked through the double doors of room 224 and saw only nine of thirty students in his 9 a. m. first-year Spanish class. Attendance had been dropping as the Christmas holiday approached, but this was worse than usual. Messman had a quick explanation. "It's raining," he said.

Class began with a brief exercise: Messman wrote a paragraph in Spanish on the blackboard and led the students through a translation of it, writing the English version on the board as they went. At 9:15, fifteen minutes into the forty-five-minute class, a boy walked in and strutted to a seat in the back, saying nothing to Messman about being late. Two minutes later, another latecomer arrived, without a tardy excuse or books.

Messman asked the class to open their books to a Christmas carol on page 204. "I don't have my book," one girl called out. A boy who didn't bring his book moved to sit next to a boy who did. Finally, Messman asked how many students had their books. Four of the eleven raised their hands.

Messman shook his head, more resigned than angry. He handed out photocopies of the song, which he had handy because he was planning to use it in another class that did not have the same book. It was now 9:20. A few minutes later, a boy and a girl walked in empty-handed. He gave copies to them. At 9:27 a. m., another girl arrived, also without her book, and he gave her a copy.

The class was twenty-seven minutes old, nearly two-thirds over, and the students had hardly done any work.

On another day, teacher Liliana G. Chiappinelli stood in front of a student's desk in her 9 a. m. second-year Spanish class, her head bowed as she read from an open book. The lights were off. One girl of the twenty-one students present seemed to be responding to her questions; the rest were doing something else.

One girl at a front-row desk was reading a paperback romance novel. Four girls were having a lively conversation, another was painting her fingernails, another was asleep, another was sipping a canned soda through a straw, and two girls near the windows were looking at separate photo albums. At 9:15, a boy arrived late, took his seat and immediately struck up a conversation with a girl next to him. A few minutes later, another boy got up, walked across the room to borrow three small photo albums from a girl, then returned to his seat.

Chiappinelli, head still bowed, continued to read. At one point she looked up and said, "I don't have many people answering questions. I only have one."

The scene in Chiappinelli's classroom that day was one of the more chaotic I saw during my year at McKinley. It was more typical to see teachers constantly interrupting their classes to deal with students who weren't paying attention.

One day during one of his French classes, teacher Vernon Williams was drilling his students on certain phrases when he heard a faint melody. He looked around. He shouted to a boy sitting in the rear, earphones on his head and Walkman on his belt. The boy did not hear him. Some students laughed. Williams shouted louder. The boy finally looked up. He took his earphones off.

"I'm really surprised at you," Williams said, confiscating the Walkman, which is prohibited in the school. At the end of class, he returned the Walkman with a warning: "I don't want to see that in McKinley any more."

On the last morning before the winter break just before Christmas, the halls and classrooms at McKinley were like a ghost town. Only fifty of the school's estimated twelve hundred students were in school. About five hundred were at the Cinema Theatre in Northwest Washington, watching the Eddie Murphy movie, "Golden Child," as part of a school fund-raiser. The whereabouts of the rest was unknown.

Movie fund-raisers were popular. The students liked them because they were a break from the classroom and because some teachers gave extra credit to those who went. The teachers liked them because they could usually choose a movie that raised important social issues, which could then be discussed in class.

But "Golden Child" was primarily a fund-raiser, not an educational tool. Tickets cost four dollars, split between the theater and the school. Most teachers didn't actively promote the fund-raiser, which was sponsored by the social studies department. In some classes, it was just written in a corner of the blackboard.

Some teachers were bothered by this link between fund-raisers and grades. Still, it seemed harmless enough; during the course of a school year, extra credit for going to a movie wasn't going to change anyone's grade. But then came the incident in which Topps asked students to help the PTA pay off a $500 debt.

It began when the PTA held a Friday night dance in the gym and fewer than one hundred students came. It was the same night that McKinley's top-rated basketball team played its archrival Dunbar at Dunbar's gym. A victory might have turned the dance into a celebration. But McKinley lost and no one felt like dancing. The PTA found itself with a band costing $1,000 and a lot of unsold eight-dollar tickets.

At school the following Monday, January 12, Topps told the faculty that "we've got to find a way" to pay off the debt. She held a round of meetings with students. The seniors, who offered to donate money, suggested that students get extra credit—just as some got for going to movies. Topps liked the idea.

She came up with the following plan: For a one-dollar donation, students would receive a "ticket" that could be exchanged for extra credit in a class of the student's choice. Limit: one ticket to a student.

The next day in Anne Harding's senior English class, students seemed even less prepared than usual. Only four of the twenty-one seniors present handed in a two-page homework assignment. Harding stapled the papers and said: "Nobody can make an 'A' if you don't pass your work in today."

At one point, a boy held a ticket aloft and said, "Mrs. Harding, I got a ticket."

She glared at him. "That doesn't mean anything to me," she said.

A few days later, an eleventh grader came to Topps' office to complain that his algebra teacher, Juliana Parker, wasn't accepting the tickets.

Topps said she could not force a teacher to accept the ticket. "Isn't there another class in which you can use it?" she asked.

"I need it in her class," the boy insisted.

Topps said there was nothing she could do. Disappointed, he said he would use it in another class.

Other teachers did accept the tickets, however, and sales were brisk. Within two days of Topps' announcement, 358 had been sold. The final count was short of the five hundred needed; the PTA sold T-shirts at a basketball game to make up the difference.

The episode created some bad feeling among faculty members, some of whom confronted Topps and accused her of "selling grades." Others, however, said they saw the plan as a way to promote citizenship and participation.

Topps said that some teachers told her that their consciences wouldn't allow them to accept the tickets. Topps said she told them: "That's fine."

In late spring, Topps and the faculty turned their full attention to preparing ninth and eleventh graders for the national standardized tests, the measuring rod that many parents use to judge the city's schools. One of Topps's primary goals was improving test scores; it was also a primary goal of the school system itself.

Topps directed her math, science and English teachers to spend part of their class time on Tuesdays and Thursdays getting the students ready. On Tuesday, April 14, English teacher Beulah Smith was having trouble with her eleventh graders.

The students were using copies of old tests to do several reading comprehension exercises. Irvin Kenny, the honor roll student who says he intentionally tries not to act smart, wasn't paying attention. He whispered in the ear of a boy who was seated in front of him. He blew big bubbles from his gum. He made no effort to do the exercises.

Other students weren't paying attention either. Finally, Smith had had enough.

"Instead of paying attention, you are doing other things," Smith said, angrily. "This is typical of what happens at McKinley. Some of you are looking around in space. The test is the fifth, sixth and seventh of May. We have not taken this test very seriously."

There was silence.

"You hurt my feelings," Irvin said, feigning a sad look.

"I'm sorry but that is the way it is," Smith snapped.

"You make me feel low," he said, placing his head on his desk.

Smith went on to another exercise. More students were paying attention now.

A few minutes later, Irvin lifted his head. He turned to several others and began talking. Smith shot him an angry glance. Irvin went right on talking.

September 13, 1987

Author's Afterword

Growing up in Virginia, I was always curious about things. I worked on the college paper at Norfolk State University, where I went for undergrad. I was an English major because they didn't have a journalism program; I had planned to go into education and become a teacher. But I fell in love with reporting and writing stories for the campus paper and for a black weekly in Norfolk, Virginia.

I had a college professor who went to bat for me in my senior year and was able to persuade one of the employees at the local newspaper, the *Virginian-Pilot*, to grant me an interview. Working for them, I went out and found stories and wrote about the decline of downtown Norfolk. It turned out to be a big story that pushed a lot of buttons in town; the business community was especially critical. After I did that, I realized that I could write stories that really made a difference or called attention to things—societal wrongs or injustices or criminal acts, even—that people walk by each day and take for granted. Until somebody writes a story, exposes the wrong, uncovers the injustice, nobody pays attention. Stories shed light. It was powerful and honest. At the end of the summer, I went off to Ohio State University to work on my master's in journalism.

When I was at Ohio State, I met an editor for the *Chicago Tribune*. Through him, I landed an internship, and I went off to Chicago to work for the *Chicago Tribune* for about five months, which gave me more clips and more stuff to add to my resume to try to get a full-time, permanent job. Unfortunately, at the end of October 1974, the *Chicago Tribune* had a hiring freeze. I wrote to every paper I could think of. I finally got an interview at the *Washington Post*, and I was hired.

Once there, I competed with veteran reporters for stories. You had to prove yourself to get attention. I was like, "Ok, I'm going to have a story in the paper every day." I fell in love with writing stories and it just went from there, covering daily stories, doing features about people who were ordinary people doing extraordinary things. I ended up covering the city for a while, and then my editor sent me out to the suburbs.

In a career of thirty-three years, there's a lot that I'm proud of. I became a Pulitzer finalist for the McKinley High School series. At the time I had the opportunity to be working as an investigative reporter under the legendary Bob Woodward. In the case of the McKinley story, we weren't out to put anybody in jail or anything; we were trying to shed a light. Those were the days

when papers allowed some of us the luxury of taking time to do in-depth pieces. McKinley had been a great high school in the forties and fifties and even in
the sixties when they integrated the school—some of the city's leaders and people in the federal government had attended the school, black and white. But in
1986, when I went there, it was falling apart. The reporting was probably the
part I liked best; the writing was a challenge.

I'm always asking questions and I'm always curious about things, so
that's part of my personality. I was lucky that I had found something that I
was passionate about and that I could develop into a career. In 2008 I took an
early retirement from the *Post*; now I'm teaching the next generation about
journalism at Georgetown University, about why it's important, about why a
commitment to it is important to a democratic society.

When I came into newsrooms, there were not a lot of women editors. I
was lucky enough to work for a place like the *Washington Post*, where the legendary Katharine Graham was the publisher. She was a great role model and
an inspiration, even though as women we were very different. The truth is, we
need diversity in newsrooms. We need minorities, we need women, we need
people who have diverse opinions, we need all kinds of people who want to
seek and tell the truth. Once you get hired, though, it's nothing about who you
are. Black, a woman, whatever you may be, all of it begins and ends with the
hard work. In the end, it's all about the stories.

Christine Pelisek

Christine Pelisek is a veteran crime reporter. She covered crime, entertainment, and national news for the *Daily Beast* in Los Angeles for three years. Prior to that, she worked at the *LA Weekly* as an investigative crime reporter. She broke the story that a serial killer who had murdered women in South Los Angeles for decades had struck again in 2007. Even though the still-unidentified killer remained at large, the Los Angeles Police Department kept the news from the public, angering family members who questioned the department's commitment to tracking down the killer of poor black women.

In 2008 Pelisek won three Los Angeles Press Club awards, one for her investigative story on the Grim Sleeper. In 2009, she received the finalist prize for her Grim Sleeper investigation by the Investigative Reports and Editors, Inc. She also received a certificate of appreciation by the Los Angeles City Council for her work in the Grim Sleeper case. In March 2014, her role in the investigation was made into a movie by the Lifetime Network.

Grim Sleeper Returns

An elusive serial killer took a thirteen-year break—
now he's back

There's a small room at LAPD headquarters where the public isn't allowed, where the door is quickly shut to the hall, where arguments erupt and frustrations fester. It's off-limits to most other detectives, no press allowed. Lest anyone forget, a memo on the wall says so. The six men inside call themselves the "800 Task Force" even though they no longer occupy room 800, having moved to a lower floor of Parker Center to make room for a sex-crimes team. Their new room is cramped, the desks piled with mounds of paperwork. What is striking about their space is its main wall, heavily papered with photographs of dead young women.

The 800 Task Force was assembled in 2007 under Chief Bill Bratton to solve eleven perplexing murders in Los Angeles dating from 1985. Police have followed several trails, made a few arrests, and endlessly theorized about the killer or killers responsible. Homicide detectives have retired, new ones have joined the investigation. Each group thought they detected patterns, each group thought they had solid leads. Each was proved wrong.

For four years, police have known that a single madman is out there, a man whose audacity and sick good luck have made him the most enduring serial killer in California history and the longest-operating serial killer west of the Mississippi. In 1988, he stopped the slaughter for more than thirteen years, then killed again in 2002 and 2003. *LA Weekly* has learned that he is actively murdering Angelenos again—and the single best clue to his identity may hinge on whether Attorney General Jerry Brown allows a controversial DNA probe of the California felon database.

"He could be some computer nerd out there for all we know," says Detective Dennis Kilcoyne, a friendly yet hardened man in his early fifties, as he sips a coffee at a Starbucks one morning in late summer. It was Kilcoyne who urged the LAPD brass to set up the 800 Task Force. "It could be anybody . . . In this case, it has gone on so long—we have to be open to any possibility."

The killing began on a warm August evening in 1985 at a desperate point in US urban history, a time filled with PCP rages and crack wars. Los Angeles's murder rate—and that of most big cities—had soared to an all-time high. Amid the bloodshed, during a three-year period, seven young women and one man were killed and left in alleyways and Dumpsters, almost exclusively along Western Avenue in South Los Angeles. Ballistics matches showed the same gun was used in each case.

Then, slayings committed with the .25 caliber gun abruptly halted. The crack and PCP era faded. Los Angeles became the second-safest big city in America, and DNA matching became the hot new crime-solving tool. Under orders from Chief Bernard Parks, in 2001, the LAPD began delving into a backlog of unsolved cases from the violent 1990s, '80s and earlier, testing bits of hair and skin saved from cold crimes. The LAPD's lab workers in 2004 and 2005 hit pay dirt. Like a long-delayed tripwire, the tests found matches between new killings in 2002 and 2003 and old human traces left at the eight Western Avenue shootings in the '80s.

A monstrous Phoenix, the 1980s killer, had reemerged. "I thought, 'Holy Shit,'" says 800 Task Force detective Cliff Shepard. "This guy is out there working. I was not expecting that."

Despite the discovery of an old serial killer back in business, detectives were spread thin on cases like that of killer Chester Turner, whose DNA was linked to fourteen deaths by strangulation. Chief Parks was forced out of his post by Mayor James Hahn, and newcomer Bill Bratton did not make the South LA serial murders a priority. In fact, detectives tell the *Weekly* that in 2004, one of Bratton's captains decided, in the wake of the two new murders in 2002 and 2003, that a task force wasn't even needed. Nor were elected officials paying any attention. The killings weren't going down in Silver Lake or Westwood, and the year was 2004: City Hall's leaders were transfixed by a three-way race for mayor between Hahn and challengers Bob Hertzberg and Antonio Villaraigosa.

Nobody with any pull—no homeowners association, no local chamber of commerce—was demanding answers to ten murders by the same guy in a poor section of town.

Last year, the disinterested Bratton got a wake-up call—of sorts. On January 1 of 2007, a homeless man collecting cans from a Dumpster off Western Avenue discovered the lifeless body of twenty-five-year-old Janecia Peters near a discarded Christmas tree. She'd been placed in a black garbage bag wrapped tightly with a twist tie. She was nude but for her gold heart pendant. Her shooting barely registered with the Los Angeles media, which misreported it, calling it a stabbing.

Janecia's mother, Laverne Peters, heard a news report that a black teenager had been found dead along Western Avenue. She never dreamed it was her own Janecia. She was in Inglewood with Janecia's four-year-old son, visiting other family members. "Her son had a Christmas present for Janecia," Peters recalls. "He wrapped it himself, in aluminum foil and red rope."

The day before, Janecia had telephoned her mom. "She just said, 'I got a place.' She was really excited . . . Whoever she was going to stay with, she felt she was safe."

She wasn't. Janecia died at the hands of the Grim Sleeper. Yet Peters and dozens of other mothers, fathers, sisters, and brothers were never told their loved ones had been killed by the same psychopath.

There has been no big press conference by Bratton, who recently weighed in on Lindsay Lohan's love life. The camera-loving Villaraigosa recently beseeched the public to eat nutritiously. Unlike city leaders who decried the "BTK Killer" near Kansas City and the "Green River Killer" who terrorized Seattle, Los Angeles's City Hall is either unaware, or has kept news of California's longest-operating killer under wraps. Local journalists haven't even assigned him a creepy nickname, like Night Stalker (Grim Sleeper was chosen by the *Weekly* to mark his thirteen years of inactivity before killing again).

Two key city council members, who learned of the Grim Sleeper's existence for the first time this week from the *Weekly*, had strong reactions.

Bernard Parks's chief of staff and son, Bernard C. Parks Jr., whose district is ground zero in the killings, accused Chief Bratton of purposely keeping former Chief Parks in the dark. "Leaving us out of the loop about something so important boggles the mind," Parks Jr. said. Councilman Jack Weiss, who has repeatedly called for DNA testing of human traces stored in the cold-case files, vowed to seek weekly LAPD updates on cases that are being linked to known serial killers and serial rapists.

Thanks to the extraordinarily poor diplomacy extended by the Villaraigosa administration and the LAPD brass to the victims' mostly working-class black families, the *Weekly* was also the first to inform some families this month that the murders are known to be the work of one sick man.

Laverne Peters had long suspected that Janecia's death was part of something bigger. Her daughter's murder case was transferred from 77th Division to the specialized detectives "downtown" in 2007, and she knew that one easily forgotten young woman would not merit such an elite investigative crew.

"It doesn't take a scientist to figure it out," she says. But when LAPD detectives paid Peters a visit, they didn't come clean with her. The city's failure to involve the families, she believes, stems from the fact that "they are poor little black girls."

A deeply frustrated Porter Alexander, who learned from this newspaper that his daughter Monique's death in 1988 was the work of the Grim Sleeper, says, "We should have some awareness that it is going on again. Nobody came to us."

Detective Kilcoyne's small unit has tried to let people know that a madman is afoot. Task force detectives working the eleven murders have informed Vice and Homicide detectives, as well as local prostitutes. "This is a pretty small area in South Los Angeles. We have been talking to the prostitutes for years . . . The word is out that the police are out there."

But neither Villaraigosa nor Bratton tried to alert the city. If they ever had, one woman who would be hyperaware of it is Minister Pat Jones of the First Church of God in Inglewood. Jones, who is also co-chairwoman of the Southeast area neighborhood council and the Southwest area neighborhood council, was stunned to hear from the newspaper about the existence of the Grim Sleeper. "How come [they] haven't involved the community? There are no fliers or nothing. In order for us to work on it to stop it, we have to be all-inclusive and involve everybody. We have to flood the neighborhood. This is serious . . . We need to have a press conference to talk about it."

The *Weekly* attempted to reach elected city officials and top Villaraigosa political appointees, but many were out of town, attending the Democratic National Convention, including the mayor, City Council President Eric Garcetti and Police Commission Vice President John Mack. Spokeswoman Eva Vega said Mack couldn't weigh in on the Grim Sleeper case. "He doesn't have the time," she said. "He's too busy right now." The *Weekly* got a nearly identical response from Bratton's office.

Such responses from City Hall feed the view held by Laverne Peters, that if eleven troubled young women had been killed in Westwood or Mount Washington by a single nut case operating over twenty-three years, it would be big news at City Hall. Instead, "It is almost hush-hush . . . [The authorities] act like the parents of those kids don't exist."

Whether through ineptness or disinterest, the silence from Bratton and Villaraigosa on the Grim Sleeper murders is welcomed by some detectives, who are happy to work without the help of Joe Citizen, because they fear that the killer could bolt or change his MO. No fliers are up in hard-hit areas. The six cops on Task Force 800 have few leads, one surviving eyewitness, stacks of "murder books" crackling with age—and a killer who leaves no fingerprints.

Betty Lowe, whose daughter Mary was killed by the Grim Sleeper in late 1987, is getting on in years. She doesn't want to hear stories about why police can't find her child's killer. She learned for the first time in 2006 that Mary was the victim of a serial murderer, and her anger came quickly. "We are not going to let this go," Lowe says. "I have wanted this case solved so I can get on with my life . . . I want to know who killed my baby!"

There is one possibility Los Angeles cops have not yet pursued: The killer has left a trail of his own DNA. Crime-scene analysts have discovered traces of his dried saliva on victims' breasts. But to the surprise of many homicide investigators, his DNA profile doesn't match anything in the state offender or federal crime database.

So Los Angeles police are hoping the Grim Sleeper has a brother, father, or cousin in prison. Experts believe that roughly 40 percent of violent criminals have close relatives in jail. If the Grim Sleeper's "familial" DNA popped up in a survey of the state offender's database of more than one million DNA profiles, the LA killer might finally be identified by family name.

"They are doing research on familial DNA" at the LAPD to prepare for such a search, confirms Inglewood detective Loyd Waters, who is informally part of the 800 Task Force because the Grim Sleeper's 2002 victim, teenager Princess Berthomieux, was found dead in Inglewood. "That's powerful stuff," says former FBI profiler Gregg McCrary of the usefulness of familial DNA studies.

But those clues are currently locked up in an obscure government crime lab 376 miles north of Los Angeles, controlled by the mercurial attorney general, Jerry Brown, who wants to be the next governor of California. In familial DNA testing, a match of at least sixteen "markers" could indicate a close relative. Brown's spokesman, Gareth Lacy, says, "It is not something that will all of a sudden crack thousands of cases." But, "if it is a lead, if you have a killer at large, if it can help, we want to work with the agency."

Or maybe not. Although Kilcoyne denies it, Inglewood detective Waters says Bratton and his underlings have requested that Brown allow a familial DNA survey—but Brown's aide stonily rebuffed the Weekly's queries, saying any such DNA comparisons wouldn't occur for months. Some civil rights groups view looking for relatives by probing the state felon DNA archive as an invasion of privacy. They also criticize such comparisons because of "false positives" that could wrongly identify somebody who is not actually a family member.

Last May, Brown publicly announced that he would allow "familial" DNA surveys of the California prisoner database—but only if all other leads had been exhausted and the criminal being sought posed a threat, a description that fits the Grim Sleeper to a T.

Kilcoyne, meanwhile, fears that the Grim Sleeper has slaughtered, and might still be slaughtering, far more people than police have turned up. "We are at number eleven," he says, "and I would venture to say that this is probably half of what he has done."

Police face an almost total mystery—such as why the suspect started up again, and why he kills quietly, unlike the notoriously media-hungry BTK Killer or California's boastful Zodiac Killer. The BTK Killer bragged in letters about his murders between 1974 and 1991. His writings resumed in 2004, after the Wichita Eagle published a story on the thirtieth anniversary of his first murders, of the Otero family.

"It prompted this guy to come back to us," recalls Richard LaMunyon, then chief of the Wichita Police Department. "If we didn't catch him, he would have called his own news conference . . . He wanted to be in the hall of fame of serial killers."

BTK turned out to be an unassuming Boy Scout leader named Dennis Rader, caught after police traced a floppy disk he'd sent them to the church where he was a deacon. "[Rader] would go for a year or two without killing," LaMunyon says. "Then he would go dormant again for almost ten years."

Could LA's killer be a family man, like Rader, whose own wife and kids are unaware of his murder spree? Or perhaps California's most enduring serial killer is closer in nature to the Green River Killer, Gary Ridgway, a prostitute-hater who led police on a cat-and-mouse hunt in King County, Washington, for almost twenty years until his DNA linked him to three of his forty-eight victims.

Is the Grim Sleeper also getting revenge on women he sees as harlots, by killing so many messed up, young, black women? Or does he merely live just down the block, like Chester Turner, who killed almost exclusively near his mother's South-Los Angeles home?

What police do know is that in August 1985, Debra Jackson was found shot to death. A year later, on August 12, 1986, Henrietta Wright was found dead. Two days later, the body of Thomas Steele was discovered in the middle of an intersection. Barbara Ware was found in a trash bag in January 1987. Bernita Sparks told her mother she was going to buy cigarettes but was found shot to death on April 16, 1987. Mary Lowe told her mother she was going to a Halloween party, and was discovered shot, on November 1, 1987. Lachrica Jefferson was found shot in January 1988. In September 1988, Alicia "Monique" Alexander asked her father if he wanted anything from a liquor store and never returned.

Monique Alexander's father, Porter, was immediately discouraged by the investigation into her death, remembering it as "a big mess . . . They didn't put forth any effort. [The detectives] didn't show no aggressiveness about it."

Even so, eyewitnesses had seen her vanish into a car, and had given a vehicle description that was to come up yet again. "She got in a car with somebody on Normandie," recalls her brother Donnell. "That was what was told to us. She supposedly got into a rust- or orange-colored hatchback . . . She was tough. It was possible she might have not known him."

By the mid-eighties, detectives had begun to suspect the killings might be the work of the Southside Slayer, a mythical, evil, single force who at one point was suspected in at least twenty other slayings in the county. Victims were found in parks, alleys, roadsides, and school yards. Most were black prostitutes working in South LA. Many had been sexually assaulted. In one recurring clue, cat hair was found on some of the victims.

Police pursued, but ultimately discarded, many suspects, and investigated numerous alleged getaway cars. They sought a black man between twenty-eight and thirty-five, with a pockmarked face and a Caribbean or East Coast accent. A 1984 dark-colored Buick Regal with a baby seat. A late-model Plymouth station wagon. A 1960 Ford pickup with gray primer. A two-door red Ford Pinto with tinted rear-window glass.

So many "body dumps" were occurring during that ugly era that angry residents lashed out at police, and in 1986 launched the Black Coalition Fighting Black Serial Murders. The coalition declared that "the low-profile media coverage and problems with the investigation are all examples of women's lives not counting and black prostitute women counting least of all."

That same year, cops formed a huge forty-nine-member task force to find the killer or killers. In 1987 they got a major break when ballistics tests clearly showed that amid the bodies piling up, eight involved the same .25 caliber handgun.

Then the LAPD got its biggest break of all, in the form of Victim No. 9. She was the sole survivor, attacked just before the Grim Sleeper vanished for thirteen years. Victim No. 9, who still lives in Los Angeles (and who the *Weekly* is not identifying to ensure her safety), provided police the first eyewitness description of the attacker and his car. She said he was a thirtyish black man with short hair, driving a rust, red or orange Ford Pinto—the very car victims Monique Alexander and Mary Lowe were reportedly last seen riding in.

In nightmarish detail, the survivor told police she was picked up by a male motorist on November 20, 1988, on the corner of Eighty-First Street and Western Avenue. But he then wielded a gun, shot her in the chest and then raped her. Seriously wounded, she persuaded the killer to let her jump out of the car.

"She was really lucky," says retired detective Rich Haro, who investigated the killings, which police at one point dubbed the "Strawberry Murders"—a street term for troubled women who casually trade sex for drugs. Surmises Haro: "It was something she said that convinced him, and he dropped her off."

And Victim No. 9 provided another solid clue: The bullets removed from her chest turned out to match the gun used on the eight previous victims.

Haro and his partner caught another break in February 1989—or so they believed. In a case that would make headlines, Los Angeles County sheriff's deputy Rickey Ross, a black narcotics detective (not to be confused with Freeway Ricky Ross, a kingpin drug dealer) was arrested in his car in the Strawberry Murders "kill area." Allegedly, he was smoking coke with a prostitute. LAPD patrol cops said Deputy Ross pulled away in an "erratic" manner as they approached his car. They stopped him, and during a search found a 9 mm gun in Ross' trunk.

The next day, Los Angeles Police chief Daryl Gates held a press conference and claimed that Ross had been high on cocaine. Amidst intense controversy, Deputy Ross was charged with murdering three prostitutes who'd been slain with a 9 mm gun. But in a development that riveted the city, Ross was released after independent experts determined that the LAPD had botched the ballistics tests on his gun. Moreover, despite Chief Gates' public claim, Ross had tested negative for cocaine.

Even so, Ross was fired from his job by Los Angeles County sheriff Sherman Block for allegedly abusing alcohol and drugs and soliciting a prostitute. In 1989, Ross filed a $400 million federal civil rights lawsuit, claiming that ballistics tests of his gun "were deliberately falsified" by LAPD, but a federal jury ruled against him. He reached a private settlement with the LA County Sheriff's Department over his firing.

When he died in 2003, Deputy Ross was still under a cloud. Until recently, the retired Haro was convinced that Ross was the elusive killer in South LA. "After he was arrested, it stopped—there weren't any killings anymore," Haro recently told the Weekly.

Had Haro only known what the LAPD was about to unearth, stored for years in its evidence rooms at Piper Technological Center downtown, Ross might have died a vindicated man. Under Chief Bernard Parks and Mayor James Hahn, a cold-case unit had been created to investigate more than nine thousand unsolved killings dating to 1960. It was a formidable task, made tougher because much of the trace evidence kept at overcrowded "Piper Tech" had been pointlessly destroyed thanks to bureaucratic buffoonery. Even so, in 2001, cold-case detectives began sifting through homicide "books"—filled with arrest reports, witness interviews, investigative leads, and possible suspects— to see if physical evidence had survived from the eight killings committed by the perpetrator that Haro and others believed to be Rickey Ross.

Laboriously digging through homicide books, Detective Cliff Shepard discovered that some physical evidence had indeed survived, awaiting the day the outside world would develop the know-how to test minute scraps of DNA. Shepard asked the police lab to compare the surviving saliva samples and other DNA to samples from more recent crimes.

"You would think that somebody involved in those activities would have been arrested and had a [DNA] sample taken," Shepard says.

In 2004, his efforts resulted in a stunning, positive hit. Saliva found on 1987 victim Mary Lowe matched DNA found on the two women murdered in 2002 and 2003. The long-accused Rickey Ross had died a month before the 2003 murder, and he clearly wasn't killing from the grave.

The cops' hunches had been wrong, the spectacular Rickey Ross story line of 1989 a red herring.

The real murderer of seven women and one man was still out there—and now had killed twice more. His first victim after his thirteen-year hiatus was a habitual teenage runaway turned prostitute, fourteen-year-old Princess Ber-thomieux. Reported missing by her foster-care mother on December 21, 2001, her body was found four months later in an alley in Inglewood. Fifteen months later, in July 2003, a month after the wrongfully accused Ross died, a crossing guard discovered the body of thirty-five-year-old Valerie McCorvey in an alley.

LAPD's Kilcoyne says there could be "one hundred different reasons" why the Grim Sleeper took a thirteen-year break from 1988 to 2002. "It could be we aren't connecting the cases . . . I am sure we don't have a lab report for everything he has done. There [could be] other cases that he has done that could drastically eliminate the gap," and perhaps solve more murders.

Former FBI profiler Gregg McCrary says serial killers who take long breaks from carnage are "the exception to the rule," and that makes LA's sociopath tougher to figure out. Authors David Canter and Laurence Alison in their 1997 book, *Criminal Detection and the Psychology of Crime*, studied 101 American serial murderers and found that the average "offending period" lasts 3.75 years. A "significant percentage" spent about a year killing. The longest active period was seventeen years.

Since that book was published, Altemio Sanchez, dubbed the "Bike Path Killer," a family man loved by his neighbors, has shattered that record. Sanchez took long breaks during twenty-five years of raping and killing before being captured in 2006. During his breaks, he hung out with prostitutes. "They liked the guy," McCrary says.

Los Angeles serial killer Chester Turner, who was given the death penalty in May 2007, killed women after he got into fights with his girlfriends, who remained relatively safe—and unaware. Says McCrary, "The stress can be a motivator. A bad day at work, or a fight with your wife."

The fact that a long-lived serial killer is operating in Los Angeles got its only headlines in 2006, *when LA Weekly* broke the news that Inglewood detective Jeffrey Steinhoff was hot on the trail of a man he thought had killed teenage runaway Princess Berthomieux. Steinhoff believed the killer of the then-ten victims was Roger Hausmann, a repo man from Fresno. But Hausmann was white. The LAPD's sole survivor and eyewitness, Victim No. 9, said she had been shot by a black man with short hair, driving an orange car.

Even so, Detective Steinhoff discovered that Hausmann had been picked up for kidnapping two black teens, who told Fresno detectives Hausmann had bragged about killing prostitutes in LA Steinhoff also learned that Hausmann was the sole suspect in a series of prostitute murders in Fresno, and one prostitute told detectives that while beating her, he had exclaimed, "You're harder to kill than the other ones!"

Steinhoff also found that Hausmann had been issued a parking ticket in Inglewood around the time of Berthomieux's death. So in June 2006, a judge issued a search warrant to obtain Hausmann's DNA. From his lockup in Fresno County Jail, he denied his involvement to the *Weekly*. DNA tests proved he was telling the truth.

Short-lived media coverage at the time explained that Los Angeles had a serial killer afoot, one who had murdered ten people. But, last year, he killed again—and Shepard and Kilcoyne don't believe his gruesome work is done. "Somehow, he has slipped through the cracks," Shepard says. "I have to think the worst, that he is going to continue. It has been going on for twenty-three years—at least."

What stands out most starkly today is how few resources the LAPD's top man, Bratton, and his City Hall boss, Villaraigosa, have applied to catching the most persistent serial killer in California history. It is shocking to the victims' families, and to the few who know about it in the community, that an active serial killer continues to operate without political outcry.

"It really hurts my heart," says Minister Pat Jones. "Come on, twenty-three years? That's a lifetime. We need to stop this person."

Laverne Peters bitterly recalls how, "[The police] went all the way to Aruba," for the widely covered Natalee Holloway murder investigation. Picking at a salad at a Denny's in Fontana, the fed-up mother of victim Janecia Peters adds, "You don't just get into your car and drive to Aruba . . . I am really starting to have a problem with it . . . Why wouldn't you offer rewards? I guess no council member is really interested. I am just a mother who wishes they would say something about my daughter, like they say about every other kid."

A little more than a year ago, Bratton finally formed the secret 800 Task Force. Kilcoyne says it was initially kept under wraps because "my instructions from the prior captain" of the Robbery-Homicide Unit, which oversees it, were, "We aren't talking to the media, and that is that."

At that time, detectives still needed to "get up to speed on the case," he says. "A year ago, we weren't sure if there was going to be a flurry of murders again." Although not his decision to make, Kilcoyne, pressed by the Weekly as to why the LAPD brass and City Hall have not warned the public, says, "I don't think it will harm us to acknowledge this. I don't think we are hiding a secret that there is a 'Night Stalker' out there."

Quietly, during the past year, the 800 Task Force has chased leads as far as Florida and Texas, tailed suspects for weeks who turned out to be dead ends, and abruptly materialized at autopsies and crime scenes involving at least a dozen newly dumped bodies. Last fall, they arrested a guy who preyed on prostitutes; his DNA wasn't right. They are combing through evidence gathered from thirty body dumps dating to the eighties, with a crime analyst inputting each clue into a giant "automated filing cabinet."

But the detectives' palpable sense of urgency—their fear that he is killing even now—doesn't seem to extend to Bratton. Last May, the 800 Task Force's six detectives were required to move, giving up their space to a cold-case sexual-assault unit. That ate up several days, as the 800 Task Force detectives transported their fat murder books, files and documents to a cramped space five floors below. Inglewood detective Loyd Waters says that unwelcome disruption "threw them off."

Lately, Kilcoyne says Bratton has grown concerned about the secrecy of the task force, concluding that LAPD has an "obligation to make the public aware." But if that's true, Chief Bratton has yet to do anything about it. Bratton has never mentioned the serial killer in a press release.

Kilcoyne says, "I have briefed Bratton four or five times. He is fully aware of what we are going through. He thinks we have our work cut out for us. Every time he sees us he says, 'Good luck.'"

A Bratton press aide on August 26 told the *Weekly* the chief was "too busy" to discuss the Grim Sleeper murders, and offered to provide comment from lower LAPD brass. On the same day, although Bratton could not set aside time to discuss the eleven murders in South Los Angeles, he got big media play at a Parker Center press conference—touting the arrest of the Westside's "Silverware Bandit," a man who had been stealing cutlery and china.

Meanwhile, the miffed Bernie Parks Jr., speaking to the *Weekly* from the Denver convention, said with obvious irritation: "We are trying to get answers from them, and hopefully get the right answer soon."

Some of those answers may come from much further north, where Attorney General Brown earned a few headlines in May by publicly backing the use of familial DNA testing. However, his spokesman, Gareth Lacy, tells the *Weekly* that Brown is still months away from allowing any comparisons to the existing one million profiles in the state felon DNA archives. Brown, who is almost certainly running for governor in 2010, has been walking a political tightrope, trying to look like a law-and-order guy when he was mayor of crime-riddled Oakland, but more recently trying to woo liberal voters as the state attorney general who most hates global warming.

Until Brown gives the go-ahead to his lab, allowing state Department of Justice scientists in Richmond to compare prisoners' DNA with saliva and other DNA taken from Grim Sleeper murder scenes, Kilcoyne says: "It will take old-fashioned police work. We just can't wait for [Brown] to give us a link." If the killer "is a family man or goes home to his wife or kids . . . we might never find him."

Victims' families are demanding more transparency—and they have words of caution for Angelenos. Mary Taylor, the aunt of Valerie McCorvey, suggests that if the eleven known victims had been relatives of a City Hall politician or police officer, authorities would have cracked these cases long ago. But her niece Valerie lived a wild life, and that, Taylor believes, damned her—first with the killer, and then with the powers that be. "Hers," Taylor says, "is going to be one of those cold cases they never solve."

Monique Alexander's father, Porter, sits in a chair in his quiet, hospitable home in South Los Angeles, wondering if the killer will strike while Brown, Bratton, and Villaraigosa hide behind their bureaucracies. "He's a guy who has the area mapped," Alexander says. "He's a guy with a mindset, who is smart enough to back off and wait. I don't think he has left. He . . . can start this mess all over again."

August 27, 2008

Author's Afterword

My family were all voracious readers. I was always reading newspapers, and I had this natural curiosity to find out everything. That's what got me into journalism.

I think the best part of my job is interviewing people. Because I'm a police reporter, I really enjoy talking to police, and I like learning about their investigations. One of the things that brought me into crime reporting was that I like finding out how the police solve crimes. I always thought that was fascinating— just how they went about doing that. I write murder stories, so I was always curious about what made the murderers tick and why they did what they did. And also, even though it was very hard to talk to the families, I liked talking to them, and I liked to get their stories out there. One of the most important parts to me was to get the information out there, especially if it's an unsolved crime, so family members don't feel at a loss. A lot of times, over the years, police forget about cases so writing the story brings the attention to the public, and I think it helps family members.

When I was doing the Grim Sleeper story, I was talking to some family members who hadn't spoken to the police for twenty to twenty-five years. They just wanted to talk; they just wanted someone to listen to them, to say, "My God, my daughter's been dead for twenty years."

My first long-form crime story was called "Two Against One," and it took place in Redlands, California. It was kind of like a lovers' triangle. It was a young girl named Kelly Bullwinkle, and she was murdered by her two best friends, a guy and a girl. Her body was found in an orange grove, and she'd gone missing for months. Her best friends went out on the search and passed out fliers, and it turned out that they were responsible for her death, and they had buried her in the orange grove. That was my first decent experience with the police, because they ended up giving me almost their entire homicide book. I was able to find out the details of what happened and how they had built their case against the two friends.

I guess my weakness is I have a need to overreport in everything I do. Which is sometimes good and sometimes not. When I worked at the *Daily Beast*, you had to write stories really quickly—but it's my instinct to want to really know everything about a story before I write it. It's hard to write a story when you don't know everything about it. I tend to overreport because I feel like I want to know every detail. Reporting is number one for me, and writing is very difficult, in my opinion, and it never gets any easier. I used to work with a guy at the *LA Weekly*, an older guy, and I asked him, "Does this ever get easier?" I thought he was a fantastic writer, but he was like, "No, it never does." I was like, "Oh, God, don't tell me that."

I'm most proud of keeping the Grim Sleeper case open with the public in Los Angeles. This case sat on the shelf for many years and then the police realized the killer had struck again. But the police didn't want to alert the public that there was a serial killer out there. I thought it was important that the families and the community knew. I mean, this guy was going after young women, some of them on the streets. I thought it was important for the community to know, including the girls on the streets, that there was a serial killer out there. Whether the girls wanted to listen to the warning or not, at least they would know. Putting that out, publishing stories about it, keeping it out there, informing the community was, I think, very important, and that's what I'm most proud of.

After they started the task force, it took the police three years to catch him; throughout that time I kept writing stories. There were press conferences that barely anyone attended except for me. I just kept it out in the public, I just didn't want people to forget, and there was a fear that they might disassemble the task force, so I tried to keep the pressure on. I thought that continued press on the subject would keep the task force going. There are so many cases that go cold and detectives move on. That's exactly what happened originally. They had detectives on the case in the eighties, because there were a slew of murders, and then they disbanded the task force, and no one realized that the killer kept killing. I think it's important to keep these stories out there so people don't forget.

It's kind of sad that people today just want short quick stories. They don't have time anymore—they don't have the attention span to sit down and read a long-form story. Any time it's out there, I think it's important, because you can't do short Pulitzer Prize stories. They take time.

Dana Priest

Dana Priest is an investigative reporter for the *Washington Post*. Prior to that, she was the newspaper's intelligence reporter and its Pentagon correspondent. She covered the invasion of Panama (1989), reported from Iraq (1990), and covered the Kosovo war (1999). She traveled with Army Special Forces in Asia, Africa, and South America and with Army infantry units on peacekeeping duty in Bosnia, Kosovo, and Afghanistan. She has written extensively about the CIA's and the Joint Special Operations Command's counterterrorism operations and has documented the proliferation of US counterterrorism agencies and the private industry they rely on.

Priest has won many major journalism awards including the 2008 Pulitzer Prize for Public Service for "The Other Walter Reed" and the 2006 Pulitzer Prize for her work on CIA secret prisons and counterterrorism operations.

She authored two best-selling books, "Top Secret America: The Rise of the New Security State" (Little, Brown) in 2011 and "The Mission: Waging War and Keeping Peace With America's Military" (W. W. Norton) in 2003.

Priest works regularly with PBS' FRONTLINE, appears on network and cable television, and frequently addresses college, military, diplomatic, foreign policy, and foreign audiences. She lives with her family in Washington, DC.

CIA Holds Terror Suspects in Secret Prisons

The CIA's extreme interrogation operations set up after 9/11 are revealed for the first time.

The CIA has been hiding and interrogating some of its most important al Qaeda captives at a Soviet-era compound in Eastern Europe, according to US and foreign officials familiar with the arrangement.

The secret facility is part of a covert prison system set up by the CIA nearly four years ago that at various times has included sites in eight countries, including Thailand, Afghanistan, and several democracies in Eastern Europe, as well as a small center at the Guantanamo Bay prison in Cuba, according to current and former intelligence officials and diplomats from three continents.

The hidden global internment network is a central element in the CIA's unconventional war on terrorism. It depends on the cooperation of foreign intelligence services, and on keeping even basic information about the system secret from the public, foreign officials, and nearly all members of Congress charged with overseeing the CIA's covert actions.

The existence and locations of the facilities—referred to as "black sites" in classified White House, CIA, Justice Department, and congressional documents—are known to only a handful of officials in the United States and, usually, only to the president and a few top intelligence officers in each host country.

The CIA and the White House, citing national security concerns and the value of the program, have dissuaded Congress from demanding that the agency answer questions in open testimony about the conditions under which captives are held. Virtually nothing is known about who is kept in the facilities, what interrogation methods are employed with them, or how decisions are made about whether they should be detained or for how long.

While the Defense Department has produced volumes of public reports and testimony about its detention practices and rules after the abuse scandals at Iraq's Abu Ghraib prison and at Guantanamo Bay, the CIA has not even acknowledged the existence of its black sites. To do so, say officials familiar with the program, could open the US government to legal challenges, particularly in foreign courts, and increase the risk of political condemnation at home and abroad.

But the revelations of widespread prisoner abuse in Afghanistan and Iraq by the US military—which operates under published rules and transparent oversight of Congress—have increased concern among lawmakers, foreign governments, and human rights groups about the opaque CIA system. Those concerns escalated last month, when Vice President Richard Cheney and CIA Director Porter J. Goss asked Congress to exempt CIA employees from legislation already endorsed by ninety senators that would bar cruel and degrading treatment of any prisoner in US custody.

Although the CIA will not acknowledge details of its system, intelligence officials defend the agency's approach, arguing that the successful defense of the country requires that the agency be empowered to hold and interrogate suspected terrorists for as long as necessary and without restrictions imposed by the US legal system or even by the military tribunals established for prisoners held at Guantanamo Bay.

The *Washington Post* is not publishing the names of the Eastern European countries involved in the covert program, at the request of senior US officials. They argued that the disclosure might disrupt counterterrorism efforts in those countries and elsewhere and could make them targets of possible terrorist retaliation.

The secret detention system was conceived in the chaotic and anxious first months after the September 11, 2001, attacks, when the working assumption was that a second strike was imminent.

Since then, the arrangement has been increasingly debated within the CIA, where considerable concern lingers about the legality, morality, and practicality of holding even unrepentant terrorists in such isolation and secrecy, perhaps for the duration of their lives. Midlevel and senior CIA officers began arguing two years ago that the system was unsustainable and diverted the agency from its unique espionage mission.

"We never sat down, as far as I know, and came up with a grand strategy," said one former senior intelligence officer who is familiar with the program but not the location of the prisons. "Everything was very reactive. That's how you get to a situation where you pick people up, send them into a netherworld and don't say, 'What are we going to do with them afterwards?'"

It is illegal for the government to hold prisoners in such isolation in secret prisons in the United States, which is why the CIA placed them overseas, according to several former and current intelligence officials and other US government officials. Legal experts and intelligence officials said that the CIA's internment practices also would be considered illegal under the laws of several host countries, where detainees have rights to have a lawyer or to mount a defense against allegations of wrongdoing.

Host countries have signed the United Nations Convention Against Torture and Other Cruel, Inhuman or Degrading Treatment or Punishment, as has the United States. Yet CIA interrogators in the overseas sites are permitted to use the CIA's approved "Enhanced Interrogation Techniques," some of which are prohibited by the UN convention and by US military law. They include tactics such as "waterboarding," in which a prisoner is made to believe he or she is drowning.

Some detainees apprehended by the CIA and transferred to foreign intelligence agencies have alleged after their release that they were tortured, although it is unclear whether CIA personnel played a role in the alleged abuse. Given the secrecy surrounding CIA detentions, such accusations have heightened concerns among foreign governments and human rights groups about CIA detention and interrogation practices.

The contours of the CIA's detention program have emerged in bits and pieces over the past two years. Parliaments in Canada, Italy, France, Sweden, and the Netherlands have opened inquiries into alleged CIA operations that secretly captured their citizens or legal residents and transferred them to the agency's prisons.

More than one hundred suspected terrorists have been sent by the CIA into the covert system, according to current and former US intelligence officials and foreign sources. This figure, a rough estimate based on information from sources who said their knowledge of the numbers was incomplete, does not include prisoners picked up in Iraq.

The detainees break down roughly into two classes, the sources said.

About thirty are considered major terrorism suspects and have been held under the highest level of secrecy at black sites financed by the CIA and managed by agency personnel, including those in Eastern Europe and elsewhere, according to current and former intelligence officers and two other US government officials. Two locations in this category—in Thailand and on the grounds of the military prison at Guantanamo Bay—were closed in 2003 and 2004, respectively.

A second tier—which these sources believe includes more than seventy detainees—is a group considered less important, with less direct involvement in terrorism and having limited intelligence value. These prisoners, some of whom were originally taken to black sites, are delivered to intelligence services in Egypt, Jordan, Morocco, Afghanistan, and other countries, a process sometimes known as "rendition." While the first-tier black sites are run by CIA officers, the jails in these countries are operated by the host nations, with CIA financial assistance and, sometimes, direction.

Morocco, Egypt, and Jordan have said that they do not torture detainees, although years of State Department human rights reports accuse all three of chronic prisoner abuse.

The top thirty al Qaeda prisoners exist in complete isolation from the outside world. Kept in dark, sometimes underground cells, they have no recognized legal rights, and no one outside the CIA is allowed to talk with or even see them, or to otherwise verify their well-being, said current and former US and foreign government and intelligence officials.

Most of the facilities were built and are maintained with congressionally appropriated funds, but the White House has refused to allow the CIA to brief anyone except the House and Senate intelligence committees' chairmen and vice chairmen on the program's generalities.

The Eastern European countries that the CIA has persuaded to hide al Qaeda captives are democracies that have embraced the rule of law and individual rights after decades of Soviet domination. Each has been trying to cleanse its intelligence services of operatives who have worked on behalf of others—mainly Russia and organized crime.

The idea of holding terrorists outside the US legal system was not under consideration before September 11, 2001, not even for Osama bin Laden, according to former government officials. The plan was to bring bin Laden and his top associates into the US justice system for trial or to send them to foreign countries where they would be tried.

"The issue of detaining and interrogating people was never, ever discussed," said a former senior intelligence officer who worked in the CIA's Counterterrorist Center, or CTC, during that period. "It was against the culture and they believed information was best gleaned by other means."

On the day of the attacks, the CIA already had a list of what it called High-Value Targets from the al Qaeda structure, and as the World Trade Center and

Pentagon attack plots were unraveled, more names were added to the list. The question of what to do with these people surfaced quickly.

The CTC's chief of operations argued for creating hit teams of case officers and CIA paramilitaries that would covertly infiltrate countries in the Middle East, Africa and even Europe to assassinate people on the list, one by one.

But many CIA officers believed that the al Qaeda leaders would be worth keeping alive to interrogate about their network and other plots. Some officers worried that the CIA would not be very adept at assassination.

"We'd probably shoot ourselves," another former senior CIA official said.

The agency set up prisons under its covert action authority. Under US law, only the president can authorize a covert action, by signing a document called a presidential finding. Findings must not break US law and are reviewed and approved by CIA, Justice Department, and White House legal advisers.

Six days after the September 11 attacks, President Bush signed a sweeping finding that gave the CIA broad authorization to disrupt terrorist activity, including permission to kill, capture, and detain members of al Qaeda anywhere in the world.

It could not be determined whether Bush approved a separate finding for the black-sites program, but the consensus among current and former intelligence and other government officials interviewed for this article is that he did not have to.

Rather, they believe that the CIA general counsel's office acted within the parameters of the September 17 finding. The black-site program was approved by a small circle of White House and Justice Department lawyers and officials, according to several former and current US government and intelligence officials.

Among the first steps was to figure out where the CIA could secretly hold the captives. One early idea was to keep them on ships in international waters, but that was discarded for security and logistics reasons.

CIA officers also searched for a setting like Alcatraz Island. They considered the virtually unvisited islands in Lake Kariba in Zambia, which were edged with craggy cliffs and covered in woods. But poor sanitary conditions could easily lead to fatal diseases, they decided, and besides, they wondered, could the Zambians be trusted with such a secret?

Still without a long-term solution, the CIA began sending suspects it captured in the first month or so after September 11 to its longtime partners, the intelligence services of Egypt and Jordan.

A month later, the CIA found itself with hundreds of prisoners who were captured on battlefields in Afghanistan. A short-term solution was improvised.

The agency shoved its highest-value prisoners into metal shipping containers set up on a corner of the Bagram Air Base, which was surrounded with a triple perimeter of concertina-wire fencing. Most prisoners were left in the hands of the Northern Alliance, US-supported opposition forces who were fighting the Taliban.

"I remember asking: What are we going to do with these people?" said a senior CIA officer. "I kept saying, where's the help? We've got to bring in some help. We can't be jailers—our job is to find Osama."

Then came grisly reports, in the winter of 2001, that prisoners kept by allied Afghan generals in cargo containers had died of asphyxiation. The CIA asked Congress for, and was quickly granted, tens of millions of dollars to establish a larger, long-term system in Afghanistan, parts of which would be used for CIA prisoners.

The largest CIA prison in Afghanistan was code-named the Salt Pit. It was also the CIA's substation and was first housed in an old brick factory outside Kabul. In November 2002, an inexperienced CIA case officer allegedly ordered guards to strip naked an uncooperative young detainee, chain him to the concrete floor and leave him there overnight without blankets. He froze to death, according to four US government officials. The CIA officer has not been charged in the death.

The Salt Pit was protected by surveillance cameras and tough Afghan guards, but the road leading to it was not safe to travel and the jail was eventually moved inside Bagram Air Base. It has since been relocated off the base.

By mid-2002, the CIA had worked out secret black-site deals with two countries, including Thailand and one Eastern European nation, current and former officials said. An estimated $100 million was tucked inside the classified annex of the first supplemental Afghanistan appropriation.

Then the CIA captured its first big detainee, in March 28, 2002. Pakistani forces took Abu Zubaida, al Qaeda's operations chief, into custody and the CIA whisked him to the new black site in Thailand, which included underground interrogation cells, said several former and current intelligence officials. Six months later, September 11 planner Ramzi Binalshibh was also captured in Pakistan and flown to Thailand.

But after published reports revealed the existence of the site in June 2003, Thai officials insisted the CIA shut it down, and the two terrorists were moved elsewhere, according to former government officials involved in the matter. Work between the two countries on counterterrorism has been lukewarm ever since.

In late 2002 or early 2003, the CIA brokered deals with other countries to establish black-site prisons. One of these sites—which sources said they believed to be the CIA's biggest facility now—became particularly important when the agency realized it would have a growing number of prisoners and a shrinking number of prisons.

Thailand was closed, and sometime in 2004 the CIA decided it had to give up its small site at Guantanamo Bay. The CIA had planned to convert that into a state-of-the-art facility, operated independently of the military. The CIA pulled out when US courts began to exercise greater control over the military detainees, and agency officials feared judges would soon extend the same type of supervision over their detainees.

In hindsight, say some former and current intelligence officials, the CIA's problems were exacerbated by another decision made within the Counterterrorist Center at Langley.

The CIA program's original scope was to hide and interrogate the two dozen or so al Qaeda leaders believed to be directly responsible for the September 11 attacks, or who posed an imminent threat, or had knowledge of the larger al Qaeda network. But as the volume of leads pouring into the CTC from abroad increased, and the capacity of its paramilitary group to seize suspects grew, the CIA began apprehending more people whose intelligence value and links to terrorism were less certain, according to four current and former officials.

The original standard for consigning suspects to the invisible universe was lowered or ignored, they said. "They've got many, many more who don't reach any threshold," one intelligence official said.

Several former and current intelligence officials, as well as several other US government officials with knowledge of the program, express frustration that the White House and the leaders of the intelligence community have not made it a priority to decide whether the secret internment program should continue in its current form, or be replaced by some other approach.

Meanwhile, the debate over the wisdom of the program continues among CIA officers, some of whom also argue that the secrecy surrounding the program is not sustainable.

"It's just a horrible burden," said the intelligence official.

November 2, 2005

Author's Afterword

I was drawn to journalism for a few reasons. One is the independence that you can have. As soon as I started working at the newspaper at the University of California, Santa Cruz, I realized I could figure out what I wanted to cover. I thought that was a lot of power for a student journalist, and that was a tremendous draw. That's sort of the lesson I took with me into my career—to be independent, not to lean on editors to figure out what I would write about. I loved that part.

The other reason I love journalism is because you go to places and talk to people who ordinarily you wouldn't have any reason to meet, people who are very different from yourself. You get to experience in a little way the lives of people you'd never have actually met. That has always been a big component for me. And the change of pace every day is another thing that really attracted me to it. You do one story, or a series of stories, and then you move on, sometimes to a completely different subject. It feeds a curious mind.

The other big thing is that journalists can actually have an effect on society. The chance to actually do something, to right wrongs, to point out injustices or illegal acts—that's really attractive to me, and possibly the strongest reason that I was attracted to investigative journalism. Unlike the traditional quick stories that newspaper writers do, investigative reporters get to dig deeper, to make a better case by finding more facts, to go places where daily journalists don't have the time to go.

Personally, my work has seen to it that I have many fewer stereotypes of people than I did before. I don't mean your typical racial stereotypes, I mean more occupational since I covered the Pentagon. I probably came to the Pentagon with a set of stereotypes about people who served in the military, and those turned out quickly to be false. At one time, I had stereotypes about certain people who worked in government—and those turned out to be false as well. So I really have learned that even though we look often at institutions and how they operate and whether they're doing what they say they're doing, whether the government is doing what it says it's doing, they really are made up of individuals who make individual decisions, and I think I've learned that in a way I didn't know was so important. It's the government, yes. But it's run by people.

I never really experienced many gender obstacles. Sometimes I was the young reporter in an older, male field because my general field is national security, but I never saw that as an obstacle for a lot of reasons. The main obstacle I face is probably pretty typical of all women *and* men in our field, which is getting people to talk, especially the ones who are not *supposed* to talk to you. The further I went into the world of national security, and then into the world of the intelligence community, the harder it became. In some instances, these people could lose their jobs and be prosecuted. So that's the real challenge, finding the whistle-blowers and the sources and coaxing them into your confidence.

In my career I'm most proud of two things. First, there were the stories that broke the news of the super prisons for terrorists and the counterterrorism role that the CIA played. The other was the series about the horrible conditions at Walter Reed Army Hospital. Those two stories both ended up creating change. They had a big effect on public discussions. The secret prisons were eventually closed, and the Walter Reed stories led to the examination of how veterans were being cared for in this country. There have been a lot of improvements since.

I feel like young students are getting a multiplatform education. But because there's such an emphasis on that, I think some students get shortchanged on the old-fashioned notion of dogged, hard-nosed, investigative reporting. That's one reason why I decided to go into teaching, which I'm doing now at the University of Maryland's School of Journalism, because I really want this generation to understand the power of reporting in its most basic, purest sense without the bells and whistles. The facts are the facts, regardless. You don't have a story without the story, and that always takes a lot of hard work and heart.

Corinne Reilly

Corinne Reilly joined the *Virginian Pilot* in 2009 as a military reporter after four years at the *Merced Sun-Star*, in Merced, CA, her first newspaper. She left Hampton Roads for the *Washington Post* in 2012 but returned to the *Pilot* in 2013. She has reported from Iraq, Afghanistan, and Haiti, and was named a finalist for the 2012 Pulitzer Prize in feature writing. A native of San Jose, CA, she is a graduate of the University of California, Santa Barbara.

A Chance in Hell

The war's worst casualties go to the NATO hospital
at Kandahar Airfield

Part 1

The doctors can hear the wailing before their patient is even in sight.

A second later, a flight medic bursts through the trauma department doors. His face is serious. He's short of breath. Outside, corpsmen rush to unload a soldier from a military ambulance that carried him here from a Black Hawk. Two dozen doctors, nurses, and surgeons have been awaiting their arrival.

"Who am I talking to?" the medic shouts.

"Here!" blurts Lt. Cmdr. Ron Bolen, the head of the hospital's trauma department. He points to the Navy doctor leading the team that will examine the soldier first.

"OK, you've got tourniquets on both legs," the medic gulps. "The right one is totally gone to at least the knee. He lost a lot of blood."

The doctor hurriedly inquires about vital signs, fluids administered in the field, and the weapon that caused the explosion that did all this.

The next question would usually be whether the patient is conscious, but this time no one has to ask.

Outside, the wailing is getting louder.

It's a Sunday morning. The soldier is being wheeled inside. Ashen and shaking, he asks Bolen if this is the day he's going to die.

"Don't lie to me," he pleads.

Bolen looks the soldier hard in the eyes. "You're not going to die," he says calmly. "And I don't lie."

Someone counts to three and the soldier is lifted in one fluid motion from the stretcher to a trauma bed. Seven people are working on him now, ripping away dirty clothes, starting IVs to replace lost blood and calling out vital signs.

"Temp is 97.9!"

"BP is 135 over 65!"

"Pulse is 117!"

A doctor cuts the tourniquet off the leg that's still intact and runs his finger down the sole of the pale foot. "Can you feel this?"

A few minutes later the soldier is in the operating room. He's writhing now more than shaking. Through the moans, he's mumbling three words over and over.

"This is bad. This is bad. This is bad."

He keeps lifting his head, trying to get a look.

On the end of the bed, the last right boot he ever put on is lying at an angle that's all wrong, a sweaty foot still inside. The calf above it is a shredded mess of uniform, flesh, dirt and grass. Nothing about it looks real.

Above that there is no discernible knee, just a thin stretch of filthy skin barely hanging onto what's left of a thigh, which looks a lot like the mangled calf, except for one thing: Among the blood and mud, there is a little white inchworm, scrunching and straightening, slowly making its way across a bit of dying muscle.

Somehow it survived an explosion the soldier may not.

Around him, a dozen people are preparing for surgery. The room smells like damp earth, rubbing alcohol, and blood.

"Hang in there one more minute, bud," the anesthesiologist says, trying uselessly to soothe his patient. "Everything's gonna be OK in just a minute."

A nurse walks in. Next to the boot, she sets down a medical form.

It says the soldier's name is Eddie Ward.

It says he is nineteen years old.

Ward was nine when the war in Afghanistan started. Like many of the men fighting here now, he hadn't finished the fourth grade when the first wave of troops landed.

Nearly a decade later, it's no wonder that most Americans just want it done, that month after month, the public opinion surveys come back the same: The war doesn't seem to be going well. We should have left by now. We're tired of thinking about it, tired of worrying about it.

"I understand that it's old news," Bolen says. "The stuff you hear about now—it's all troop withdrawals and winding down."

He closes his eyes for a moment and rubs them. It's been a while since he slept. "All I can say is we got nineteen new traumas yesterday. Nothing is winding..."

He's interrupted by the beeping of the pager that never leaves his side. He unclips it from his waist and reads the message.

"IED blast," he says. "Three patients en route."

In military parlance, this place is called a Role 3 medical treatment facility, meaning that its role is to save the war's most critical casualties.

Role 1s are typically battalion aid stations. Twos are usually more advanced than civilian urgent care clinics. Role 3s are essentially hospitals, but unlike 4s and 5s, such as the military medical center in Landstuhl, Germany, or Walter Reed in the United States, they are not designed to provide long-term care or rehabilitation.

Instead, Role 3s operate close to the front. Their doctors and nurses deal nearly exclusively with trauma. They take the worst of what a war dishes out, and for the twenty-four to forty-eight hours that a soldier or Marine is theirs, they do whatever it takes with whatever they have to stave off death until he can be flown out of the fighting.

In the case of this Role 3, the worst casualties are worse than they are anyplace else.

Owned by NATO and run by the US Navy, the hospital is staffed in part by personnel from Portsmouth Naval Medical Center. It is in the heart of Taliban country at Kandahar Airfield, a sprawling, heavily fortified southern NATO base that's attacked with rockets so routinely that no one bothers to panic anymore when the sirens sound.

Even staff members who've served multiple combat tours say they've never seen injuries as devastating—or as numerous—as those they witness here. Nearly three-quarters of their patients come directly from the battlefield, the vast majority of them victims of insurgent-made bombs—what the military calls improvised explosive devices, or IEDs. Their signature wounds are double- and triple-limb amputations with severe injuries to the pelvis and genitals.

NATO established the hospital after the start of the war, and for years it consisted of interconnected plywood shelters and tents. A little over a year ago, it moved into a seventy-thousand-square-foot building. The outside is made of two-foot-thick, rocket-resistant concrete. Inside, it looks like a small version of any modern Western hospital.

The only difference, aside from the camouflage scrubs and the sound of C-130 cargo planes taking off in the distance, is that this place is far better prepared to treat Afghanistan's brand of serious trauma.

"If these soldiers landed in the same condition at any major hospital back home instead of here, there is no doubt in my mind that many more of them would not live," says Capt. Mike McCarten, a fifty-nine-year-old Navy doctor and the hospital's commanding officer. "We can't do everything. We can't treat cancer. But when it comes to war injuries—to IEDs, to gunshot wounds—I believe we are the very best there is."

Indeed, the Kandahar Role 3 is among the most advanced hospitals ever to operate in a combat zone. With a core trauma staff of roughly one hundred doctors, surgeons, nurses, and corpsmen, it sees an average of about two hundred patients a month—fewer in winter and more in the spring and summer Taliban fighting seasons. Besides US Navy personnel and a few doctors from other American service branches, the staff includes NATO clinicians from Canada, Britain, and the Netherlands.

Patients come from across Afghanistan's southern half, almost always by helicopter because of the steep surrounding mountains, the dangers of traveling by road, and the need to get them here fast. In addition to coalition soldiers, they include Afghan civilians, members of the Afghan national army and police, and enemy combatants wounded in the fighting.

Incoming casualties arrive at the trauma department. Down the hall are three operating suites, twelve intensive-care beds and a thirty-five-bed intermediate care ward. The hospital's dozen surgeons include three orthopedic specialists and a neurosurgeon—one of two in Afghanistan. There is also an interventional radiologist adept at snaking catheters into places surgeons can't reach to stop bleeding, and a sixty-four-slice CT scanner that is more advanced than most in the United States.

For service members who arrive here with a pulse, the survival rate is between 97 and 98 percent, a remarkable record given the severity of their wounds.

The hospital owes this success as much to its people as to its equipment and specialties. Their skill and efficiency are products partly of all the medical lessons that a decade of brutal insurgent war teaches, and partly of the sheer volume of trauma that comes through their doors.

"When you see the same things day in and day out—patients with two or three extremities blown off, with really bad burns, or almost all their blood gone—you get very good at treating it," says Cmdr. Jim Sullivan, a Navy reservist and ER doctor from Southbridge, MA. "It sounds strange, but like anything else, practice makes perfect. And we get a lot of practice."

It is not uncommon for half a dozen category Alphas—the most critically wounded patients—to land here at once, or for doctors to go a month without a day off because of the unrelenting flow of casualties.

Sometimes it's clear what injury takes priority—the missing arm or the hemorrhaging femoral artery. Sometimes the worst wounds are hidden—internal bleeding or a snapped third vertebra. Some patients are unconscious. Others are excruciatingly aware.

The details are different every time, but once a patient lands, some things are inevitably the same.

There is always the initial rush to ease the pain, to assess the damage, to remove tourniquets, and to replace lost blood. There is almost always a hurried trip to the CT scanner, then an emergency surgery, and then the moment the patient wakes up.

That, too, tends to unfold predictably.

He is usually groggy and confused with little recollection of how he got here. His eyes search for a person. They settle on a doctor or a nurse. And then he strains to ask whatever question comes to his mind first.

Where am I? How long have I been here? Will I walk again? Do I still have knees?

For those who are there to answer, none of it ever feels routine.

"We meet a lot of people on the worst day of their life," Sullivan says.

It is a job that has existed for as long as there has been war. With every new medical advancement, it should get easier.

It never does.

Most of the staff volunteered for this. They trained for it. They asked colleagues who've done tours here what to expect.

But none of it truly prepared them for the physical and emotional slog.

On good days, it is pulling nails and rocks from the wounds of a soldier who still has all four limbs. It is taking the crumpled piece of paper he has carried on every patrol, dialing the scribbled numbers, and handing him the phone so he can hear his girlfriend's voice.

Other days, it is unfolding a flag and draping it over a body. It is standing at attention on the tarmac outside as nine caskets are loaded onto a US-bound cargo plane.

"There are some things you can't unsee," Bolen says.

There are no designated breaks, no nights off. If it sounds bad enough when the staffwide page goes out, everybody drops what they're doing—showering, sleeping, working out at the gym across base—and literally runs to beat the helicopter.

Time loses meaning unless it's counting down to a patient's arrival; days and weeks tend to blur into one another, because at the end of a shift, there is no going home. There are only long-distance phone calls and conversations over Skype in which they brush past questions from husbands and wives about what they did that day. They all learn early on that trying to explain it only causes worry, and the people on the other end never know what to say anyway.

And in the back of their minds, hanging over it all, one nagging thought persists: the people they treat are not, in fact, the war's worst casualties.

Because the worst ones never make it here.

"That's where the real sacrifices are happening—out there," says Cmdr. Joseph Taddeo, a general surgeon from Portsmouth. "What we're doing in here, inside this hospital, this is nothing. You see the stuff we see and all you can really think is, 'I've got it good. I've got it easy.'

"Compared to the guys out there, I'm just a tourist here."

Ward is unconscious on the operating table.

He's on his back with both arms out straight. There's a breathing tube in his mouth. His eyes are taped shut.

Looking at him now, quiet and still for the first time since he arrived, you begin to notice things about him besides his terrible wounds.

You notice how young his face is. You notice that he's tall.

You notice his muscles, how lean and toned he is.

You figure he has to be an athlete.

Maybe he is—was—a football player.

You notice the two words scrawled on the back of his forearm, and you wonder whether, after this, he'd get them tattooed there again: "No regrets."

Then you start to think about everything that lies ahead for him, assuming he survives. You think about how he's going to feel when he wakes up after this surgery and realizes that it wasn't all a nightmare. You think about how it will hit him all over again just as hard after the next operation.

And the next.

And the next.

You wonder whether he has a wife. You wonder what he'll say when he makes the first phone call home, and what the person on the other end will say back.

You think about the long recovery, all the rehab, the prosthesis. You wonder what he dreamed about doing after the Army and whether he'll still be able to do it.

Then you realize you've seen him before.

"I recognize this guy from the gym," says one of the staff who is about to operate on him, a Navy lieutenant and orthopedic physician assistant named Joelle Annandono.

She stops her preparations and stares hard at Ward's face.

The room falls quiet. No one knows what to say.

A few seconds later, a Canadian surgeon leading the operation breaks the silence.

"We need to start," he says.

July 31, 2011

Part 2

For the weight of what the surgeon is about to do, it seems like it should take more than a few snips.

But just like that, in two easy squeezes of the scissors—three or four seconds maybe—Lt. Cmdr. Kirk Sundby severs the thin stretch of tissue connecting Eddie Ward's calf and thigh, and the soldier's right leg is no longer his.

Sundby, a Canadian orthopedic specialist, turns to a Dutch army nurse who is standing by with a large red plastic bag. They place the leg inside, the boot still on it.

"Anything else?" the nurse asks.

Sundby drops in a stray, five-inch piece of femur. Broken and jagged at both ends, it's been stripped clean of flesh by the upward force of the blast. "That's it for now," he says.

The nurse nods, then sets the bag on the floor near the door.

The half-dozen doctors in the room survey what's left. With no skin to contain it, the pile of loose muscle that is the end of Ward's thigh is spread out wide on the table. Before it can be packed back inside, it must be thoroughly cleaned. A surgical technician passes Sundby a bottle of saline. With one hand he pours it over the mess of flesh, and with the other he begins massaging out all the dirt and grass that the explosion blasted in.

Three others help, picking out bits of rock and gravel as they go.

"This is one of the dirtiest wounds I've seen," says Navy Lt. Joelle Annandono, an orthopedic physician assistant based in Bremerton, WA.

Several bottles of saline and iodine later, the first wash is done, and the doctors move on to the next step: cutting away all the tissue that is dead or dying. Pink and red are good colors. Purple and blue must be removed.

This time, there is a lot of the latter—at least several pounds.

"This is getting really high," Sundby says, meaning the amputation. "I didn't think it would be this high when I first saw him."

Nearly three hours after they started, the surgical team begins to wrap up. The Dutch army nurse picks up the red bag. He seals it with white tape, then places it inside another red bag and seals that too. As he carries it out of the operating room, his back hunches over with the weight. He sets it down on the floor in a nearby office. In a couple of hours, it will be transferred to the military morgue next door for incineration.

The doctors pack Ward's wound with rolls of wet gauze, then fold over skin they saved to cover it. Sundby loosely stitches it all together for easy reopening; in a day or so, when Ward lands in Germany, everything will be washed out again.

The surgery is done now, but Annandono is not.

She removes her blood-soaked gown, then wets a blue cloth and rubs a few spots of red off Ward's chest. She places her hand over his heart and holds it there a few moments while she wipes bits of dirt from his face. Then she rewets the cloth and scrubs the yellow iodine stains off his remaining foot.

"I don't want it to be a funny color when he wakes up and looks down," she says.

"What he's not going to see will be hard enough."

Ask about his toughest day here, and Lt. Cmdr. Ron Bolen answers with a name.

"First Lt. Daren Hidalgo," he says. "He's the first one I lost."

He pauses for a moment, then says Hidalgo was twenty-four, and his injuries just weren't survivable.

He pauses again, this time for several seconds, and then he repeats himself, as if he's just gone over it again in his head to confirm that nothing more could have been done.

"Yeah, they just weren't survivable."

A forty-one-year-old Navy reservist and nurse from Nashville, Tenn., Bolen got here in February. Since then, he's rarely been away from the hospital for longer than a few hours at a time. He heads the trauma department. It's among the most demanding and critical positions here, though he rejects that suggestion. "Every job here is the hardest job," he says.

He has a round, pale face, soft gray hair, and bright blue eyes made brighter by the matching color of his scrub top, which he usually pairs with desert-camouflage pants. He's unassuming and thoughtful—the kind of person who can soothe a patient just by squeezing his hand or uttering a few calm words. In his pocket he keeps a small, green notebook where he jots down things he wants to remember. Hidalgo's name is there, along with every other service member who has died on his watch.

"I feel like if I write them down, they won't be forgotten," he says.

It's clear he feels every loss; he makes no attempt to deny the overwhelming emotional impact of the job. Instead, he lets it in and makes sense of it the best he can.

"Yeah, war is terrible and people die here," he says. "But their sacrifices mean something, and at least this hospital gives them a chance. It's what I always have to come back to."

It's a perspective that many members of the staff embrace: As bad as Afghanistan is, it would be worse if they weren't here. It comforts some more than others. There are days when it helps and days when it doesn't.

"The things we see routinely here, they aren't natural. They're not supposed to be part of the normal human experience," says the hospital's commanding officer, Capt. Mike McCarten, who has been a Navy doctor for twenty-eight years. "We're not wired to make sense of stuff like this, so it's not in our best interest to become emotionally involved.

"Of course, we all do it anyway."

Many members of the staff experience flashbacks and nightmares. A lot are on Ambien to help them sleep. Tours at the hospital used to last a year, but after too many caregivers returned home with symptoms of post-traumatic stress disorder, the Navy reduced rotations to six or seven months.

"There are a few holdovers who've been here almost a year," says the hospital's director of surgery, Capt. Tim McCullough, who's from Suffolk. "You can tell who they are."

Sometimes staff members ask to stay longer. McCarten almost always says no. "If they're gonna have a shot at making it home roughly the same person they were when they left, they have to go," he says.

Then he adds, "For me, this is the capstone of my career, and I think a lot of the staff would say this is the single most important thing they'll ever do in their professional lives.

"But it can also be hell on earth."

A little while after Ward's surgery, three soldiers are standing at his bedside in the ICU. They're talking softly so as not to wake him, though he's so heavily sedated that even shouting probably wouldn't do it.

None of the soldiers knows Ward personally; they're liaisons from his division. They say he's a mortarman with the 2nd Brigade Combat Team, 101st Airborne Division, based at Fort Campbell, KY. His unit has been in Afghanistan nearly a year. Ward is not the first of its members to end up here. His visitors don't know much about what happened, just that it was a land mine, and that he was on a hilltop in an area where Americans don't usually operate when he stepped on it.

One of them hands a zip-lock bag to Ward's nurse. It contains everything he had on him at the time of the explosion: an iPod in a purple case, a watch with dried blood on the face, his military ID, and a neatly folded twenty-dollar bill.

"Can this stay with him?" the soldier asks. "There's nothing too valuable, no wedding ring or anything."

The visitors leave, and Ward is alone except for the nurse, who is carefully monitoring his heart rate, blood pressure, temperature, and respiratory rate. She adjusts his breathing tube to a position she thinks is more comfortable. She presses her hand around the toes on his remaining foot to make sure they're warm, an indication of good blood flow.

Then she summons another nurse to help her change his bedding. "He already bled through the sheets," she says.

A few hours later, a general arrives with an entourage to present Ward's Purple Heart. He says it's OK that Ward is still asleep; often when medals are awarded here, the recipients aren't conscious.

The general leans in and speaks softly into Ward's ear. "I don't know if you can hear me now," he says, "but I'm going to talk to you anyway, just in case."

He tells Ward that the Purple Heart is the oldest medal awarded to US service members, that it was established by George Washington. He says he would have rather done this when Ward was awake, but presenting it to him here, before he's flown out of Afghanistan in a few hours, seemed more important.

Ward is still on a ventilator. He's got at least half a dozen tubes running to his mouth and arms. He isn't wearing a shirt, so the general pins the Purple Heart to the bedsheet.

Everyone stands at attention while the orders are read aloud. Then the general leans in again, and someone in the entourage snaps a few pictures.

"So the soldier can see what happened," the photographer says.

The general gently places a hand on Ward's forehead. "Thank you for your valor and your courage," he says.

The group leaves, and Ward is alone again.

A few minutes later, his nurse returns to his bedside.

"I never stay anymore when they do the Purple Hearts," she says. "I always end up crying."

It's dark out when the call comes in.

You can see the exhaustion on Bolen's face. It's been an especially long day.

It started early with three American soldiers with the 10th Mountain Division. They were inside a fifteen-ton armored vehicle when an IED flipped it upside down. The truck commander got away with surprisingly minor injuries. The driver literally dug his way out. The gunner wasn't as lucky; he spent more than an hour trapped underneath in the turret and suffered burns to his legs and torso.

Soon after the soldiers landed, the pagers all buzzed again. More than forty Afghans were injured in a bus crash, possibly precipitated by an IED blast, and the six most critical patients were flown here—serious spinal and head injuries, several bone fractures, multiple intubations. Nearly the entire trauma staff was summoned, and it took them all day to get the last patient stable and into the ICU.

Now Bolen's pager is buzzing again. It's been less than an hour since the rest of the haggard staff dispersed to eat, sleep, or Skype relatives waking up in the States. Bolen was just about to do the same.

He reads the message. It's another IED. Two Americans this time, one with a suspected traumatic brain injury and the other with both legs amputated.

"The bird's thirty minutes out," he says. "Call a team back."

He walks to the board and writes it in:

> Trauma bay 1, category Alpha, double amp., U. S.
> Trauma bay 2, category Alpha, TBI, U. S.

Then he waits.

Back home, he's a flight nurse for Vanderbilt Medical Center, a civilian hospital. He earned a living as a paramedic while attending nursing school. Before Vanderbilt he worked as a critical care and ER nurse at Johns Hopkins and the Shock Trauma Center in Baltimore. He spent time in the Air Force and Army Reserve, then switched to the Navy eight years ago.

He has three kids. The youngest is ten. She worries a lot that he won't come home.

"All I can tell her is that I'm being careful and that I wouldn't have come here unless it was important," he says. "I think she gets it."

Twenty minutes pass, and then there's an update. Only one patient is coming now. The double amputee just died in the helicopter.

Bolen looks at his shoes. He needs a few seconds to take it in. Then he says the on-call team may go. No one else speaks.

McCullough, the director of surgery, clasps his hands on top of his head and looks to the ceiling.

A physician assistant in workout clothes—she was getting ready to go to the gym across base when her pager went off—shakes her head and walks out.

Then a corpsman who'd been out of the room when the update came asks what's going on.

"The double amp's an angel," Bolen says.

The corpsman's face tightens. He balls his right hand into a fist and punches it into his left palm. "We don't even get a chance to try?" he says. "That's bullshit!"

Bolen walks to the board.

He reaches for the eraser.

August 1, 2001

Author's Afterword

After college I was a bank teller for a couple of years. It was horribly boring. In college I'd been intrigued by two speakers I'd seen, both journalists, Sebastian Junger and Philip Gourevitch. Both wrote amazing books; I guess that planted a seed. I always thought of journalism as an unrealistic career, or something not a lot of people got the chance to do or to do well. But I was feeling stifled at my job, so I decided to give journalism a try. I took a news writing class at a junior college and I guess I never looked back.

In 2010, I embedded with a photographer in Afghanistan in order to tell the story of the NATO hospital at Kandahar Airfield. It took awhile to get permission—the military told us the longest a reporter had stayed on the airfield was three or four days, which was ridiculous to me—just to travel there took three to four days. Eventually I got permission to stay for two weeks.

Within two or three days the staff seemed comfortable about us being there. I was blown away by how trusting they were, actually. Within a couple of days they were allowing us into operating rooms to observe and photograph surgeries. The agreement was that we would get service members' permission at a later time, when they were well enough to consent. Based on other experiences I've had covering the military and reporting in health care settings, that's an amazing level of trust. We couldn't have done anything like this if we didn't have their trust. We lived in a modular building about a five-to-ten minute walk from the hospital on the base. Except when I was eating or sleeping or writing, I was at the hospital.

Originally, I envisioned the story as a topical series about the hospital. For example, they treated members of the Taliban; I thought that could be a story, what it's like to do that job. But within a couple of days, I knew that everything I was seeing didn't fit into nice categories. The entire place and everything happening there was the story.

My favorite thing to do is to tell the story of regular people in a way that makes other people care. Any time I feel like I've actually done that, I feel especially proud.

Being a journalist has changed me in so many ways. Being exposed to so many different people—I've learned a ton that I would never have learned in another job. I've become a more empathetic person, but it's also made me a tougher person. When you're writing about real people in desperate circumstances, the toll is both terrible and enlightening. You see things and make connections that you never could have known were there.

Over time, I've learned the value of putting myself in other people's shoes, especially the people I am writing about. In the beginning, I thought the right approach was to be sort of cold about things, but I've given up trying to do that. I think my stories are better for it.

Loretta Tofani

Loretta Tofani grew up in an apartment in the Bronx, the granddaughter of Italian immigrants. At age eleven she decided to become a journalist; she enjoyed writing and wanted to learn about the world firsthand. She became editor-in-chief of both her high school and college newspapers. At Fordham University, where she received her bachelor's degree, she learned about the role of journalist as social conscience. Inspired, she later wrote stories—including her series on jail rapes that won a Pulitzer Prize in 1983—that helped change broken systems. Loretta was a staff writer for the *Washington Post* from 1978 to 1987, and a staff writer for the *Philadelphia Inquirer* from 1987 to 2001. At the *Inquirer*, she was a foreign correspondent based in Beijing for four years, where she moved with her husband, John E. White MD, and her then-infant daughter, Nicole. Since leaving the *Inquirer*, Tofani has worked as a freelance writer and a businesswoman. A Fulbright scholar, Tofani has a master's in journalism from the University of California, Berkeley. In addition to the Pulitzer Prize, she has won numerous other national, regional, and local journalism awards. She lives in Oregon with her husband and children.

American Imports, Chinese Deaths

Chinese workers toil in dangerous factories
to make cheap products for export

Part 1

GUANGZHOU, China—The patients arrive every day in Chinese hospitals with disabling and fatal diseases acquired while making products for America.

On the sixth floor of the Guangzhou Occupational Disease and Prevention Hospital, Wei Chaihua, forty-four, sits on his iron-railed bed, tethered to an oxygen tank. He is dying of the lung disease silicosis, a result of making Char-Broil gas stoves sold in Utah and throughout the United States.

Down the hall, He Yuyun, thirty-six, who for years brushed America's furniture with paint containing benzene and other solvents, receives treatment for myelodysplastic anemia, a precursor to leukemia.

In another room rests Xiang Zhiqing, thirty-nine, her hair falling out and her kidneys beginning to fail from prolonged exposure to cadmium, which she placed in batteries sent to the United States.

"Do people in your country handle cadmium while they make batteries?" Xiang asks. "Do they also die from this?"

With each new report of lead detected on a made-in-China toy, Americans express outrage: These toys could poison children. But Chinese workers making the toys—and countless other products for America—touch and inhale carcinogenic materials every day, all day long. Benzene. Lead. Cadmium. Toluene. Nickel. Mercury.

Many are dying. They have fatal occupational diseases.

Mostly they are young, in their twenties and thirties and forties. But they are facing slow difficult deaths, caused by the hazardous substances they use to make products for the world—and for America. Some say these workers are paying the real price for America's cheap goods from China.

"In terms of responsibility to Chinese society, this is a big problem for Americans," said Zhou Litai, a lawyer from the city of Chongqing who has represented tens of thousands of dying workers in Chinese courts.

The toxins and hazards exist in virtually every industry, including furniture, shoes, car parts, electronic items, jewelry, clothes, toys, and batteries, interviews with workers confirm. The interviews were corroborated by legal documents, medical journal articles, medical records, import documents, and official Chinese reports.

Although these products are being made for America, most Chinese workers lack the health protections that for nearly half a century have protected US workers, such as correct protective masks, booths that limit the spread of sprayed chemicals, proper ventilation systems, and enforcement to ensure that the employees' exposure to toxins will be limited to permissible doses measured in micrograms or milligrams.

Chinese workers also routinely lose fingers or arms while making American furniture, appliances, and other metal goods. Their machines are too old to function properly or they lack safety guards required in the United States.

In most cases, US companies do not own these factories. American and multinational companies pay the factories to make products for America. From tiny A to Z Mining Tools in St. George to multinational corporations such as Reebok and IKEA, companies compete in the global marketplace by reducing costs—and that usually means outsourcing manufacturing to China. Last year, the United States imported $287.8 billion in goods from China, up from $51.5 billion a decade ago, according to the US Commerce Department. Those imports are expected only to increase.

Worker health and safety are considered basic human rights. But in the global economy, responsibility to workers often gets lost amid vast distances and international boundaries.

"This is a big-picture problem," said Garrett Brown, an industrial hygienist from California who has inspected Chinese factories that export to America. "Big-picture problems don't have quick or easy solutions."

The International Labor Organization (ILO) publishes international standards for workplaces. China agreed to many of those standards and also enacted a 2002 law setting its own rigorous standards. Under Chinese law, workers have the legal right to remain safe from fatal diseases and amputations at work.

But the law hasn't been enforced, Chinese and international experts agree. Economic growth has been a more important goal to China than worker safety.

Even the World Trade Organization, which maintains some barriers to trade to protect consumers' health, does not concern itself with issues of workers' health. As a result, enforcement of health and safety standards has been left to the governments of developing countries and the companies that outsource to those countries.

Often, smaller companies never even visit the factories where their products are made. Larger companies try with only limited success to audit operations, often complaining that their efforts are failing. Records are falsified and unsafe machines are used after audits. Safety guards are removed so workers can produce faster.

"Through auditing tours, we can make good improvements and changes, but those changes are not sustainable," complained Wang Lin, a manager for IKEA based in Shanghai. "Chinese government law enforcement is greatly needed," added Wang. "Without that, companies cannot sustain a good compliance program."

The Chinese Ministry of Health in 2005 noted at least two hundred million of China's labor force of seven hundred million workers were routinely exposed to toxic chemicals and life-threatening diseases in factories.

"More than sixteen million enterprises in China have been subjecting workers to high, poisonous levels of toxic chemicals," the ministry said at a conference on occupational diseases in Beijing, which was reported by the state-controlled media. The ministry particularly blamed "foreign-funded" enterprises that exported goods.

China has more deaths per capita from work-related illnesses than any other country, according to the International Labor Organization. In 2005, the most recent year for which data are available, 386,645 Chinese workers died of occupational illnesses, according to Chinese government data compiled by the ILO and cited in the July 14, 2006, *Journal of Epidemiology*. Millions more live with fatal diseases caused by factory work, other epidemiologists estimated in the article.

The number of workers living with fatal diseases does not include those who suffer amputations. Primitive, unsafe machines with blades that lack safety guards have caused millions of limb amputations since 1995, according to lawyers for Chinese workers.

The scale of the fatal diseases, deaths and amputations challenge the common wisdom—recited in both the Chinese and American press—that US trade with China has helped Chinese factory workers improve their lives and living standards. "If I had known about the serious effects of the chemicals, I would not possibly have taken that job," said Chen Honghuan, forty, who was poisoned while handling cadmium to make batteries for export to Rayovac, EverReady, Energizer and Panasonic in the United States.

China's 2002 Occupational Disease and Prevention Control Act established limits on workplace poisons, which in most cases are as strict or nearly as strict as US regulations.

But it hasn't helped much. After the law was enacted, for example, the average benzene level in Chinese factories reported in twenty-four scientific journals from 2002 through 2004 was more than eleven times the allowable level, according to scientists from Fudan University of Public Health in Shanghai, writing in the November 2006 *Journal of Regulatory Toxicology and Pharmacology*.

Scientists reached the same conclusion about workers' exposure to lead in the manufacture of paint, batteries, iron and steel, glass, cables, and certain plastics.

"The data demonstrated that many facilities in the lead industries reported in the literature were not in compliance with the OELs [occupational exposure limits]," wrote Xibiao Ye and Otto Wong in a 2006 medical journal article. "Similarly, there appeared to be only a minor impact of the 2002 Act on the reduction of occupational lead poisoning in China. The current overall occupational health-monitoring system appears inadequate, lacking the necessary enforcement."

Most American businesses that import from China are small- and medium-sized, US shipping records show. Unlike large companies, they ordinarily do not visit the factories or check on factory conditions.

"I found the factory on the Internet two years ago," Michael Been, owner of A to Z Mining Tools in St. George, said of a factory he uses in Guizhou Province. "They have someone who writes English."

Been has never been to the factory and has no plans to visit.

Some larger companies, however, pay auditors to monitor conditions in the factories they use. But auditors' visits provide merely a "snapshot in time," business owners say. Chinese workers suggest those snapshots often are staged, with the number of toxins reduced before the visits and workers reassigned to new and safer tasks. The glimpse that visitors get of Chinese factories often is incomplete for other reasons: Many large factories have small satellite "workshops," which are much smaller factories nearby that visitors never see, according to Chinese workers interviewed for this story.

"These Americans visited the large factory, but never visited the workshop where I worked," Chen Faju, thirty-one, said as she pointed to numerous photos in her factory's magazines of visiting Americans. "If they had visited, they would have smelled the poisons."

Chen and colleagues from the workshop were hospitalized for chronic anemia and myelodysplastic anemia, beginning in 2002, a result of brushing toxic glues for years onto the soles of New Balance and other sport shoes sold in the United States. The shoes were made by thirty thousand workers in the Yue Yuen industrial park in the city of Dongguan.

Chen's medical record, dated February 14, advises that she be removed from a job of "working with organic chemicals." A manager from Chen's workshop, Du Masheng, said toxins are not used anymore.

In addition, auditors typically have been more concerned with fair wages than worker safety.

Derek Wang, a former auditor for Reebok, recalls that he and his former boss lurked outside factories at night to see if workers were working overtime so they could make sure they were paid for the additional work.

But asked for the ingredients of glues the factories used to make the shoes, Wang said he didn't know. He never had glues tested for carcinogenic benzene or n-hexane.

Chinese provincial governments are responsible for checking compliance with Chinese law. But too often, officials have a financial stake in businesses, leading to corruption and twenty-four-hour warnings before rare inspections occur, said Liu Kaiming, executive director of the Institute of Contemporary Observation, a Chinese think tank.

There are too few inspectors in China to monitor safety, experts say. There is one inspector for every thirty-five thousand Chinese workers, Brown, the American industrial hygienist, calculated in a journal article. Local governments in China also do not fully understand the "adverse effects on workers' health" of occupational hazards, according to an article this year in the journal *Regulatory Toxicology and Pharmacology*.

"Chinese labor law is not that bad," said Dominique Muller, the Hong Kong director of the International Confederation of Free Trade Unions. "The problem is the implementation."

Added Guo Jianmei, a law professor at Beijing University who represents workers injured in factories: "The problem is that the Chinese government does not have an incentive to reform the enterprises."

In most countries, trade unions help ensure that employers abide by occupational health and safety regulations. The unions also help train workers in proper use of machines and protective equipment.

China has only one trade union, controlled by the central government. Its function is to enhance production and maintain labor discipline. Workers who try to organize or establish their own free trade unions are arrested and face lengthy prison sentences. Lawyers who have tried to help them also have been imprisoned.

"In China, there is absolutely nothing you can do," said Au Loong- yu, a researcher for the nonprofit organization Globalization Monitor in Hong Kong. "Workers have been robbed of the basic tool of self-defense, forming independent unions. And the government is biased in favor of the business sector, so it cracks down on workers who try to speak up for themselves."

Indeed, the Chinese government treats issues related to workers' rights as sensitive matters of state security. Even those workers with diseases or amputations who try to help other workers with similar conditions—by forming independent nongovernment organizations (NGOs)—have had their organizations shut down by state security police, they said in interviews.

"Now we pose as a business, as a consulting firm," said Zhu Qiang, an underground NGO leader in Shenzhen who lost his arm in a crude machine while making plastic bags for America.

China's failure to permit free trade unions translates into additional cost savings for American consumers and profits for American companies, reducing the cost of manufactured imports from China from 11 percent to 44 percent, according to Columbia University law professor Mark Barenberg.

The lack of unions also makes it even more lucrative to use Chinese workers to make goods.

"In the US, if you are a manufacturer, you have to contribute to unemployment insurance and worker compensation insurance, you have to buy workplace environmental insurance and liability insurance, and you have to comply with the occupational health and safety law," said David Welker, research coordinator for the International Brotherhood of Teamsters in Washington, DC.

US businesses, while adamant they don't want Chinese workers to get sick or hurt, know their costs are lower because the regulatory environment is more lax.

Meanwhile, the shipping containers from China arrive every day.

October 21, 2007

Part 2

Factory workers in the small industrial city of Foshan, China, made parts for Char-Broil grills and gas stoves without wearing respirator masks with charcoal filters. The factory had no special ventilation systems. No ear plugs. No chemical wash units.

All of these safety protections were standard equipment when workers in Columbus, GA, built and assembled Char-Broil stoves until their factory closed last year.

Another difference? Some of the Chinese workers are dying.

In a barracks-like building with a tin roof in Foshan, Wei Chaihua and other workers operated the machines that sanded and polished the steel for Char-Broil stoves. Now Wei's lungs are filled with microscopic metal specks that created nodules that make it difficult to breathe. Wei has silicosis, a fatal lung disease he contracted because the Bai Xing factory here had higher levels of silica dust than allowed by Chinese law, according to his medical records and a local government inspection report of the factory air.

The factory provided Wei and other workers with only thin gauze masks.

Similarly ill-equipped factories in China make jewelry, utensils, tool and die casts, ceramic tiles, dinner plates, and marble tiles for US and worldwide export. Epidemiologists estimate about 4.4 million workers in China have silicosis from working in these industries without adequate protection, although most have not been diagnosed.

"I know my days are numbered," Wei, forty-four, said, raising his left hand to his heart after the exertion of talking. "I cannot believe this has happened to me."

The story of Wei's high expectations in taking a factory job compared with the actual grim consequences of his work is a story common throughout China. It suggests that US media reports that globalization has lifted millions of Chinese out of poverty have not taken into account the widespread loss of health and life from occupational diseases.

Wei spent nearly all his life working in a farming village in a mountainous part of Hubei Province. He, his wife and two children raised corn, potatoes, and Chinese cabbage on a half acre of land. The air was clear, unpolluted. There were no factories.

For most of his life, Wei said, he felt relatively satisfied. He was a subsistence farmer, but felt secure in the knowledge his family would not go hungry. Throughout the 1990s, however, Wei could not help but notice friends and neighbors leaving for jobs in distant cities. They spoke of educating their children, improving life for their families. Wei decided he should try this new route, too.

"I hoped to give my children a better future," he said.

In October 2002, Wei said goodbye to his family, not knowing when he would see them again. He traveled for thirty-six hours by train to southern Guangzhou Province, arriving first in Shenzhen. The heavy traffic, the noise, the loud blaring music in the streets, the tall buildings, and the many factories all surprised him. The air looked like gray lint, thick with industrial dust and chemicals.

In Shenzhen, Wei initially worked in construction, but ended up seeking factory work in Foshan, only a few hours away by bus.

He found a job in the Bai Xing factory, which transformed raw steel into polished, shiny stainless steel for charcoal and gas grills. It also made "Dutch ovens," cast iron pots overlaid with bright orange, red, blue and green enamel.

The discipline, rigor and monotony of factory work surprised Wei. "I missed home, my old life, a lot," he said.

But he forced himself to adjust.

Most workers, like Wei, didn't even know what they were making, having never seen an outdoor gas oven before. When asked to name the object he made, Wei insisted he did not know. "Waiguo dongxi," he said. "Foreign thing."

Wei operated one of four machines that sand and polish steel, each machine producing metallic dust as it sanded with ever greater refinement. His machine was last in line, producing dust containing the finest particles.

A manager told Wei the thin gauze mask he wore would protect him. Wei said he thought, simply, it would protect him from getting dust in his lungs. He did not know it was supposed to protect him from an actual disease that could kill him.

At work, Wei would open the door of the large machine that did the sanding, put the steel in its proper position, close the door and press a button. The machine made a swishing sound as it sanded; then the noise stopped. When Wei opened the door, metal dust flew out, covering his hair and face with a gray film. He'd take the steel out, put it aside, and start the whole process again.

After three years, by April 2006, Wei had difficulty breathing and suffered frequent nausea. He became tired easily, even after just two hours of standing at work. He could not walk more than a few yards without feeling breathless.

Four months later, lacking stamina, Wei stopped working and sought medical treatment. He hasn't returned to work since.

Meanwhile, the Foshan Nanhai Disease Prevention and Control Center investigated Wei's medical complaint. An inspector from the center visited Wei's factory on December 8, 2006, according to an inspection document, and found the concentration of silica dust exceeded the maximum short-term exposure limit by 56 percent over fifteen minutes, and exceeded the maximum permissible time weighted-average concentration over eight hours by 144 percent.

A spokesman for the Desheng Enamel Development Company in Guangzhou, which owns the Bai Xing factory where Wei worked, said he knew about Wei's illness but did not believe it had resulted from his work in the factory. "We always have followed the law and regulations of the country in what we do for the worker," Zhang Li Tao said. "He only worked for the factory for one year, so we're not sure if it's the factory's fault that he has this disease or a factory where he worked previously."

Wei's identity card from the factory shows he worked there for three years. Wei says he did not work in any other factory.

Zhang said Char-Broil was the company's largest customer. The Bai Xing factory sends its products to Char-Broil using the Guangzhou Trademaster and Creation Company.

Shipping documents show that on May 15, 2007, Guangzhou Trademaster sent $44,258 worth of barbecue parts in seventy-two hundred cartons through the Port of Long Beach to Char-Broil. On May 21, Char-Broil received $58,407 of "brass burners" from Desheng Enamel's shipping company.

W. C. Bradley Company, which moved its manufacturing to China in stages over the past decade, requires all overseas vendors to sign agreements saying they and any subcontractors will comply with their country's health and safety regulations, Chief Executive Steve Butler said. "We don't want to be part of a system that creates a problem for workers," he said.

But monitoring the manufacture of the Char-Broil gas stoves from Georgia has been a challenge. W. C. Bradley employs Chinese agents to help the company operate in China. "They are responsible for sourcing our products, and for compliance—making sure the products conform to design specifications, and the materials conform to design standards," Butler said.

Butler said he did not know how agents made sure that factories comply with China's health and safety regulations, and acknowledged independent auditing may be necessary.

"How do we look over their shoulders?" Butler asked, referring to agents and factories. At a recent meeting, the company decided to include money in its budget for "plane tickets to China" so employees can conduct their own audits, he said.

In January 2007, Wei obtained his diagnosis from the Guangzhou Occupational Disease and Prevention Hospital. A physician there told him he had silicosis and needed treatment.

Wei had never heard of the disease but was happy it could be treated. He assumed he'd get better. Instead, he got worse.

On March 19, Wei was admitted to the Guangzhou Occupational Disease and Prevention Hospital, which provided him with an oxygen tank to help him breathe.

Wei asked a physician when he'd be cured. The physician, Wei recalled, looked at him apologetically. "He told me, 'There is no cure,'" Wei said.

A medical report from the hospital dated March 27 noted Wei had "second stage silicosis." The third stage is terminal.

Now, unable to work, Wei lives in a one-room apartment rented for him by the factory. He receives a "maintenance allowance" of about fifty-five dollars per month, seventy-five dollars less than he earned while he was working. Someone from the factory brings him his meals. Under Chinese law, workers with medical records certifying that they have occupational diseases are entitled to sick pay, hospitalization, and medical expenses from the employer. The employer also must provide them with housing and meals.

If the state later determines that an employee cannot work, the employer or the employer's insurance must pay them disability compensation—in most cases no more than the equivalent of two years' salary, usually not more than $5,000. But many employers succeed in not paying it, according to lawyers.

Although Wei's employer must feed and house him for now, Wei is afraid of the factory's bosses. Like most factories in China, his factory employs a team of security guards. They are backed up, Wei believes, by gang members. Indeed, other Chinese workers interviewed for these stories who argued with their employers over back pay or overtime pay had physical evidence of severe beatings.

In one case, worker Hu Yongxian, thirty-nine, a carpenter at a factory that exported furniture to the United States, pulled up his shirt to show wide black marks across his back and similar markings on his scalp.

"They used iron pipes," Hu said, referring to the factory's security guards, who settled a dispute over Hu's back pay. "I fell to the ground and they kept beating me."

During one of several interviews in a restaurant, Wei's cell phone rang jarringly six times, at intervals of fifteen to thirty minutes each. He did not answer, but he did glance at the number on his phone each time. "It's the factory again," he said. "They keep calling me. They are watching me. They know

I'm not in my room. They don't want me to talk about my disease, about what happened to me."

At one point, Wei considered leaving the restaurant in Foshan and cutting the interview short. "The factory has a gang," he said. "I'm afraid they will have me killed."

The factory's spokesman, Zhang Li Tao, said the factory protects itself from outside troublemakers with security guards, but he says it does not use those guards against employees.

Every day now, Wei, who has trouble eating anything more substantial than soup, wakes up around 11:30 a. m. and goes to sleep at 6 p. m. He spends most of each day in bed, listening to the radio. Sometimes, if he is feeling well enough, he walks down the block and back to his apartment.

He is waiting for the social security bureau to decide the severity of his disability so he can ask the factory for disability money. The degree of the disability, factored in a formula with Wei's salary, will determine the amount of compensation Wei can receive. He hopes for a few thousand dollars.

Wei does not intend to go to court, he said, adding that he wants a quick resolution.

Workers who go to court, usually because their employers refuse to pay compensation, tend to receive much more money than those who do not, according to a spokesman at China Labour Bulletin, a nongovernment organization in Hong Kong. On December 22, 2005, the Huidong County People's Court awarded a silicosis patient, Feng Xingzhong, thirty-three, a record amount: nearly $60,000. Approximately half the amount was to cover long-term medical treatment. It was the first time a court had awarded compensation for long-term treatment to an occupational-disease patient.

Wei wants to return home to die. But he does not want to leave Foshan until he has some disability money to take home with him. As it is, he has given up his dreams of sending his children to high school and college.

"My only dream now," said Wei, "is to be at home with my family when I die."

October 22, 2007

Author's Afterword

I wanted to be a journalist even as a child and as a teenager. Initially, the impulse was that I was a good writer and I enjoyed writing. I felt that I wanted to do something with writing, but in my family, which was lower middle class, it was not acceptable to say that you were going to write a novel or do something artistic, you needed a *real job*, meaning a regular paycheck. I thought journalism would be acceptable, because you could get a regular job and salary in those days. At first, this logic didn't matter to my father, who thought my idea was ridiculous. In time I won him over to my way of thinking, but we had many stormy years along the way, especially when I was a teenager. I'd grown up in the Bronx in the 1960s in a very sheltered, Catholic environment. As a teenager especially, I longed to explore the world beyond the shelter that school and family were providing. It was wonderful and comfortable, but I just knew in my heart there was something more out there for me. I believed journalism would open up the world to me. I saw it as a means of exploration and adventure, a way to be able to see things for myself.

In college at Fordham University, I met professional woman journalists. They inspired me; they were smart and sensible women who could see when things were and were not true. You could see that they had lived and had explored the world for themselves; they had a real independence about them. They were very strong mentally. I admired that very much. I also had male professors at Fordham, in particular a priest, Raymond Schroth, who let me understand the responsibility of journalism as a sort of moral mission—this is what sparked my fire for investigative reporting.

It seems like I've been doing journalism my whole life. I thought about it a lot in grammar school and did all the writing activities I could. In high school I wrote for my high school paper and became the editor in chief. Later, I became the editor in chief of Fordham's paper, the *Ram*. It's almost as if I were born to be a journalist, as silly as that sounds. But when I think about it, there was never a time in my life when I didn't want to do this job.

The main obstacle I faced in starting my career was actually my father, an old-school Italian who felt journalism was no career for a woman. I am deeply indebted to the women's movement and all the newswomen who came before me—all those talented women who suffered writing for the society pages, the "women's ghetto" of the newsroom. It was those women who paved the way for me to go to the *Washington Post* and be on the night police beat and work from 4:30 p. m. until three in the morning, running after homicides and fires in the middle of the night, and no one thinking twice about my gender. Those beats—police, courts, local government—really give you the basics of journalism. For me, it was my foundation for everything else that I did later as a journalist.

Of course, I'm proudest of the series for which I won the Pulitzer. It brought attention to the problem of jail rapes and helped repair a broken system. I'm also very proud of the fact that I was a foreign correspondent in China for four years; the Chinese government at that time made it very difficult to be a foreign journalist in China, as it still does. Yet, I was able to do some wonderful stories. The story behind the story of working in China is just plain doing your job, despite harassment, detention, and other limitations placed by the Chinese government. I also feel proud of the series that's excerpted here, "American Imports, Chinese Deaths." I did that story as a freelancer, putting together travel funding from the Pulitzer Center and the Center for Investigative Reporting, and convincing editors at the Salt Lake *Tribune* to edit and publish it. I made five trips to China for that series; it was a very difficult reporting adventure because I was not supposed to be in China—as a freelancer, I was not accredited by the government as a journalist, so I was flying in on the sly to do my reporting. However, I would not have been able to do that series had I not worked previously as an accredited foreign correspondent in China. After four years working in the country, I knew how the system worked. I knew how to get access and find what I wanted most of the time without being detected.

Over the years, there have been some times when I've felt that being a woman was to my advantage. I do feel that women are often seen as softer, gentler, and so, consciously or not, I often come across that way when I'm doing my interviews. I empathize easily with people; I'm not the confrontational type of reporter. I know how to draw people out; I understand timing. There is a rhythm to asking questions. You have to be sensitive to when you can ask certain things. You have to build up to it.

In terms of investigative reporting, I think women have made a lot of progress. At the *Philadelphia Inquirer*, there was really a lot of support for investigative reporting under Gene Roberts, the editor who hired me. Gene left in the nineties, but especially under him, the paper was well known for its investigative reporting. It felt like a special time: a lot of great colleagues bouncing story ideas off each other and talking techniques and strategies. It was a wonderful environment for men and women reporters, both. That's the kind of atmosphere you dream about being in, fabulous mentoring and strong friendships. It's really inspiring.

Eileen Welsome

Eileen Welsome graduated from the University of Texas, Austin and spent the early years of her career as a newspaper reporter. Gradually, she moved into investigative reporting and books. In 1994, while working as a reporter for the *Albuquerque Tribune*, she won the Pulitzer Prize for national reporting for a series of articles about eighteen people injected with plutonium during the US Government's Manhattan Project. She left the newspaper to write a book about that experiment and others that occurred during the Cold War. She is the author of four nonfiction books and is at work on a fifth.

The Plutonium Experiment

America's secret medical experiments
on average citizens during the Cold War

At 3:30 p. m. on July 18, 1947, doctors in a San Francisco hospital gathered around a patient's bed and explained an experiment they were about to perform. The patient, a railroad porter with an eighth-grade education, nodded his assent. Doctors later would describe him as "fully oriented and in sane mind."

A bull's-eye was drawn in ink on the hard, smooth calf of the man's left leg. A hypodermic needle loaded with plutonium, a silvery, manmade metal considered one of the most toxic substances on Earth, was plunged into the center. The needle sank nearly an inch. There was no bleeding when it was withdrawn and no pain or discomfort "whatsoever" six and a half hours later.

Three days later, the left leg was amputated at midthigh for what was believed to be a pre-existing bone cancer. Tissue samples were sent to a laboratory where researchers conducting a secret experiment were eager to find out how, among other things, plutonium distributed itself in the human body.

The patient was Elmer Allen. He was the eighteenth and last person to be injected with plutonium in an experiment conducted between 1945 and 1947.

Elmer, who was thirty-six at the time, returned with his wife to her small hometown of Italy, Texas, where a bleak future awaited him. He would suffer epileptic seizures, alcoholism, and eventually be diagnosed as paranoid schizophrenic—a mental illness his family doctor said centered partly on his feelings about how he had been used.

It was the summer of 1944 when Fredna Hadley met a strapping young porter named Elmer Allen in a West Texas train station. It was a romantic beginning in an era of romance—a time of sad farewells and sweet homecomings in a democracy caught up in a global war.

Fredna, a young graduate of Tillotson College in Austin, Texas, was in the El Paso train station waiting for the train that would take her to Los Angeles to see her aunt.

"People were pushing to get on the train. This woman had some children, a little baby in her arms and two small children. I stepped back and let her go in front of me, and they closed the gates," Fredna recalled.

She began to cry. Elmer, a porter for the Pullman Company, noticed her distress. "I can get you on the next train," he said.

Their love affair began. Not long after that, Elmer followed Fredna to her hometown of Italy, Texas, a small farming community forty-five miles south of Dallas.

After a brief courtship, Elmer and Fredna were married on September 10, 1944. They moved to Oakland, CA, and later to nearby Richmond. Their first child, Elmerine, was born a year later. A second child, William, was born two years after that.

Elmer continued his work as a railroad porter while Fredna worked as an aide in a health clinic. Like Texas, the postwar Bay area was still segregated, but the African American couple felt happy to be working. "We were optimistic about the future," Fredna recalled.

But an accident occurred on September 3, 1946, a minor accident really, which would set in motion events that would forever alter their lives. Elmer was trying to get off a train in Chicago when it jolted and threw him to the side, injuring his left knee.

When he got back to Oakland, a company doctor took an X-ray. The film revealed a fracture. Elmer was advised to wrap the knee in an Ace bandage and apply heat, but that didn't help. He was referred to another doctor.

A second X-ray showed a lesion in the knee area had grown. A biopsy was done. The pathologist found no evidence of abnormal growth or tumor. "The principal picture is that of newly forming bone, organizing hemorrhage and chronic inflammation," he said.

Elmer was unable to work and the Pullman Company refused to accept liability for the accident, saying the injury didn't appear to be "on a traumatic basis." He couldn't afford further treatment and was referred in June 1947—almost a year later—to the outpatient clinic at the University of California hospital in San Francisco.

By then, Elmer's physical and financial situation was desperate. His knee had swollen to three or four times its original size and was so tender he couldn't put weight on it. He was taking pain medication and had been out of work for six months. According to a hospital application form, Elmer had sixty dollars in debts. And twenty-five dollars in cash. (His rent alone was thirty-five dollars a month.)

Elmer's diagnosis worsened, and he later was admitted to the San Francisco hospital. His medical records show the following:

- June 25, 1947. A doctor examining one set of X-rays suggests the changes in Elmer's knee could stem from an infection superimposed on a surgical defect, but he says the possibility of bone cancer "must be seriously considered."
- July 3, 1947. The doctor examining the June 25 X-rays does another set and reverses his opinion. Elmer, he said, "probably" has a cancer in the cartilage or bone. He doesn't rule out infection.
- July 14, 1947. The hospital's pathology department does a second biopsy. Elmer definitely has a form of bone cancer, a pathologist said.

The doctors decided the only way to prevent the spread of bone cancer through his body was to amputate his leg, a treatment still used today. Bone cancer is a rare disease that is usually fatal by the time it is diagnosed. Eighty percent to 95 percent of patients who have it die within five years of its discovery.

The days and weeks after Elmer's amputation are a blur in Fredna's mind. What she remembers most is how scared she was—two babies to support and a husband with an amputated leg.

"I was so far away from my people," she said.

They were both far from home and about to be hurtled into a more alien world—an experiment conducted by scientists of the Manhattan Project, which produced the atom bomb.

While scientists at Los Alamos National Laboratory were designing the bomb itself, other research was being done at the Metallurgical Laboratory at the University of Chicago, the William H. Crocker Radiation Laboratory at the University of California in Berkeley and other labs.

Much of the health and safety research centered on new, radioactive elements that were capable of sustaining a nuclear chain reaction. Of great interest was plutonium, named after the planet Pluto.

"It really should have been called 'plutium,'" Glenn Seaborg, a co-discoverer of plutonium and Nobel laureate, said from his Bay area home. "But we liked how 'plutonium' rolled off the tongue."

Plutonium was discovered in 1941 on the University of California campus in Berkeley. Plutonium 239 has a half-life of 24,065 years, the time it takes for half of its radioactive atoms to decay.

The military potential of plutonium, a material so secret that it was referred to during the war years as "the product," was recognized. Scores of young scientists recruited into the secret Manhattan Project went to work, trying to figure out how to manufacture plutonium and other radioactive isotopes in large enough quantities to be harnessed into an atomic bomb.

By the fall of 1942, enough plutonium had been made to be visible to the naked eye. As the amount of plutonium increased, so did concern over its toxicity.

In 1944—a year before the human experiments were to begin—11 milligrams of plutonium (about the size of the head of a pin) were set aside for animal studies by physician and researcher Joseph Hamilton at UC-Berkeley. Col. Stafford Warren, the chief medical officer of the Manhattan Project who authorized the experiment, described plutonium in 1946 as the "most poisonous chemical known."

Plutonium had properties similar to the radioactive element radium. The human toll wreaked by radium was well documented, and the federal government wanted to avoid a similar tragedy in its laboratories.

Young women who had worked in factories painting luminous figures on watch dials with radium-laced paint in the 1920s were developing cancer. It was discovered that many had swallowed lethal amounts of radium when licking their paint brushes.

Unlike radium, which decayed to radon and could be detected in the breath, the only way to measure plutonium in the body was through urine and stools. And the only way to extrapolate how much plutonium a person may have been exposed to, researchers figured, was through an experiment in which a known amount of plutonium would be introduced into the body and carefully measured in the urine and stools.

"Studies conducted on man involving the introduction of known quantities of the element into the human body were viewed as the only solution to the problem," states a report by the Atomic Energy Commission, which investigated the experiment in 1974.

The injections began in 1945, just three months before J. Robert Oppenheimer watched the atomic bomb near Alamogordo and recalled an ancient Hindu quotation: "I am become Death, the destroyer of worlds."

The first patient, injected on April 10, 1945, was an African American suffering from severe auto injuries and hospitalized at the Manhattan Engineer District Hospital in Oak Ridge, TN. The patient walked out of the hospital several weeks later, giving rise to a long-held belief by some researchers that the plutonium actually had promoted a rapid healing of the bones. "They gave him a whopping dose of plutonium," recalled Karl Morgan, the former director of Oak Ridge's health physics division. "They were surprised a Black man who had been scheduled to die had walked out of the hospital and disappeared."

Three patients were injected at Billings Hospital at the University of Chicago; three patients, including Elmer, were injected at the University of California Hospital in San Francisco; and the remaining eleven patients were injected at Strong Memorial Hospital, the teaching hospital of the University of Rochester in upstate New York.

Wright Langham, a group leader in radiobiology at Los Alamos, went to Rochester to help coordinate the experiment on the eleven Rochester patients. Langham, who was later known as "Mr. Plutonium," may have escorted the numerous samples shipped back to New Mexico by train. Los Alamos did the chemical analyses of the urine, stool, blood, and tissue samples taken from patients.

Scientists were looking for patients suffering from chronic diseases that made survival for more than ten years unlikely. Two reasons lay behind this thinking, one humane and one utilitarian.

First, they wanted to avoid the possibility of radiation effects, such as cancer, showing up later in life. Second, early death improved the chances of obtaining what a Los Alamos report called "postmortem material"—body parts.

Livers, spleens, gonads, kidneys, hearts, ribs, intestines—virtually every organ—would be harvested and measured for plutonium in patients who died soon after the injections.

Three patients were African American, and fifteen were white. Five—including Elmer, Albert Stevens, John Mousso, and Eda Schultz Charlton—lived for more than twenty years after the injections.

That alone is reason to condemn the project, some scientists say. "I find that when people play God, when they find somebody's terminal and therefore it's all right to do something to them you wouldn't do to other people, I find that rather obnoxious," said Berkeley scientist John Gofman, considered one of the world's leading experts on low-level radiation.

Had they lived fifty years, the plutonium patients would have received an average of forty-four times the radiation the average person receives in a lifetime from background and medical X-rays. But three patients received much more.

Elmer received the smallest dose, but he received plutonium 238, a "hotter" form that is more unstable and more radioactive than plutonium 239. About half remained in the amputated leg, giving Elmer about six times the radiation the average person today receives in a lifetime.

Scientists today disagree on whether the plutonium would have increased the patients' pain, worsened their conditions or hastened their deaths. "I think any of these exposures could cause excruciating pain in the person who would suffer the consequences," health physicist Morgan said.

But Roland Finston, a health physicist who just retired from Stanford University and helped the *Tribune* calculate the radiation doses, said it's unlikely the doses would have caused any immediate acute effects. The real danger, he said, would have been the development of leukemia or solid tumors in later life. "It would not have caused any measurable effect on the patients at the time or shortly thereafter," he said.

The government said later deaths were unrelated to the plutonium injections and said there was no evidence to suggest the plutonium influenced the patients' diseases or caused cancer.

"The observation that cancer did not, apparently, develop in any of these eighteen injected patients does not mean that the doses given were too small to cause cancer," said John C. Cobb, a retired physician living in Corrales. "The plutonium may indeed have caused a cancer to start in any, or all, of these patients, but the patients' own immune systems could have eliminated the cancer cells."

Cobb is a former chairman of the University of Colorado's department of preventative medicine and served on a governor's task force that looked at health effects from plutonium and other problems at Colorado's Rocky Flats nuclear weapons plant.

Cobb said plutonium's irradiation of the bone marrow also could have damaged the patients' immune systems and made them more susceptible to diseases. "Immune deficiency can contribute to a great variety of symptoms," he said.

Many years later, when Elmer was back in Italy, Texas, he would tell his old friend Joe Speed about the doctors who raced in and out of his hospital room the summer his leg was amputated.

"They were practicing to be doctors," Speed recalled. "They were students. Different young men would come in, telling him to do this and that."

"He told me they put a germ cancer in his leg. They guinea-pigged him. They didn't care about him getting well. He told me he would never get well."

Doctors at the clinic were immediately interested in Elmer. "Of great teaching value," a medical official wrote on Elmer's chart after an early visit.

Patricia Durbin, a scientist at Lawrence Berkeley Laboratory in California, said the patient selection was both "personalized and random."

"The bulk of the people were just people," she said.

Durbin was in a second generation of scientists who "rediscovered" the plutonium experiment and lobbied in the early seventies for follow-up studies. In 1946, she was a young student working in the lab of scientist Joseph Hamilton, one of the experiment's architects.

"They were always on the lookout for somebody who had some kind of terminal disease who was going to undergo an amputation," Durbin said. "There are not very many of them. But they had colleagues at UC-San Francisco and San Francisco General who were kind of on the alert for potential cases."

About a month before Elmer was admitted to the hospital, a Chinese boy described in documents as "CAL-A," underwent a similar injection and amputation. The sixteen-year-old boy was injected on June 10, 1947, with americium, another radioactive element, at what records described as the "Chinese Hospital" in San Francisco.

Two days later his leg was amputated. He was taken to the University of California Hospital in San Francisco for studies before and after the amputation. He died eleven months later and is buried in San Francisco. "There was no evidence of disclosure in the chart of this patient," said DOE records obtained under the Freedom of Information Act.

When asked if she knew anything about that case, Durbin said, "His guardian couldn't speak English. He got treated in a good hospital as a consequence."

On July 18, 1947, the white cast placed on Elmer's left leg after the biopsy was split down the side and removed to prepare for the "tracer injection."

"Some throbbing pain but no other discomfort," a doctor wrote in Elmer's records.

At 3:30 p. m. that day, medical people gathered at Elmer's bedside. He was told of a procedure they were about to perform.

"The experimental nature of the intramuscular injection of the radioactive tracer sample was explained to the patient, who agreed upon the procedure. The patient was in fully oriented and in sane mind," his medical records state.

Three doctors and a registered nurse witnessed the explanation, assisted in the injection and signed their names at the bottom of Elmer's consent form.

One doctor who signed his name was Bertram V. A. Low-Beer, another early nuclear pioneer who used radioactive substances in medical treatments. Low-Beer's name shows up in Elmer's medical records only on the day he was injected. The consent form also appears to have been written by Low-Beer.

Elmer is the only patient for whom there is documented evidence that he was told of the injection. The consent form, however, does not describe what he was told. Even then, Elmer's consent didn't come close to today's strict guidelines for informed consent, which require written acknowledgement by the patient after full disclosure of the research, its risks and benefits.

Fredna questioned why doctors did not include her when they discussed the experimental procedure with Elmer. "It seems like they should have told me about it," she said.

Elmer's daughter, Elmerine, said her father, with his limited education, would not have understood the explanation. "If they told my father that he was injected with plutonium, that would be like telling him he was injected with ice cream," she said. "He would not know the difference."

The injection of plutonium into Elmer was conducted despite orders to the contrary. On December 24, 1946, the Manhattan Engineer District learned "certain radioactive substances were being prepared for intravenous administration to human subjects" in Berkeley. An immediate halt was ordered.

Then, on April 17, 1947, four months before Elmer's injection, the US Army Corps of Engineers, Manhattan District, sent a memo to the Atomic Energy Commission reiterating the prohibition and going one step further.

"It is desired that no document be released which refers to experiments with humans and might have adverse effect on public opinion or result in legal suits. Documents covering such work should be classified 'secret.' Further work in this field has been prohibited by the general manager."

In that same memo, officials ordered that three documents involving human experimentation be upgraded from "restricted" to "secret" and that a search be conducted to make sure no other agency had gotten any of the records.

A month later, commission officials refused to declassify a paper titled "A Comparison of the Metabolism of Plutonium in Man and the Rat," written by Hamilton and others in Berkeley. "It contains material, which in the opinion of the management of the United States Atomic Energy Commission, might adversely affect the national interest," a May 23, 1947, letter states.

Some historians have said experiments with critically ill patients were common in the 1940s. And in fact, radioactive isotopes of strontium and radium, as well as massive doses of radiation to the whole body from X-rays, were given to patients at hospitals throughout the country, records show.

Scientists and doctors working for the Manhattan Project, and later under contract with the AEC, frequently stated the experimental therapies were part of the patients' normal treatment and that they were simply gathering data on physiological changes.

In one case that was similar to the plutonium experiment, eight very ill cancer patients in the early 1940s were exposed over a month to an average of 300 rads of whole-body irradiation from X-rays in a New York hospital. Five died within six months. Scientist L. F. Craver blamed their deaths on their diseases and said such doses should be "well-tolerated" by healthy people.

About 300 rads of whole-body irradiation delivered in a week or less will kill 50 percent of its subjects. Some 420 rads delivered in a one-month period will kill 50 percent of those exposed, according to Finston, a health physicist who recently retired from Stanford University.

Scientist Robert Stone, one of the experiment leaders, admitted the true purpose of the experiments with X-rays in a 1948 letter found at the Bancroft Library at UC-Berkeley:

"I freely admit that in 1942 when we started this work, I was influenced by the fact that we needed to learn as much as we possibly could concerning the effects of total-body irradiation on people with relatively normal blood pictures. At that time, I was confronted with the problem of building up the morale of the workers on the new atomic bomb project, many of whom were seriously worried about the effects of prolonged whole-body irradiation."

The records also show that scientists and doctors knew the ethics of such experiments were questionable and were sensitive about the experiment. In later documents, the AEC itself admitted that a policy of informed consent was well established by 1947.

As late as 1983, the DOE was still sensitive. Nathaniel Barr of the DOE's Office of Energy Research, put it this way: "The issue of informed consent, if raised, will be difficult to deal with in the light of recent DOE and federal policies and procedures regarding human subjects."

Elmer was a cooperative patient. Only a week after the amputation, he was eager to get up and around. "Has been up in wheelchair with great joy," Dr. Raymond S. Mullen wrote nine days after the surgery. Mullen was one of the doctors who witnessed the injection.

"In wheelchair most of day. No pain from stump. Eager to find work after convalescence—not depressed," Mullen wrote the next day.

Elmer was discharged from the hospital August 7. He was fitted for a prosthesis and got regular chest X-rays at an outpatient orthopedic clinic. In an entry dated May 11, 1948, a doctor wrote: "This pt. had radioactive stuff injected prior to amp." (The first four words are underlined.)

Elmer's last visit to the clinic appeared to have been July 6, 1949. "Gaining weight and feeling fine. No difficulty with stump. Walking (with) aid of cane," an entry states.

As an amputee, Elmer no longer could work as a railroad porter, so he turned to other ways of making a living. He learned how to repair shoes. He haunted the wharves in San Francisco, where he would get and sell fish. For the rest of his life he felt phantom aches and pains in the missing limb. "He said they kept the leg. They didn't bury the leg," Fredna recalled. "When his toes would start hurting, he'd say, 'I guess they're working on that foot of mine.'"

A couple of years later, with Elmer wearing a new prosthesis from the California's vocational rehabilitation department, the couple bundled up their two young children and returned to Italy. "He wanted to make a good living for his family," Fredna said. "After he lost his leg, he just gave up all hope."

The move back to Italy, despite its boast of being the "biggest little town in Texas," demoralized Elmer. In the summer, when a furnace-like heat drives all but the heartiest behind air-conditioned doors, Italy's Main Street looks like a deserted movie set. Elmer had not wanted to leave the hills or the cool breezes that rolled in from San Francisco Bay, but he needed family support. And Italy was home to Fredna's family.

In the early 1950s, Italy attracted national attention because of its approach to race relations: "Two mayors and two city councils—one for African Americans and one for whites. He was disgusted. He never wanted to come back here. He had many hopes and dreams for his family," Fredna recalled.

He cleaned bricks in nearby Dallas, repaired shoes at Goodwill Industries, upholstered chairs and sometimes plowed the rich, dark soil farmers called "black gumbo," friends said.

Mostly, it was up to Fredna to hold the family together. For thirty-five years she taught school, much of the time at Stafford Elementary, which was within walking distance of their small house.

Fredna, a poet in her spare time, thinks she never lived up to her potential, in part because of the pressure of raising two children and taking care of Elmer. "It took something away from me. I haven't done all the things I could have done."

Elmer's now-married daughter, Elmerine, said her father got the best of care. "Anything he wanted, he got it. He had an automobile to drive; it wasn't always a new one. Whatever he had, my mother provided it."

Elmer made toys for schoolchildren, kites from brown paper bags, lampshades from popsicle sticks, and flower baskets from egg cartons. His son, William, and his granddaughter, April, would go on to become engineers. "He could do anything. But there was nothing for him to do," recalled Speed, Elmer's friend.

A job at Goodwill ended when Elmer began having epileptic seizures and it was no longer safe for him to commute to Dallas. Fredna would put a tablespoon in his mouth when he had a seizure in the middle of the night. "He would chew the spoon to pieces—his tongue, too," Elmerine recalled.

He had other problems. He drank alcohol "very, very heavily" until ten or twelve years before he died. Elmerine said. He began taking Thorazine, a drug used in the treatment of various mental disorders. For some reason, it halted the drinking, she said.

David Williams, a physician in nearby Waxahachie, was Elmer's family doctor for the last twenty years of his life. Williams said he diagnosed Allen as a paranoid schizophrenic.

"This paranoia was certainly helped and did center around his feeling that he had been utilized as a younger man with this exposure to plutonium," he said.

"What I saw was a fellow who had a loss of limb and became an emotional cripple because of it. He took to the bottle and then got off that. He probably had paranoid schizophrenia all of his life. As far as doing things, I thought he was using this possible exposure as a crutch, a reason, rather than quite doing as well as I would have liked to have seen him do."

Elmer told Williams on his first office visit that he had been injected with plutonium. "It was difficult to tell whether to believe him or not. I wondered." Williams said. "I also wondered if it was a portion of his paranoia and whether or not it was a crutch for him not to function as he should have functioned. His conscience needed a salve to where it was OK for his wife to be teaching and earning and so forth."

Williams said he never saw evidence that the plutonium had any physical effect on Elmer. He said he didn't encourage Elmer to talk about the experiment. "I didn't think there was a lot of gain there. Do you follow? In other words, I didn't turn him off; I'd listen, but I felt like he had other, more ongoing problems that were more pressing that we needed to deal with day to day rather than going back to that."

It was the evening of June 9, 1973. Elmer and Fredna were in Car 1635, Drawing Room D of the "Texas Chief," an overnight train bound for Chicago. Elmer had worked as a railroad porter many years earlier, so the sway of the train and the clacking rhythm of the rails must have cradled him like an old rocking chair.

Then there was the view from his window. Weedy back lots and wash hanging from clotheslines as the train pulled out of Fort Worth. Cows, horses, and barns hurtling by. Green pastures unspooling like dreams. And later, the lights. Everything chattering of those old railroad days.

The next day, they were met in Chicago by a limousine driver at Union Station and whisked to a Ramada Inn, where a bouquet of flowers awaited them.

The Allens were on the trip of their life, a 19-day whirlwind that would take them to Chicago and then hundreds of miles northeast to Rochester. Limousines, fresh flowers, private train compartments and immaculate hotel rooms awaited them. And the government scientists were actually going to pay them $140 for participating in follow-up studies plus $13 a day.

On the day after their arrival in Chicago, Fredna went sightseeing. Elmer went to a sprawling national lab near Chicago. There he was placed in a whole-body counter, and his urine was collected and studied for traces of plutonium from a long-ago injection.

Against the festive backdrop, Elmer's unwitting participation in the second phase of an experiment launched almost thirty years earlier began. A new generation of researchers carried forward a cover-up initiated by the Manhattan Project scientists.

Neither Elmer nor Fredna nor their family doctor learned of the real purpose of the trip until a year later, formerly classified documents show. Eda Schultz Charlton and John Mousso, two other patients injected with plutonium many years earlier, also were unknowing participants in the follow-up studies, which involved the collection and chemical analyses of urine, stool and blood samples. Relatives of deceased patients whom scientists also wanted to exhume were duped, records show.

"My mother thought this was big stuff coming from Italy, Texas," Elmerine said of her parents' trip. "She thought she was the queen of England. It wasn't like they said, 'We're testing you guys because we injected you with plutonium.'"

Chicago, the place Elmer and Fredna were bound that warm summer night, was the city where it all began. While working as a railroad porter many years earlier, Elmer fell from a train and injured his leg, which eventually led to an amputation.

Doctors said the leg had bone cancer, a disease which is normally fatal in five years. But Elmer was to live another forty-four years, which makes the original diagnosis suspect, one scientist said.

"If the diagnosis had been correct, by rights he should have been dead in five years or something like that," said retired scientist John Rundo. "Bone cancer is normally fatal, not universally, but usually. He didn't die, as you know, so one can conclude that he probably didn't have bone cancer." Rundo oversaw the chemical analyses done on the excretion samples taken from Elmer and the others in 1973.

Durbin, the scientist from Lawrence Berkeley Laboratory in California who reviewed Elmer's medical records, also said she doubted the accuracy of "CAL-3's" diagnosis.

"I think the diagnosis of the bone cancer was questionable," she said. "The cells were not convincingly tumorous, at least on my reading of the pathology report."

But in a later interview, she said she believed "CAL-3's" leg still would have required amputation. "They were going to have to take the leg off anyway because the knee was so badly shattered. It hadn't healed well."

In 1967, Durbin learned that at least one patient injected in the 1945–47 experiment had lived at least twenty years, and she began a concerted effort to find out what happened to the rest.

Two decades earlier, she was a young student washing beakers in the laboratory of Hamilton, one of the country's savviest scientists, about the biological effects of plutonium.

Durbin, a plain-spoken scientist in her mid-sixties, is a staunch defender of the project and says the data saved countless people from being overexposed in the workplace. She said the international community still uses the data to set limits for human exposure to plutonium.

"These things were not done to plague people or make them sick and miserable," she said. "They were not done to kill people. They were done to gain potentially valuable information."

"The fact that they were injected and provided this valuable data should almost be a sort of memorial rather than something to be ashamed of. It doesn't bother me to talk about the plutonium injectees because of the value of the information that they provided."

In late December 1972, Durbin turned the information she had gathered over to the now-defunct Center for Human Radiobiology at Argonne National Laboratory near Chicago. This was the organization that had followed the radium dial painters, the women who died of cancer after licking the radioactive brushes they used to paint watches.

It was decided that survivors' urine, blood, and stools would be gathered on the metabolism unit of the University of Rochester's Strong Memorial Hospital. The Center for Human Radiobiology would do the chemical analyses.

Scientists also wanted to study the remains of deceased patients. Over the next five years, they exhumed three bodies and obtained the ashes of a fourth patient.

The MIT Radioactivity Center in Phoenix was in charge of getting permission for the exhumations from relatives. The staff there had done similar work in tracking down radium dial painters and other people exposed to radioactive elements.

The arrangement suited officials at Lawrence Berkeley Laboratory just fine. "The introduction of exhumed bodies into the politically charged Berkeley atmosphere might even result in picketing of the laboratory by students," a worried official is quoted as saying in the AEC report.

Los Alamos National Laboratory, which played a key role in the first phase, took a supporting role in the 1973 follow-up. Some samples from the 1973 studies were sent to Los Alamos, but Los Alamos scientists, particularly Langham, wanted to keep out of it the second time.

Langham, who performed the initial chemical analyses from eleven Rochester patients and an Oak Ridge accident victim, had grown weary of being identified with the experiment, Durbin wrote in a 1971 letter. He was distressed in particular that the Rochester patients had never been told they were the subjects of an experiment and resented the pervasive influence the project had on his entire professional life, Durbin wrote. "He said if such material were available, the Los Alamos group would be interested in participating, but that they did not want to be directly responsible nor in direct contact with whomever was actually obtaining samples," the letter states.

Elmer and Fredna's trip to Chicago and Rochester began with a March 7, 1973, letter to their family doctor, A. O. Dykes, from Argonne National Laboratory.

"We are trying to locate a patient of yours by the name of Elmer Allen in order to do a follow-up study on treatment he received for a sarcoma in July 1947," wrote Austin Brues, medical director of Argonne's Center for Human Radiobiology.

"We are especially interested in cases of this sort, and his is of particular interest since he has this unusual malignant tumor and has shown such a long survival time," Brues wrote.

"Please assure him it would only be for observation and collection of excreta," he added. Nowhere in the letter is plutonium mentioned, a substance an AEC official later would point out dryly was not given for therapeutic reasons.

Elmerine, grown and with a family of her own at the time, remembers her parents' excitement. "It was like it was going to be an adventure. My mother called. She said, 'You know, I got this letter from this doctor that was one of your dad's doctors when he had has leg amputated in California. When she found out your father was still alive, she was just amazed and what they wanted to do, they wanted to see if we will come to the University of Rochester in New York to run some metabolism tests.'"

Scientist Rundo recalled seeing the patients. "I looked at them. I saw people who were in reasonably good states of health, considering their ages, considering one had lost a leg twenty-seven years earlier. These were normal people, nice people." The plutonium in Elmer was barely detectable. "His excretion rate was extremely low," Rundo said.

After the tests at Argonne, the Allens rested a day and then boarded a bus to Rochester, where another limousine took them to their hotel. Elmer spent fourteen days in the metabolic unit at Strong Memorial Hospital. Fredna kept several souvenirs of the trip, including a Polaroid snapshot of Elmer with a doctor she identified as Christine Waterhouse. A couple of the medical people even gave her their autographs. One was a scientist whose name appears in scientific papers describing the plutonium found in the hair and bones of exhumed corpses.

Fredna said she had no idea what the doctors were doing. "Every time I went to see him, he was in bed. They would study the food he would eat," she said.

For two weeks, Elmer ate the same kind of food. His urine and stool samples were gathered regularly. On the day he was to be discharged, he had a seizure. They stayed an extra day.

On April 17, 1974, more than a year after Elmer had been sent home, the AEC's Division of Inspection and the Biomedical and Environmental Research Division began an investigation. The reasons for the inquiry are not clear.

A detailed report of the findings later was prepared and classified "Official Use Only." The DOE now says it doesn't have the report, but the *Tribune* obtained a copy from a former Capitol Hill staffer. In the report, the DOE deleted the names of patients, doctors, scientists, and investigators. The internal inquiry focused mostly on:

- Whether patients in the 1945–47 period had given their informed consent for the experiment.
- Whether the survivors in 1973 were properly informed of the true purpose of the follow-up studies and gave their informed consent.
- Whether the relatives of the deceased patients were properly informed about the exhumations.

The answers were no, no, and no.

Investigators fanned out across fourteen cities, examining records and talking to scientists involved in both phases of the experiment. More than 250 documents were copied and brought back to AEC headquarters. The

investigation uncovered a web of deceit that dated back fifty years. The investigators found:

- No written evidence that any of the patients were informed of the original plutonium injections or gave their consent. Witnesses claimed
  some patients were told orally they were going to receive a radioactive
  substance, but plutonium was a classified word at the time. Elmer was
  told only that he was to receive a radioactive substance.
- In 1973, survivors Elmer, Eda Schultz Charlton, and John Mousso were
  not told the true reason scientists were interested in studying them.
  They also did not give their informed consent for the studies even
  though Argonne National Laboratory, as contractor with the AEC, had
  agreed to abide by regulations requiring such consent for human studies. Robert Loeb, spokesman for the University of Rochester Medical
  Center, said the hospital didn't require patients to sign informed consent forms because they were involved in excretion studies only.
- The relatives of the dead patients also were deceived or lied to about the
  true purpose of the exhumations.

One of the documents that illustrated the extent of the cover-up was the last
paragraph of a December 21, 1972, memo written by Robert Rowland, a retired
scientist who at that time was director for the Center for Human Radiobiology:

"Please note that outside of CHR we will never use the word plutonium in
regard to these cases. 'These individuals are of interest to us because they may
have received a radioactive material at some time' is the kind of statement to
be made, if we need to say anything at all." (The words "never" and "plutonium"
are underlined in the memo.)

Rowland, who still lives in the Chicago area, said in an interview that he
was given those instructions "orally" by officials in Washington, DC. "We were
not in any way, shape, or form to allude to plutonium," he recalled.

A. F. Stehney, another scientist from the Center for Human Radiobiology
involved in the follow-up studies, said the plutonium patients weren't told the
truth because everybody was "leery of getting these people all excited.

"We were told these people were pretty elderly and might get very upset if
we started talking about radioactivity in their bodies."

While scientists were contacting living survivors about follow-up studies,
others were trying to secure permission from relatives of deceased plutonium
patients for exhumations. Here's what they agreed to tell relatives:

"An appropriate approach would be to say that the center was investigating
the composition of radioactive materials that had been injected at an earlier

date in an experimental type of treatment; and that since the composition of the mixture was not well known, there would be considerable scientific interest in investigating the nature of the isotope and the effects it may have had."

On September 24, 1973, the body of a twenty-year-old woman identified in official records as "HP-4" was exhumed. The patient's sister had given permission for the exhumation. "Since the sister did not inquire as to the reason for the injections, the issue was not broached," the AEC report revealed.

The relatives of seven deceased patients eventually were contacted. None was told the real reason, AEC investigators found. "Disclosure to all but one of the next of kin could be judged misleading in that the radioactive isotopes were represented as having been injected as an experimental treatment for the patient's disease," the report says.

After the investigation, the AEC ordered that survivors be told the truth. Relatives of the deceased patients also were to be recontacted and told.

In May 1974, Brues, the medical director of the Center for Human Radiobiology, took a night flight to Dallas. There, he met another AEC official and the two of them drove to Milford, Texas, to tell Elmer's physician the truth behind the studies done a year earlier.

"I told him we found that the patient had received plutonium into the muscle of the sarcomatous leg three days before it was amputated, not enough in our belief to cause any trouble or to have any effect on the tumor, but that he should be carefully followed in any case because of the very small number of such cases that are living," Brues said.

Elmer's physician, Dr. Dewey H. Roberts, who was then eighty years old, thought the plutonium might have cured the cancer, Brues said. "Dr. Roberts was quick to form the belief that the injection may have cured the tumor: We tried to cool this but with questionable success. (I had given warning of this possibility before accepting the assignment.)," Brues wrote.

The Center for Human Radiobiology was "extremely anxious" to do an autopsy when Elmer died. It also wanted permission to check him again at intervals, Brues told Elmer's doctor.

Roberts assured the Chicago scientist he would be happy to cooperate and wanted advice on whom to call in case of serious illness or death. "He said these old fellows with hypertension, in his experience, are likely to go to sleep some night and not wake up," Brues said.

"We asked Roberts to tell the patient about the nature of the injection as he has a right to know. The records seem to indicate only that he gave voluntary consent to an injection of radioactive material," Brues said.

After the visit with Roberts, the two officials paid a "social visit" to Elmer. "Our visit was welcome; his wife was taking her grade-school class to the zoo in Dallas; he is moving into the new house, finest in the area, apparently somewhat financed by his two children he visited when in the North," Brues said.

The two scientists didn't tell Elmer of the plutonium injection but advised him to talk with Roberts about a discussion they had had with him. Elmer told the two officials he would be happy to return for a "recheck" provided he didn't have to fly.

In a follow-up discussion, Elmer's doctor confirmed to AEC officials that Elmer had been told of the injection. "The patient was aware of the injection and wasn't much concerned although he did not know what it was that had been injected," the AEC report quotes Elmer's doctor as saying.

In the spring of 1974, James Liverman, a DOE official, met with Robert Berry, Army general counsel, and Brig. Gen. R. W. Green, the deputy surgeon general of the Army, to tell them they planned to inform the plutonium survivors of the long-ago injections.

"General Green was considerably concerned that no good was to be achieved in his view by surfacing a whole series of issues when nothing could in fact be done at this point in time with regard to changing those issues and that the patients or their relatives might in fact be worse off because of the public, social, or psychological trauma," Liverman stated.

AEC officials also became worried in the midseventies about how to explain the experiment—should it ever become public.

But word eventually got out. In 1976, the experiment was reported in a Washington, DC-based newsletter called *Science Trends*. The *Washington Post* also reported the story on the front page on February 22, 1976.

In the *Post* story, an unnamed official said the department "had no plans to launch an investigation to try to learn more about the injection program." What the unnamed energy official didn't say was that an investigation had just been concluded two years earlier.

The DOE records dwindle after 1974. Unsigned, handwritten slips of paper kept score of how many patients were still alive as the years went by. The decision to discontinue the almost fifty-year-old experiment remains, in some ways, as mysterious as the decision to launch the project.

Stehney, one of the scientists involved in the later studies, said things just became too difficult. "There were things we didn't feel comfortable with. We thought we had done as much as could be done at that point."

Rundo, also involved in the follow-up studies, said it was his "vague" recollection that DOE told scientists to stop their investigation. "I think it was the lawyers who were concerned. They were afraid the families might sue," he said.

But Berkeley scientist Durbin tells a different story. "Someone went to talk with one family and made misrepresentations.

"Those of us when we heard about that concluded the waters had been muddied, and we needed to let more time pass, let tempers cool. I was very angry that had happened," she said.

The plutonium experiment topped a litany of human experiments in a report issued in late 1986 by the US House of Representatives subcommittee on Energy, Conservation and Power. US Rep. Edward J. Markey, a Massachusetts Democrat who chaired the subcommittee, compared the tests conducted by the DOE and its predecessors to the "kind of demented human experiments conducted by the Nazis."

"Documents provided by the Department of Energy reveal the frequent and systematic use of human subjects as guinea pigs for radiation experiments," the opening sentence of the report says.

Markey urged the DOE to make every effort to find the patients, follow up on radiation-associated diseases and to compensate "these unfortunate victims" for damages. The AEC, after its 1974 internal investigation, also recommended survivors be given medical surveillance, with the AEC or Department of Defense picking up the tab.

But there was no pot of gold waiting for Elmer Allen, no government men who came to Italy in his waning years to try to make good.

Fighting his real and imagined ghosts, Elmer lived almost another five years after the subcommittee published its findings. Elmer died on June 30, 1991, of respiratory failure caused by pneumonia. He was eighty years old. On his death certificate, his occupation was listed as Pullman porter.

He spent some of his last days in silence at Italy's nursing home, a quiet place shaded by a large cottonwood tree. There, among the other aged residents, the cheerful nature of the amputee described by surgeons so many years ago was still evident.

"I knew he didn't want to be here, but he wasn't mean to us because he didn't want to be here. He tried to do quite a bit of stuff for himself," said Alithea Brown, a licensed vocational nurse at the Italy Convalescent Center.

"He wasn't a conversation starter. He would talk to you if you talked to him. I just never asked him how he lost his leg."

November 15, 1993

Author's Afterword

I was in a bookstore and someone mentioned that there might be a job down at this little newspaper. At the time, papers were still made the old-fashioned way, using hot type. There was a whole process that ended up with these metal plates they used to put on the presses to make the newspapers. Part of the process included something called a copy camera. They had an opening for somebody to run it. I didn't know what that was, but I applied. The job was a night thing—it was a morning paper. At first they didn't want to hire me because I was a woman, but I guess I was persuasive. They hired me anyway; that's how I got started.

After working there a while, I knew I had found my place. I went back to school at the University of Texas in Austin, and I got a degree in journalism. My first reporting job was at the *Beaumont Enterprise* in Beaumont, Texas. I started as a police reporter.

I think women are more empathetic and therefore they develop a better rapport with their sources; oftentimes, they tend to get people to open up in ways that they might not ordinarily do. I think that's one reason why women make great journalists. Another reason is that a lot of journalism, especially investigative reporting, is very, very detail oriented and very tedious. And, for some reason, women can tolerate that tedium more, in my opinion. That said, I think that historically, investigative journalism has always been a "more macho" form of journalism, and thus there were probably more men than women in the field. And I'm thinking, if you go back to the heyday, at the time of Watergate, and you look at some of the reporters back then, they were all men. It was men who were really making gains and breaking stories.

Even so, I consider myself part of the club. I would describe myself as an investigative journalist and author, but I've done all kinds of journalism. I've been a police reporter, a labor reporter, a courthouse reporter. I've written feature stories. I've done everything. But I've always gravitated into longer-form journalism, mainly because the stories were long and complicated. It just happened that way. I would start doing my reporting, and A would lead to B would lead to C would lead to D and so on. I found that I was really good at chasing paper—going to courthouses, filing of Freedom of Information Act requests, doing whatever could be done. I've always found that one piece of paper leads to another, which leads to another. I would say that I'm most proud of the investigative work that I've done, mainly because, in some small way, it has changed the world for the better.

I've always been a rather defiant person, and I think that was really important in daily journalism. To be a good journalist, you have to follow your gut. You have to know that you've got a good story, and not let anyone deter you from following it. In this way I think my personality was well suited for journalism, especially investigative journalism. That said, my personality was also ill suited for journalism. Over the years what I've learned is that most bosses want people who are go-along, get-along types, though there are exceptions. The politics of the newsroom have always been irksome for me. Bottom line, as a staff writer you have to walk the line, do the grunt work, do the stories that need to be done. Then, in your spare time, you can follow your dreams and your heart. I've known a lot of great reporters who could have been greater, but they always just did what they were told. On the other hand, maybe their lives were a little bit easier than mine was. I always wanted to do what I wanted to do. I followed my gut. That doesn't always go over so well in an institution. Inside the building, they want you to be great but more than that, they want you to do what you are told.

But all of us know first and foremost, we are in it because of our gut instincts, our desire to pursue a story to its logical conclusion. In the end, that's the thing that makes you great. The instinct. The follow-up. The inspiration and the perspiration.

Permissions

About the author

Joyce Hoffmann is an associate professor at Old Dominion University. Prior to that, for twenty years, she was a daily and freelance journalist. Her book, *On Their Own: Women Journalists and the American Experience in Vietnam*, published by DaCapo Press in 2008, reflects her long interest in the role of women in American journalism.

She has a PhD in American studies from New York University. Her dissertation, *Theodore H. White and Journalism as Illusion* explored the political journalist's career role in shaping the coverage of presidential campaigns in the last four decades of the twentieth century. It was published by the University of Missouri Press and won the 1995 Frank Luther Mott Research Award.

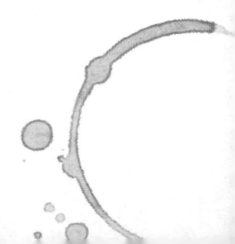

About the Interviewers

Kaylen Ralph is *The Riveter*'s editor in chief and cofounder. She is a graduate of the Missouri School of Journalism and currently resides in Minneapolis, MN, a city that demands recognition beyond its extreme climate. Right now, it's the perfect place for the woman with the bright orange fur coat who enjoys drinking for warmth while reading, writing, and editing. She's an early bird by necessity but enjoys late nights dancing with friends. You can follow her on Instagram and Twitter at @kaylenralph.

Joanna Demkiewicz is *The Riveter*'s features editor and cofounder. She graduated from the Missouri School of Journalism in May 2013, just two months after colaunching *The Riveter* with Kaylen, and she now resides in an Uptown brownstone with a fainting couch in Minneapolis. When she's not working publicity for a local theater/bowling alley/restaurant/bar or drooling over Jack McCoy circa "Law & Order," she is researching for The Sager Group and assisting with *OF NOTE* magazine's editorial duties. Her favorite lady journos are Ariel Levy, Sarah Nicole Prickett, and Maureen O'Connor. Creep on her via Twitter @yanna_dem or Instagram @yannademkiewicz. Call her Yanna.

The Riveter is a women's long-form lifestyle magazine in print and online, dedicated to exposing the power of women as long-form journalists. It is an effort to fill the void that exists in women's media and to diversify the narrative surrounding women in publishing. *The Riveter* publishes stories that can't be summed up in a sell line because women, as writers and readers, deserve more from a women's magazine. For more information, please see www.TheRiveterMagazine.com.

About the Publisher

The Sager Group was founded in 1984 by author and journalist Mike Sager. In 2012 it was chartered as a multimedia artists' and writers' consortium, with the intent of empowering those who make art—an umbrella beneath which makers can pursue, and profit from, their craft directly, without gatekeepers. TSG publishes e-books and paper books; manages musical acts and produces live shows; ministers to artists and provides modest grants; and produces and distributes documentary, feature, and web-based films. By harnessing the means of production, The Sager Group helps artists help themselves. For more information, please see www.TheSagerGroup.Net.

Made in the USA
Columbia, SC
17 October 2017